ICELANDIC FOLK MAGIC
WITCHCRAFT OF
THE NORTH

About the Author

Albert Björn Shiell grew up in the shade of the South Downs of Sussex, England. He spent his days there walking ancient chalk hills, full of burial mounds and folklore. Trading it all in 2017 for cold and seemingly desolate Iceland, Albert picked up his life and moved North.

He now lives in downtown Reykjavík, writing and researching, translating old Icelandic books. He spends his days walking the land around him, learning and conversing with the many plant and land spirits of Iceland. Focusing now on an animistic framework of Nordic magic combined with the Sussex cunning of his homeland, Albert aims to deliver practical folkloric magic inspired by both his homes.

Find him on social media @ Sussex_Pellar.

ICELANDIC FOLK MAGIC

WITCHCRAFT OF THE NORTH

ALBERT BJÖRN

Chicago, Illinois

Paperback ISBN: 978-1-959883-28-9
Hardcover ISBN: 978-1-959883-89-0
Library of Congress Control Number on file.

Disclaimer: Crossed Crow Books, LLC does not participate in, endorse, or have any authority or responsibility concerning private business transactions between our authors and the public. Any internet references contained in this work were found to be valid during the time of publication, however, the publisher cannot guarantee that a specific reference will continue to be maintained. This book's material is not intended to diagnose, treat, cure, or prevent any disease, disorder, ailment, or any physical or psychological condition. The author, publisher, and its associates shall not be held liable for the reader's choices when approaching this book's material. The views and opinions expressed within this book are those of the author alone and do not necessarily reflect the views and opinions of the publisher.

Cover design by Wycke Malliway.
Typesetting by Gianna Rini.
Editing by Lee Anderson.

Published by:
Crossed Crow Books, LLC
6934 N Glenwood Ave, Suite C
Chicago, IL 60626
www.crossedcrowbooks.com

Printed in the United States of America.
IBI

OTHER TITLES BY THE AUTHOR

Icelandic Plant Magic (Crossed Crow Books, 2023)

Dedication

This work has been a true labour of love: hours of sitting and translating texts in a language so deep and expansive, full of so many archaic words and so much magic, that I don't think I'll ever be fluent in it, no matter how much I speak it. I want to thank my friends, our little makeshift coven from all over the world, the witch fam. Without our blóts, gatherings, and shared magic, this work wouldn't have been anything more than a dream.

I want to thank Ísvöld, my teacher and sibling, whose guidance has been crucial. I want to thank Alda, my sporadic podcast co-host, foraging partner, and general light. Hrafnhildur and Sigurboði, who, without their friendship and support, I wouldn't feel confident to speak on these topics, let alone write books on them. To Giorgia and Kári, thank you for your academic eyes, keeping me in check and guiding me to act more like the scholar I wish I was.

I want to thank my amazing illustrator, Striga Artist, Živa; I'm so eternally grateful that you've given your time and talent to this project. Thank you from the bottom of my gay little heart. To Jóhann, Regn, Hrafnsunna, and everyone who has given their time to help me with translation questions here and there: without you all, I'd be fumbling in the dark.

To Galdra Tommi, for your knowledge and our talk about Agrippa. To Gabriel, my heart, who stands by me and supports whatever weird niche witchy project I find for myself, all my love to you. To Jón Árnason, Matthías Viðar Sæmundsson, Ólafur Davíðsson, Sigurður Nordal, and all the other sources of inspiration, practice, and written evidence to back up what we do and why we do it. This work isn't just the work of myself but the work of countless hours of talks, voice notes, ceremonies, random shared thoughts on plants and staves, and all the other parts that bring together the community we have on our beloved rock in the North Atlantic. Without you, none of this would be possible. *Ég elska ykkur öll nornir.*

Contents

GALDRABÓK: GRIMOIRE

APPENDICES AND GLOSSARIES

· KYNNING ·
INTRODUCTION

Introduction

Icelandic folk magic is a vast subject, much argued and as fleeting as the weather of the land from which it comes. It takes as many forms as there are practitioners. This book is intended to give the reader the tools they need to add elements of Icelandic folk magic and witchcraft (Fjölkynngi) to their own practice, to connect or reconnect with the magic of the island, and to build up their own craft with magic taken from both folklore and living practice. From the harsh and rugged Westfjords to the forest of the east, the stark peninsula of the southwest, the glacial southeast, and the deep fjords of the north, Iceland is home to old magic. The stories of the past tell us that since its settlement in the year 874, this land has been home to gods, giants, elves, trolls, ghosts, and more sea monsters than one can count. Wizards, priests, and the devil have all staked their claim on every corner of this wild and, at times, desolate island.

Various influences have helped shape the unique magical culture of the island, from Viking settlers to Catholic priests, Irish monks, and potentially Sámi sailors. Much of the North has had an influence over the island at one point or another. First, Iceland was ruled over by Norway, then Denmark gained sovereignty in 1918, and finally, it sneakily gained independence in 1944. The settlers often came from Scandinavia and Viking-besieged Ireland, with enslaved people taken from these regions. Due to this, Icelandic men can trace about 25% of their genome to Scotland

and Ireland, and Icelandic women can account for 62% of their genome (Ebenesersdóttir et al.). This mix of cultures can be seen in some of the folklore and myths found around the island, as well as seeping into a few spells found in both regions.

The seasons and weather have also helped shape the magic of the island. Winter is ruled by snow, ice, and darkness, along with all that comes with it. Tröll (trolls) and the darker creatures that retreat during summer return now. We look at this change as if it were a breath: the inhale of summer and retraction of these spirits to the uninhabited places is now flipped to the exhale of winter and the retreat of mankind back into our homes and barns as the *vættir* again rule the land. Winter in Iceland was very much the time of women. The men and workers often came from spending summers outside of the home (besides sleep) into this female-dominated space. We see examples of travelling *völvur* going from farm to farm to tell fortunes.

As Terry Gunnell perfectly states in his article "The Season of the Dísir: The Winter Nights and the Dísablót in Early Medieval Scandinavian Belief," "Winter was a time when people moved inside the farmhouse, when food was preserved, and weaving, brewing and spinning played a central role" (138–9). Iceland is very much a land of duality and contradiction. This often plays as prominent a role within folk magic in Iceland as it does within the land itself. Winter is ruled by the *dísír*, female forces of fate and often death—appropriate for this often bitterly cold and deadly season of snows and starvation. Skaði, the giantess, takes power here. Don't get too comfortable, though: this is the time when the infamous ever-hungry giantess Grýla and her hellish cat, known as Jólakötturinn (the Yule Cat), walk the land.

Summer is the season for foraging. Fertility reigns, and Freyr and his life-giving virility are felt everywhere. In contemporary magic, this is a time for working with the traditionally masculine, which I name *projective* or *aggressive*, so as to not get stuck within a gender binary. In the old days, this was the time for commerce, farming, shepherding, and courting. Projective and aggressive forces abound, and midsummer's twenty-four-hour sunlight brings an energetic high point. Inspired by nineteenth-century folklore, the morning dew of summer, especially on *Jónsmessa*, is rolled in for luck and fertility. Brúða (poppets) are stuffed with herbs for all sorts of magical workings, and the herbal supplies needed for winter are gathered from all around the island.

The spirits of the land play a key role in all folk magic, and in Iceland, this is no different. Spirits abound. The jötnar, tröll, draugur (ghosts), landvættir (*genius loci*), and huldufólk (hidden people) all have their role to play and are all still relevant in contemporary folk magic. Where we could say that the jötnar diminished in power, shrinking into trolls, the elves have held steady power and belief in Iceland. These spirits and their contemporary roles will be discussed in more depth later.

After the Reformation in Iceland, many priests were believed to have secretly recorded or contributed to books of magical staves and healing that we know and work with today. We see a reference to Agrippa's *Three Books of Occult Philosophy* found in the library at Skálholt, as well as a few schoolboys being reprimanded for possessing books of magical staves. Later, in eighteenth- and nineteenth-century folklore, we find Grimmi Gottskálk credited with having written the infamous *Rauðskinna*, one of the legendary black books of Icelandic magic, as well as Galdra-Loftur going mad trying to find it. Said to be bound in human skin, this tome supposedly contained spells shared by kölski, the devil himself.

It is worth mentioning, however, that the devil wasn't much of a big player in the world of Icelandic sorcerers. Sure, the folklore of the nineteenth century tells us that some Lutheran priests were attending a black school in France, hidden in caves. This school was said to be ruled over by the devil, with trolls and demons for teachers. But the devil wasn't the scary big bag that he was over on the continent. This was maybe due to the mixing of Christianity and Paganism that occurred in Iceland even until recently. Without the Catholic wizard priests recording their spells and charms, we would have little to work with nowadays. I wonder how many "Viking" enthusiasts would be lacking a Vegvísir tattoo?

It wasn't all about wizard priests. Other forms of magic and practice played a role in the pre-Christian past of Iceland and the other Nordic countries. Galdur was, and still is, regarded as the more structured magic of staves, songs, and chants. The word itself comes from the verb *að gala* (to call up or make noise). This vocal aspect is very important to galdur, and throughout this book, I refer to spoken charms as *galdur*, as we do here in Iceland. This sort of magic has often been assigned to male practitioners, though galdur is not something only for men. We use the terms for *galdramaður*, *galdrakona*, and the modern term *galdrakvár* for non-binary practitioners of this art. Galdrastafir and many types of charms fall into this category, though we shouldn't get caught up in categorising all types of magic under these two terms. Keep in mind that these two subjects are vast and I encourage the reader to research them deeper within a historical and academic context to better understand them. The other magic practiced was *seiður*. In the simplest terms, seiður often involves prophecy, divination, and the calming of land spirits and magic, which affects the landscape. An example of this magic in the Viking age is the prophecy of Þórbjörg Litlivölva, as well as acts like creating magical fog and summoning fish to fill a fjord. We see both men and women engage in seiður during pre-Christian times.

Often, the men carried the taboo of being considered *ergi*, a term that might be interesting for queer readers to research further. These seiðmenn are sometimes said to work seiður for destructive ends, such as calling storms and göringaveður to wreck ships. This othering of men practicing a magic that was often considered outside of their traditional role was enough justification for King Harald Finehair of Norway to have his own son put to death. Let it be noted, however, that Óðinn was also known to practice this form of "women's magic." I highly recommend reading Ellora Nimbkar Rich's MA thesis, "Seið the Magic Words: Two Case Studies in Old Norse Etymology," for a good linguistic breakdown of these words and their possible roots.

In contemporary practice, and as a queer practitioner myself, I can guarantee that anyone can engage in both these types of magic. We are no longer subject to being ostracized for stepping outside of this Viking age norm. In modern practices, many are now doing away with gender-bound concepts in magical work. It pays to keep this in mind when reading folklore written and recorded by men of their time. Galdur and seiður are, in many ways, two sides of the same coin. Just like all magic, both these techniques may be worked for good or bad, and indeed, the very idea of good or bad magic is a Christian concept that we can't accurately apply to Viking-age mentalities and magical practices.

That brings us to animism, a central part of all Icelandic folk magic. As I've now mentioned, spirits dominate the landscape here. Dragons slumber beneath the earth, emerging as plumes of lava. Hrímþurs (frost giants) bring winter storms and control the winds. Draugar of all forms don't behave like the dead should. Icelandic magic focuses heavily on spirits, be they plants, ghosts, landwights, and more. Even up until the 1970s, the tradition of leaving the last of the year's hay, or even burning it, for the landvöttir to ensure the next year's harvest was still observed.

Known as *álfkonufang*, this practice very likely has a pre-Christian root that people retained until half a century ago. All these spirits need to be considered when performing workings in certain places, for example.

Even the view of the soul is sometimes contradictory in Icelandic tradition. Many follow the three souls theory, which tells us that our being is made up of three aspects: the upper, middle, and lower soul (I will go into detail on this later). But there are also ways of thinking within Nordic traditions regarding upwards of seven parts that make up a being. All together, Icelandic folk magic is as interesting as it is complicated, and it is very much my hope that by discussing the techniques and workings we use here, the reader will be able to enrich their practice with some of what the island has to offer. This book will draw comparisons to neighbouring Scotland, Norway, Denmark, and Sweden. By comparing and making connections with our neighbours, we can see how traditions spread. This includes how some old Gaelic spells came to be found in Iceland, possibly due to enslaved Scottish people being taken here from their homeland. The spákonur of Iceland are no doubt related to the spaewives of Scotland. Norwegian and Icelandic black books work similar techniques, and the Gotlandish faerie folk have much in common with the hidden people of Iceland.

I will use a few words interchangeably to describe the practitioner as best fits the context. But it is worth noting that in Iceland and Icelandic tradition, one doesn't simply call themselves a "Völva" just because they wish to pick up a Nordic title or add a feather to their cap. Being a Völva takes training, experience, latent skill, and ability, as well as, most importantly, having a community to serve and people to aid. This is not a book that teaches how to become an Icelandic Völva, as that can only be taught within the land and by another who was called that before you. Some of the words I will use within this book include *seiðkona, spákona, galdramaður, seiðkarl, særingamaður,* and, finally, *norn. Norn* is the most all-purpose word. It means "witch" in the exact same way that the word *wicce* derives from *wyrd:* fate. A norn is one who weaves and manipulates their own fate. The rest of these words are sadly binary, and as with much of Icelandic, it has been a bit of a struggle to modernize them. *Seiðkona* or *seiðkarl* can mean artist, brewer, conjurer, weaver, creator, and many other things; within the context of this book, I use it to describe a person who works seiður. *Spákona* or *spákarl* refers to a diviner or someone who looks into the future, past, or present. *Galdramaður* is a word that is often translated as "wizard"; in

Iceland, this word has been used to describe priests and peasants alike. Individuals such as Jón Lærði (Jon the Learned), a famous self-taught wizard, and the infamous Grimmi would have been given this title. The distinction for us is that galdramenn tend to work galdur in the form of staves and songs over seiður and the more subtle arts. *Kvár* is used as the modern non-binary suffix. For example, a non-binary person practicing seiður would be a seiðkvár. One other term that fits all would be *seiðberi:* one who bears or carries seiður.

Many aspects of witchcraft found throughout Europe don't pop up in Icelandic folklore and tradition. The Witches Sabbat, for example, is not a part of Icelandic lore. Covens, in general, were never a part of Icelandic folklore, as the island's sparse population meant that specific nighttime gatherings on hills would have been unfeasible and likely dangerous. There is no specific hill or spot where witches gather, although there are plenty of magical hills, mountains, mounds, and more within the landscape. Esjan, the mountain seen across the bay of Reykjavík, is one such magical mountain (as well as being a nice hike), named after the Irish witch who was said to reside there in *Kjalnesinga saga*. Another famed magical hill is Spákonufell, which rises above Skagaströnd in North Iceland. This spot is well worth a pilgrimage. Take any big questions one might have and ask them to the spirit of Þórdís, the Seeress who once resided on the hill. The local Museum of Prophecies is also worth a look.

Iceland is peppered with magical hills, but no one hill is the counterpart to the Swedish Blåkulla, host of the sabbat. Along with the absence of the sabbat, the devil himself played a much lesser role in Icelandic magic and was not feared until later, during and after the Protestant Reformation. The devil in Iceland plays a similar role to the devil in Romanian folklore, running schools of black magic and handing out degrees and powers to priests who wish to learn magic. This sort of exchange could be viewed similarly to the selling of the soul and the signing of the black book, but that sort of deal doesn't pop up. Due to this, I would suggest that a lot of lore surrounding schools run by the devil most likely comes from post-Reformation anti-Catholic propaganda.

Wise people and wizards were called upon to settle disputes, curse land and livestock, and more in Iceland's history, sagas, and folklore. This aligns with the same role that wise people of mainland Europe also played. The fact that many magical texts traveled all around Europe didn't go unnoticed in Iceland, and from what evidence we have of the galdrabækur (magic books), we see influence from texts such as Agrippa's *Three Books of Occult Philosophy* and *Le Petit Albert*. Iceland is connected with these magical undercurrents and is still very much influenced by them. Its unique worldview and animistic lens, as well as religious history, have helped shape that into a true blend of old and new magic going back into the distant past. The importance of records in Iceland has also helped its magical traditions to survive, no matter how filtered down. Many grandmothers will still know of a few simple herbal charms and never thought of it as witchcraft, but it is witchcraft nonetheless.

Interestingly, in Iceland, the belief in huldufólkið (the hidden people) was similar to the belief of the fae of Ireland and Scotland. These beings are feared and respected, and roadworks are occasionally still halted by machinery malfunctions believed to be the work of the elves that live within the rocks and boulders that sit in the way of new roads. People in the countryside are known to still leave food at certain álfasteinar as offerings in exchange for help through hard winters. The name *huldufólk* replaced elves in the nineteenth century as the most common name used to describe these beings, although there have been a few others through the centuries.

There are even specific festival days that relate to the huldufólk. The twelfth night (the sixth of January) is one in particular. Álfabrennur (elf bonfires) used to be held on this night. It was common for whole communities to gather and party in costume and masks so as not to know who is and is not an elf. This tradition has changed in recent years, with the sixth being a night of fireworks and occasionally still bonfires. Jónsmessu (midsummer) is arguably the most important day in the calendar of an Icelandic folk practitioner. It is used for many things, especially work involving elves and crossroads. On this night, the practitioner should go off to a crossroads in the middle of nowhere and engage in útiseta (sitting out). The elves are said to come and tempt those who do with food and other such things. If the practitioner can resist any temptation laid before them, rewards are guaranteed.

The hidden people were said to be the original children of Adam and Eve, expelled from the Garden of Eden and left invisible to the other children of God. They live in the mountains and rocks of Iceland. Certain places are known as their churches and halls, but the most famous is their capital city, located in Ásbyrgi in North Iceland. This impressive canyon houses an old forest, one of the only forests of large trees in the country. Protected from the weather by the horseshoe canyon itself, this area is truly magical. Its mystery becomes most apparent when visited at dawn and dusk. I've spent many nights there in late summer, and at dusk, the light shifts, causing many "faces" to appear on the grand walls surrounding you. This canyon was said to have come about from the footprint of Óðinn's eight-legged horse, Sleipnir. The faces that appear and the way the echoes dart around the canyon add to the credibility of this indeed being the capital of Iceland's hidden elf community.

Tröll and jötnar exist in folklore and in the landscape in the form of giant stone features, which draws attention to them and, often, looks very much out of place. Folklore tells us of trolls coming down from the mountains in the darkness of winter, knocking on windows and doors, and tempting unfortunate people outside and into their jaws. Trolls in Icelandic folklore, to me, represent the forces of chaos that abound on this windy island. The weather can present a real danger in the winter (and, indeed, all year round), changing quickly and somewhat unpredictably. It was and continues to be a serious hazard.

Many stories of trolls include luring people up to their mountain abodes during winter. These people are never seen again, and if they are, the state they are found in is gruesome (worse still, if they themselves have become a troll). Stories of trolls also often include futile attempts to outsmart their victims. This common trope is no different in Icelandic folklore. The Thurs are a little more dangerous. Often conflated with the jötnar and much envied by the Æsir and Vanir, the Thurs are spirits closer to the primordial chaos and much more aligned with what we would call "trickster spirits" from a Traditional Witchcraft perspective. To many of us in Iceland, these are seldom invoked, if ever worked with at all. Only a fool plays with fire.

To many of us in Iceland, the jötnar are the embodiment of primordial chaos. In relation to modern Traditional Witchcraft traditions, Icelandic folk magic can be seen as a somewhat less visited but fond cousin. Many people with Catholic or Christian heritage are beginning to feel more comfortable working with and invoking saints and angels, and some follow the ways of the European wise folk, working planetary times and snippets of high magic into their practice. Icelandic magic is very much like this, working as a mishmash of Catholic, Protestant, Pagan, and, dare I say it, "Viking" Nordic folk practices. As such, many of the techniques, tools, and workings I will discuss in this book can easily be slotted into the folk magical practice of many readers. My aim is not to recreate or fabricate an entirely authentic ancient Icelandic folk magic practice. Thanks to the brennuöldin and Kristintakan, this is sadly impossible, but nevertheless, it is my intention that the reader is able to pick and choose aspects of Icelandic sorcery to utilise as they see fit.

Kristintakan—the taking on of Christianity—happened officially in the year 1000. (It pays to remember the settlement started in 870 or so.) The process was difficult, and many Pagans, though baptised, still retained their beliefs alongside Christianity. This dual faith is common in many folk practices and is central to much of Icelandic folk magic. The Catholic period in Iceland lasted from around 1050 to 1550, with the two dioceses of Skálholt and Hólar. These two centres became places of magical myth after the reformation, said to be home to secret schools of magic and the sites where infamous black books were written in Iceland.

Catholicism officially ended with a civil war and the eventual beheading of the bishop Jón Arason and his sons in 1550. The Lutheran church took over, and Catholicism was outlawed. Some outlawed and exiled Catholics moved to Scotland for safety. Catholicism only really returned in 1855 with the new Catholic church being established on the island. The demonisation of Catholics and Catholic bishops could be partially responsible for the legends and stories of wizard priests and their unsavory antics.

The five-hundred-year period of Catholicism left a large mark on Iceland's magical landscape. Catholic mysticism was undoubtedly popular within the Icelandic priesthood. Solomonic magic and the works of Agrippa had a clear influence on some of the priests who could very well have created many of the staves we still use today. Lingering folk belief in the old gods also trickled into the workings of learned and literate men. We see this in the instructions for some spells involving Latin and the names of Christian figures alongside the old gods and giants.

These priests knew of the magic of planets, angels, and many other aspects of high magic that the common folk would have likely had little to no knowledge of. Planetary and angelic aspects of staves, timings, and the diffused and diluted influence of Agrippa's *Three Books* present themselves to those who can see them. Even the magic of the early 1800s, with its revived interest in these strands of high magic, shows us the importance of timings in gathering plants and materia. Magic, outside of herbal work and any lasting family traditions and lineages, was mainly performed by men, especially learned men. One such man was Jón Lærði (John the Learned).

Though called "Lærði," he had no formal education but was a self-taught scholar, writer, and craftsman. He was also a competent galdramaður, most famous for his exorcism of two ghosts. There are many stories about him, some of which we will discuss later. Another infamous character within Icelandic folklore is Grimmi, a previous bishop of Hólar and supposed author of the legendary *Rauðskinna* grimoire. His nickname means "cruel," and stories of him confirm this. Even two hundred years after his death, his infamy influenced a student at a Latin school in Hólar, Loftur Þórsteinnsson, to go in search of *Rauðskinna*. Sources vary about what happened to him, but many say he was driven mad in his search and rowed out into the ocean, never to return. *Rauðskinna* is still sought after, and many practitioners on the island have their theories about where it lies and who or what protects it.

In more modern times, galdur is still very much practiced and recorded. The folklorist Jón Árnason recorded not just stories but many staves and examples of magic from all around the country. His collected works are still available, although they haven't all been translated into English, which is great motivation for those who wish to learn Icelandic. His work is central to much of modern folk magic in Iceland, and without him, we would have lost so much of the history and practice. An article by Ólafur Daviðsson from 1903 is also to thank for popularizing many staves, as well as being heavily drawn from by a few modern authors on Icelandic magic. Matthías Viðar Sæmundsson's book *Galdrar á Íslandi*, published in 1993, is, in my opinion, the best summary of the magic of this country; my own explanation of the subject is nothing but a candle in the wind to his writing. Sadly, this has never been translated into English.

In terms of modern practice, Ásatrú has grown in Iceland in the last century, with the ongoing building of a temple to the old gods in Reykjavík. Ásatrúarfélagið has been growing as a group, with many more open rituals encouraging new members. The persisting belief in elves hasn't died out, and animism is becoming much more of a focus in the larger witchcraft zeitgeist worldwide, which aligns with how Icelanders have viewed their natural world since the settling. Iceland has always been a magical land. The spirits here make themselves known and heard. If we wish to work with them, it is time for us to listen and learn.

᛫ÞJÓÐATRÚ ᛫
FOLK BELIEF

1

Planetary Timings

In my opinion, much of modern Western occultism owes its depth to the work of Heinrich Cornelius Agrippa von Nettesheim. His work, *Three Books of Occult Philosophy*, outlines the ruling planetary forces and elements of all things. Agrippa's work on natural, celestial, and ceremonial magic has been adored by occultists the world over since it was first printed in 1535. His name became so commonplace when referring to the occult that many grimoires were often simply referred to as "Agrippas." Through the lens of planetary natural magic, we can dissect all things under the sun and work them into our own sympathetic magic. I'd go as far as to say that his work aligns with Icelandic animistic thinking, though on a somewhat "zoomed out" scale, whereby our vættir are the planets themselves. For these reasons, I work off his writing, including planetary timings and rulers in all aspects of my sorcery, and with his work found in the libraries of the very places that likely produced many magical staves, I see Agrippa's work as influential to the magic of Iceland from the sixteenth century onwards.

The influence of high magic through the learned priest class in Iceland, Agrippa, and the general similarities between Solomonic seals and galdrastafir is arguably why planetary timing is still so important within Icelandic magic today. This, as well as what I would call a "macro-animistic" mentality around planetary intelligences and spirits, makes it important for us to know when and where we should be gathering materia as well as what materia we should be working with. Understanding the world through the lens of the seven planetary virtues compliments animistic work very nicely.

We don't look at the planetary powers as gods, just larger spirits working within the same spirit ecology, but on a much grander scale. This helps us to both memorise and understand why we do what we do. Learning that certain plants are ruled by the planet Venus, for example, tells us many ways we may be able to work with them. Indeed, a plant we recognise in contemporary practice as being ruled by the planet Venus, such as Vallhumall (*Achillea millefolium*), also falls under the rule of Freyja, Mary, Frigg, and deities, as well as spirits, that we can work with towards Venusian ends, such as love, friendship, and healing. Learning these planetary forces and their correspondences gives us a simple knowledge base we can use to pull together various materia, as well as tells us which time they should be gathered and worked with for the greatest potency.

Planetary forces, as well as elemental forces, connect all things. The planets rule over certain things, such as plants, days, hours, and minerals, and each of these may convey the virtues of its ruler when used in magic or medicine.

As an example, we could look at the sólblóm (sunflower, *Helianthus annuus*). This dramatic and clear emblem of the Sun shows us its alignment and connection with Solar virtues. It grows straight up, reaching towards the sky, in full sun. Its flower reflects its planetary ruler's appearance as its bright yellow petals reflect the colour of the Sun. Its seeds are a food source, one sunflower producing hundreds of nurturing seeds just as the Sun produces life on this planet. This is not a subtle example of the correspondences we would do well to learn.

Like I included in my previous book, *Icelandic Plant Magic*, Agrippa's descriptions of each planet can be found along with each of their planetary symbols and letters.

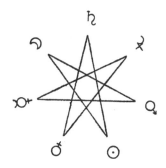

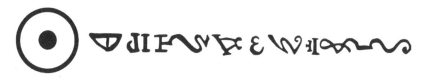

THE SUN: As the king of the heavens, the Sun represents kingship and supremacy within many Western occult frameworks. It is most often associated with the divine; godly, righteous power, and might. Solar materia includes gold amulets, sunflower seeds, dandelion flowers, tiger's eye, amber, and yellow roses. As one might imagine, yellows, gold, and all tones that inspire warmth belong to the Sun. The numbers of the Sun are 6, 36, 111, and 666.

THE MOON: As the Sun is king, so the Moon is queen. Within a binary method of magic, we see the Moon as the Goddess, though this is limiting. The Moon holds power over the unconscious mind, all workings held by moonlight, secrets, and divination. Lunar materia includes chickweed, silver, yarrow, seashells, moonstone, many white stones and flowers, and Lunar waters used for cleansing and purification. Lunar colours are white, silver, and grey, and the numbers of the Moon are 9, 81, 396, and 3321.

Mercury: Mercury is the messenger, the winged and swift ruler of communication and exchange. Within Western occultism, Mercury stands alone, not part of any planetary pairings such as the Sun and Moon. Mercury standing alone gives it unique powers over mental matters. All stones that concern stealth, thievery, communication, and wisdom fall under Mercury. Mercurial materia includes the feathers, bones, and remains of birds that fly long migratory routes and are adapted to hide and steal valuable, shiny trinkets. Corvids are especially Mercurial birds for their nature as thieves. The colours of Mercury are yellows and oranges, but some people ascribe greens to Mercury as well. The numbers of Mercury are 8, 64, 260, and 2080.

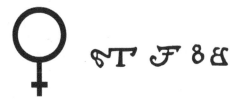

VENUS: Venus, queen of love, persuasion, and beauty, stands opposite and adjacent to Mars. Typically, she is seen as the hostess, one all wish to conquer or become. Venus displays fury, rage, and vengeance, especially when wished upon unfaithful lovers. Venus is the rose: beautiful from afar, but act the fool, and you'll feel the sting of her hidden thorns. Stones of Venus include, most famously, rose quartz, as well as jade and emerald. Venusian plant materia includes roses and all fruits and flowers. Venus is the bounty of the Earth and the fruits of one's labour. The colours of Venus are greens, pinks, and reds. Copper is the most Venusian metal. The numbers of Venus are 7, 49, 175, and 1225.

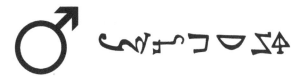

MARS: Near Venus, we find noble Mars. Martial energy is the curious young one, prematurely believing oneself ready to venture into the world. Martial energy is the self-righteous warrior, the sharp spear in the heat of battle, the scorpion's stinger, and the turtle's hard shell. Mars rules protection, fiery passion, anger, violence, and much of what we would associate with the patriarchal world. Stones of Mars include carnelian, also aligned with Fire, as well as ruby, which overlaps with Venusian virtues. Martial materia includes blood, bones of beings killed in fights and war, soil gathered from battlefields, bullet casings, and other materia relating to Martial weapons. Phallic imagery, as well as any phallic materia, is often ruled by Mars. Iron is also ruled by Mars, as it is the blood of the

Earth and is most often concerned with protective and offensive work. Martial plants include all those owning spikes and stinging defences. The colours of Mars are red, orange, and crimson. The numbers of Mars are 5, 25, 65, and 325.

♃ ᚠᚢᚤ ᚪ⊕⊞ᚔᛁᚾᛂᛒᛏ᛬ᚢᚲᛣ

JUPITER: Jupiter stands opposite and adjacent to Saturn. Another king within the heavens, Jupiter is concerned with wealth, and Jovial powers offer expansion. He is the king of the scene, offering connections and opportunity, allowing wealth to flow freely. Jupiter brings influence and social power, and we see this overlap of Jovial and Venusian powers of social prowess coming from two different paths to reach the same goal. Jovial plants are abundantly found colonising spaces and striving towards the light. Sweet and decadent-smelling plants, as well as those we often dismiss as common, are often ruled by Jupiter. Stones of Jupiter include lapis lazuli, malachite, and some agates. Jovial materia includes roots, leaves, and remains of materia that attract; the remains of hoarding animals, such as squirrels and rodents, are also Jovial due to their high rates of reproduction. The colours of Jupiter are purples and greens, and the numbers of Jupiter are 4, 16, 34, and 136.

♄ ᚔ᛬ ᚴᛘᚹᛁᚷᚧᛦ

SATURN: Standing opposite Jupiter, Saturn is the misanthropic old man, the great binding force of the heavens, and he knows and values the limits of all things. Saturnine powers are concerned with binding and control, the limits of life, and Saturn stands at the end. We see this very clearly in Saturn's frequent role as the ruler of toxic plant materia, which often has the power to end life. Where this may all sound negative, it is wise to remember that though death and the end of things may be sad, it is essential for the continuation of all cycles. Saturn watches over these cycles and is the firm hand guiding that which may have had its time. Stones of Saturn are often also toxic.

Remains of Saturnine animals can follow this toxic trend, such as the fangs of venomous animals, though simply working with bones as the symbols of death is Saturnine in and of itself. Saturnine animals are those who rely on cunning and ambush. Skulls as a medium for spirits are Saturnine, both because one can only utilise them after the death of the owner and because skulls act as limiting vessels that can contain a spirit, making it easier to communicate with. The colours of Saturn are purple, dark blue, black, and dark grey. Saturn's numbers are 3, 9, 15, and 45.

In terms of gathering materia adhering to planetary timings, the hours of the day are broken down into chunks assigned to each planet. The seven days of the week are each ruled by one planet: Monday to the Moon, Tuesday to Mars, Wednesday to Mercury, Thursday to Jupiter, Friday to Venus, Saturday to Saturn, and Sunday to the Sun. It is best to gather materia for workings within the day and hour most relevant to the work. For example, for a spell to encourage new love with a focus on clear communication, we can gather materia on a Friday, the day of Venus, during the hour of Mercury. This gives us plenty of ways to combine certain planetary days and hours for the most appropriate combination of virtues.

In Iceland, the following poem dictates other virtues to the days of the week. This verse can be used to focus on and highlight specific magic in ways other than those of the traditional planetary days.

In this translation of *fjár*, I've substituted for "money" in English, as the connection between wealth and livestock—*fehu* and *fé*—is better translated in modern witchcraft practices as "wealth." This poem is found in Christopher A. Smith's *Icelandic Magic: Aims, Tools and Techniques of the Icelandic Sorcerers*.

"Sunnudagur til sigurs,	"Sunday for victory,
Mánudagur til mæðu,	Monday for trouble,
Þriðjudagur til þrautar,	Tuesday for trials,
Miðvikudagur til moldar,	Wednesday for Earth,
Fimmtudagur til frama,	Thursday for fame,
Föstudagur til fjár,	Friday for money,
Laugardagur til lukku."	Saturday for luck."

Within the Icelandic galdrastafir tradition, we find two staves designed as seals of the Sun. These two sólar innsigli (depicted on pages 212-213) show us how planetary magic was likely worked alongside other aspects of high magic within Iceland's past. From these sólar innsigli, I have designed planetary seals for each of the remaining planets. These seals can be worked into discs of wood, stones, or metal to use as platforms from which to perform all sorts of workings. Each includes circles, which make useful points on which to place small candles. These candles should be anointed with planetary oils. The staves themselves, once created, should be reddened with blood as is traditional.

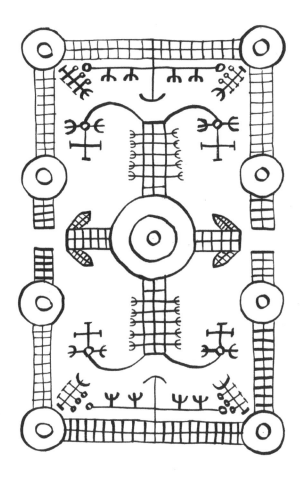

Lunar Innsigli

Merkúrius Innsigli

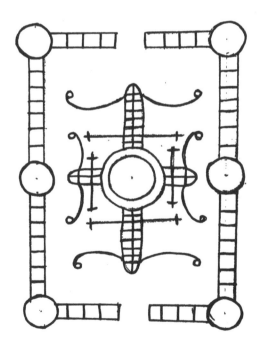

Venus Innsigli

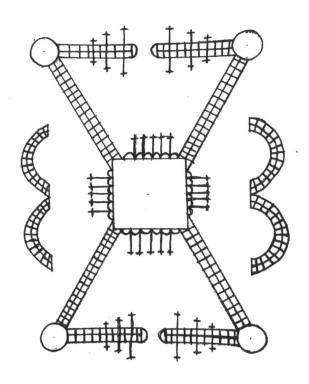

Mars Innsigli

Júpiters Innsigli

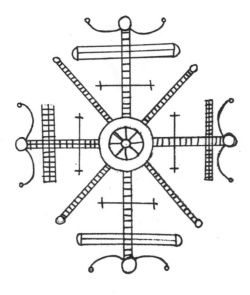

Satúrnus Innsigli

FOUR MAGICAL FOCI

Like many other magical traditions, Iceland draws on magical quartets. Below is a brief overview of each element and one of my personal quartets before we move on to discuss the four protectors of Iceland.

Earthly materia emphasises sturdy, rational virtues, and are plants, stones, and remains that ground us. This includes plants that live close to the earth, growing low and slow; stones that ground us and help centre our focus; and remains of animals that live slow and long lives or live within holes. Moles' feet, as amulets of protection, make for a good example of these Earthly virtues. So do plants like blóðberg (*Thymus praecox*) that help ground us and provide slow, solid healing, and stones like tourmaline and onyx, which help ground our energies and focus us in the physical.

Watery materia concerns itself most often with emotions, healing, and the subconscious realm of dreams. The materia we can work with that emphasises the virtues of Water may be plants that grow in water or close to it, stones that aid in dream work and the opening of the mind and flow of emotions, and remains of animals that either live in water or spend time living near it. The bones and remains of sea birds, amphibians, and more—especially whale bones—can be worked for their Watery virtues. Plants such as vallhumall (*Achillea millefoloum*), as well as willow species (*Salix spp.*), work well to align us with Watery virtues. These plants often grow in wet locations, showing us their alignment with this element. Some stones ruled by Water include agates and coral.

Airy materia reveals itself as materia that aids in communication, opens paths, and governs intellect and speech, as well as aids in memory and other mental concerns. Materia that aids us in emphasising Airy virtues includes the bones and feathers of birds; remains of animals known for cunning, such as the fox; stones that inspire and aid in the realm of study and thought, such as amethyst and sunstone; and Airy plants include those which grow in high places, such as the Icelandic highlands and areas above the treeline. Augnfró (*Euphrasia frigida*) is a good example of an Airy plant we can work with for virtues ruled by Air, as the plant reveals truth and aids in thought, memory, and improving mood.

Fiery materia is that which concerns itself with Martial power, heated emotion, and, oftentimes, emotions and qualities that tend to be put down as sinful or bad if uncontrolled. Fiery materia includes objects like hrafntinna (obsidian), the remains of many reptiles which rely on the heat of the sun to live, and plants concerned with lust, war, and might. Sunflowers are ruled by the Sun as well as Fire. Einir (*Juniperus communis*) is another example of a Fiery plant, showing us the strong protective virtues of this element. Other stones include carnelian, which inspires lust, and amber, which entices and allures.

Taking it a step deeper, I work with four magical foci; these sigils cover four main goals towards which we most frequently work magic. Each focus can be used to focus and empower materia towards a relevant end. The sigils can also be worked as individual talismans, carved or etched in various materials, and carried to focus on these goals. I use them mostly to empower materia within a certain day and time, working planetary magic alongside these symbols. They are part of my unverified personal gnosis (UPG)—beliefs based on my relationship to and understanding of folk magic—and I have found them effective and complimentary to my practice for well over a decade. Our own unique relationships with spirits, tools, and practices are valuable, though we must remember not to state our own experiences as fact. Even more "verified" group gnosis should be rooted in folklore, or at least draw heavily from it, should we want to make greater claims. Throughout the book, I mention my own design and UPG, what comes from group gnosis, and what is directly from folklore. Please feel free to use all of these UPGs and workings: try them, test them, and tweak them if you want. All good UPG should, at the very least, inspire us to create or find and develop our own gnosis.

The first was designed for workings of healing, aiding, increasing, and receiving. It can be used to empower materia concerned with Venusian healing, Jovial increase, and Solar luck, to name a few. Work herbs and charms for healing with this focus.

The second focus concerns workings of decrease, harm, and hexing. This focus should be used to empower all materia used for active malefica. Where the fourth focus might be the most appropriate for binding, this focus is best used for active offense. All Martial works of protection with outward spikes should utilise this focus.

The third is a focus I created to balance. This focus is worked to centre, focus, balance, and ground. It can be included in spells for stability or for grounding energy as an aid for returning to one's body after intense spirit flight. It can be worked to aid in the creation of magical medicine to realign oneself after periods of illness, stress, or change, or it can be worked into spells to make things remain as they are.

The fourth focus aids in change, transformation, and fluidity. It is concerned with spells of manifestation, worked alongside materia that encourages communication, change, and new beginnings. It is mainly concerned with work that utilises Mercurial materia, though there are many crossovers that we can utilise this sigil for. Moving from one state to another can involve the influence of any planetary power. We could use it to empower materia designed to bring in business if our business is struggling, or bring about a new relationship, friendship, or lover.

I also work with an altar cloth that I have created to combine all these foci, along with the planetary septagram. The following diagram shows the way I position these symbols on one altar cloth. I opted to paint this, but if you have the time and patience, you could embroider or print this out.

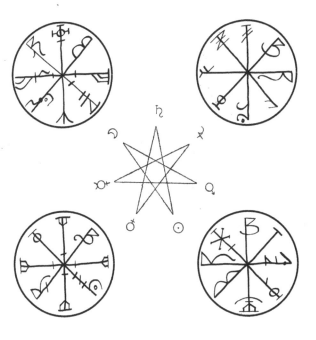

This layout allows me to place the object I wish to empower within the centre of the cloth. Alongside it goes a small candle, anointed with a planetary oil on the most appropriate planetary symbol, along with materia to be focused on the circle of the most appropriate magical foci. I work this cloth as my main ritual space when empowering herbs, enchanting talismans, and creating charm bags.

For example, creating a talisman for clear communication can be worked by placing the talisman in the centre of the septagram, anointing a small candle with a Mercurial oil and placing it on the symbol of Mercury, then placing the relevant materia on foci number four (for fluid change and communication). An invocation of the spirits of Mercury is then read aloud, and the enchantment to be made is spoken over the talisman, burning incense and utilising any tools you wish to use in the space around you. When speaking what you wish, use wording such as:

"Lord Mercury, I ask that you empower this materia,
Through this focus, combine and align your powers of
communication into this talisman.
Bring about that which I ask,
Lord of communication, travel, and thieves,
I ask this of you, humbly…"

This sort of working can also be performed within one of the two examples of simple magic circles found on page 133. This sort of planetary invocation can also be performed using the planetary innsigli presented previously. Each can be worked with candles, herbs, and other materia to focus and empower planetary virtues.

2

Landvættur: The Giant, the Dragon, the Eagle and the Bull

Many magical practices and systems include an elemental and directional aspect as a central theme. Agrippa shows us the place for the classical four elements in *The Philosophy of Natural Magic*, providing the importance of the elements relating to planetary forces and as rulers over all the material world. Many magical frameworks equate the elements to directions, with the Wiccan four watchtowers being one of the best-known examples. Water belongs to the West in this idea, ruling over emotions, psychic powers, and the subconscious, among other things. Air belongs to the East, bringing mental powers, invention, inspiration, and more. The Earth belongs to the North, grounded and realistic, concerned with wealth and the physical. And Fire belongs to the South, ruling, among other things, passion and all things fuelled by it.

Within Icelandic folk magic, as well as more formal Ásatrú, the four corners of the sky (cardinal directions) are held aloft by four dwarves. Their names are Austri (East), Vestri (West), Suðri (South), and Norðri (North). It is both good practice and beneficial to call upon them before performing any ceremony, though we could also work with Skírnismál, and call upon the forces and spirits, "Heyri jötnar, heyri hrímþursar, synir Suttungs." This hails the giants and natural forces to be present while we do our work and ceremonies.

During ceremonies, we sing out to them, chanting their names in rhythm and building our voices until we loudly call before falling silent and listening out (and often feeling out) to see if they offer any resistance to our work or intentions. If they do, we know that this is not the time and place for whatever we wish to work. If they allow us, we go ahead, recognising that we, as mere mortals, are subject to the will of these spirits as forces of nature and rulers of the sometimes harsh environment we live in.

While we recognise these four directional forces as important, we also recognise four other rulers of the land. These four landvættir are known throughout the island, appearing on both the coat of arms of the country as well as being depicted on the back of all Icelandic kronur coins. Their use likely stems from medieval heraldry and the resurgence in interest in this aspect of the past, but their spirits are indeed felt throughout the country. These four beings also each rule a direction, as well as being the rulers of their own legions of nature spirits, land spirits, and, depending on sources and situations, sometimes more. These four landvættir are as follows.

Gammur, the eagle of the harsh North. He is a giant eagle who rules the sky and all spirits of the wind, weather, and more. King of the bird and winds, he is called upon for much of the weather magic we work, as well as anything relating to Air. The word *gammur* is an older word for "eagle."

In the South lives a stone giant known as Bergrisi. His court of spirits includes all those of earth, stone, rock, and soil. Within folk magic, we call upon him and his court for works regarding typical Earth elemental associations such as wealth, strength, material possessions, and fortitude. He rules the giants—Jötnar—within Iceland, standing higher than the hilltops with his great iron staff. We know his name as Járngrímur (iron mask).

In the West, a great Bull, Griðungur, is the ruler of Water and all aqueous spirits. *Griðungur*, like gammur, is an old word meaning "bull." Although many consider the bull and cow animals of the land, in Icelandic folklore, mermaids, seas-dwelling spirits, and gods also rear cattle, occasionally giving them as gifts to fishermen and farmers. Many other animal spirits fall under Griðungur.

A giant dragon, Dreki, rules the land and sky of the East. Dreki is the king of all the volcanic spirits of the island, as well as the ruler of all spirits that resemble serpents and lizards. While he rules Fire and all it entails, the East is a lot less volcanic and geothermally active. We call on Dreki as the King of Fire.

These four landvættir are regarded as the protectors of the land and have been called on time and again to defend it. One such tale goes as follows: long ago, the Danish king Harald Bluetooth asked his court wizard to travel to Iceland in the form of a great whale spirit, attempting to consolidate power over the people and land. The spirits of the land rose about the island, and each time he tried to find a place to land ships, they appeared to scare him off. He first came to the East, but upon nearing the shore, Dreki, the giant dragon, flew down from above. His piercing cry rang out, and soon, the mountainside was filled with all the spirits of his court. His hoards of serpents and lizards, spitting poison and volcanic fumes, flooded down the mountainside, driving the wizard-whale away.

He then swam West, deep into Eyjafjörður, home to Akureyri, the capital of the North. The water of the deep fjord rippled. Suddenly, he heard a great roar from Gammur, the giant eagle of the North, whose wings were so wide they touched opposite sides of the mountain at the edge of the deep fjord. Soon, the sky was filled with his court of birds and Air spirits. The whale-wizard swam on, skirting the dramatic peaks and fjords of the Northwest and into the many small uninhabited islands of Breiðafjörður.

From a deep mist, he heard a deep, angry bellow. The giant bull Griðungur and his court of animal and water spirits appeared, blocking the way of the wizard. The whale-wizard swam further West, then South, around to the Reykjanes peninsula. He tried to come ashore at Vikarsskeið but stopped when the final ruling landvættur appeared. Bergrisi, the giant of the South, ruler of all Iceland's Jötnar, an impressive mountain giant higher than all the hills, loomed over the whale-wizard with his iron staff in hand. The whale-wizard was bested; he couldn't find anywhere to land on such a desolate island. So, he swam back and told the king of Denmark that this was an unworthy wasteland, saving his own pride (as well as Iceland) as he did so.

From a modern perspective, we could say these four spirits watch over this island and can be felt if you so choose to work with them, though we do recognize many other varied landvættir. It is also worth remembering that these spirits may well be inspired by the four evangelists, and where they can be worked with as any spirit, those who wish to be more purely folkloric in their approach may do better simply acknowledging the land spirits in general. Iceland's older animistic worldview plays a central role in the way we perform and practice our magic, knowing that all spirits who dwell here deserve respect and should be worked with, not against, lest, just like the forces of nature they rule over, they turn on us and return the island to its rightful inhabitants.

The island's attitude of animism is infrequently fully realised nowadays by many of its inhabitants. *Andartrú* (animism), or spirit belief, was likely so commonplace that now it's more likely to be overlooked. People here still acknowledge the álfar and vættir (as fun folktales or not), heed warnings of destroying nature, and commonly speak on the repercussions. I believe this is animism persisting. Though people may not be acutely aware of the spirits, their land and homes are still respected. A word we have coined for contemporary animism in Iceland is *náttúrutrú* (nature belief). This is not in common use as much as we would like, but it encompasses the animistic ideals and mindsets of those who live in Iceland. These ideals are often confirmed in folk tales as well as written sources, for example, mentions of landvættir in Landnámsbók and sagas.

These spirits are often present before the settlers move in to build farms and must first be appeased. Deals and pacts, one aspect of magical work common the world over, would likely have been involved. For those of you who live within their small local areas, landvættir are to be approached for your own sake; they rule the land around you and, to the minds of many animistic spiritual folks, can just as easily harm those who live there as well as help them.

Specific spots are also tied to landvættir. In both sagas and in living practice, we acknowledge specific rocks, waterfalls, hills, and more as their homes. Something that carries into, and often was blended with, later elf beliefs. Older ideas around this, for example, those of *Úlfljótslög*—the first set of laws recorded in Iceland in 930—include the removal of the heads of ships before approaching land so as not to incite fear or anger from the landwights. The landvættur of farms and fields have much in common with the later beliefs of Tomte and Nisse in Scandinavia.

3

Undir Haugnum: Under the Mound

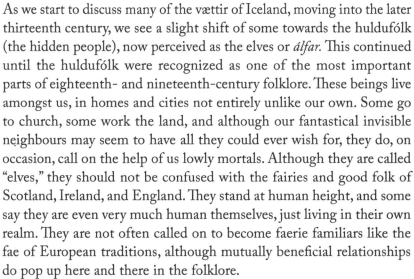

As we start to discuss many of the vættir of Iceland, moving into the later thirteenth century, we see a slight shift of some towards the huldufólk (the hidden people), now perceived as the elves or *álfar*. This continued until the huldufólk were recognized as one of the most important parts of eighteenth- and nineteenth-century folklore. These beings live amongst us, in homes and cities not entirely unlike our own. Some go to church, some work the land, and although our fantastical invisible neighbours may seem to have all they could ever wish for, they do, on occasion, call on the help of us lowly mortals. Although they are called "elves," they should not be confused with the fairies and good folk of Scotland, Ireland, and England. They stand at human height, and some say they are even very much human themselves, just living in their own realm. They are not often called on to become faerie familiars like the fae of European traditions, although mutually beneficial relationships do pop up here and there in the folklore.

Huldufólk can be solitary or living within cities, such as their capital, the dramatic U-shaped valley of Ásbyrgi, said to be formed by the footprint of Sleipnir (offspring of the god Loki and steed to Óðinn). A visit to this impressive valley around dusk during the time of year when day and night sit equal is sure to give one all the evidence they need that the hidden people inhabit the valley. Belief in the álfar is a central part of Icelandic folklore, and the respect and, in my opinion, a healthy amount of fear held for them is a necessity. Prone to both vengeance and sometimes outright cruelty, the álfar have always manipulated and punished those who do them wrong, especially if this has come as a betrayal after one has previously gone to some lengths to help them. One story involving the secrets of the hidden people, which plays a role in the use of magical ointments in Icelandic tradition, comes from folklorist Jón Árnason.

One night, a woman with some skill as a midwife received a knock on the door to her farm. She thought it odd that such a thing should happen due to the late hour and location of her home, which was somewhat out of the way of others. She answered and was greeted by a man asking for her aid in a birth. The woman agreed to help and went along with him. During the journey, she noticed a few peculiarities about the man, but being a good Christian woman, she reserved judgment. The man led her to a large stone boulder that stood quite dramatic in the landscape in the middle of a neighbour's field. He knocked three times on the stone, and suddenly, the stone was no longer a stone but a rather beautiful, stately-looking home.

The woman was ushered inside and was soon surrounded by a handful of the most beautiful people she had ever seen. In the centre of the room lay a blonde-haired woman who was about to give birth. She was in great pain and thankful that the woman had arrived in such good time. After a difficult but successful birth, the woman was handed a green ointment. She was instructed to anoint the new babe's eyes with the ointment and then thoroughly wash her hands so no trace of it was left on her. Knowing that these hidden people often had great wealth and secret knowledge, the woman made sure to sneak a small amount of the ointment for herself. After all this was done, she was thanked and led out of the house, down through the field, and home. When she got home, she made sure to anoint herself with a little of the ointment, then promptly fell asleep.

Upon waking, she didn't believe the events of the previous night and thought they were a dream until later that day when she went into the village. She now saw beautiful people walking amongst the people she knew. Thinking herself very cunning, she made a great effort to pretend she didn't see the hidden people around her. For many years, she watched them, learning from their actions, how to predict the weather, and eavesdropping on their conversations. She learned a great deal from them, heard their beautiful singing in church, and watched their curious ways.

She used this knowledge to help the local farmers predict the weather and always knew which crops to grow after seeing what the hidden people had planted. She maintained her secret for many years until one day she saw the woman she had played midwife to wandering about the village. Forgetting herself for a moment, she approached her and spoke to her. But once the elf woman knew she had been seen, she spat into the eyes of her former midwife, rendering her magical sight powerless. The woman lost her gift to see the hidden people and all that they were doing from that day on.

Blending folklore such as this with our own practical magic, we make use of a few ointments for similar purposes, mainly to help us connect to the spirits of the land (and sometimes to check in suspected cases of the hidden people meddling with our business). A recipe for a practical ointment to help us engage with spirits can be found on page 298.

Though the huldufólk were seen as elves through nineteenth-century folklore and into modern times, this is not the way they've always been understood. Just as with Óðinn, we see how scholars' ideas and understanding of the álfar have changed over time in Iceland. Terry Gunnell, in his paper "How Elvish Were the Álfar?" gives explanations as to how many of these elf beliefs were assimilated with those of landvættir and dísir in Iceland and reminds us, as I will mention later, that we need to remember the context of Snorri's *Prose Edda* and who exactly he was writing this for. The elves of today may well be the dísir, landvættir, and dvergar of yesterday; elves and bergbúar (rock-dwellers) may not have always been lumped into the same category either.

Ointments, magical stones, and other objects (*náttúrur,* as we call them) need to be collected on special days at special times, and even sometimes only appear to you once the land spirits have left them as reciprocated offerings in appreciation of your desire to build a relationship with them. St. John's Eve (*Jónsmessa* in Icelandic) is one such day when special náttúrur are to be gathered. On that night, certain stones can be found to grant invisibility, bring protection, and much more. Sometimes, álfar may leave these out for you, though be wary of tricks.

One similarity that many huldufólk share with the fae of the Gaelic world is that they sometimes live underneath or within mounds, hills, and boulders. We have already heard of the elf woman living within the boulder. Visiting their realm is sometimes only a dream away, although one need not dream when there are other methods of consulting spirits within Icelandic tradition. Útiseta (sitting out) is a technique with many different practical applications. There are many ways we can engage with this practice, but keep in mind that it is reserved for use at various liminal times and specific times of the year, such as Jónsmessa and those liminal moments between days. For the purpose of guiding, I will lay out the details of how I engage with it.

Firstly, good tools are essential. Although the ability to directly connect with spirits is something we can all achieve, some may take to it more naturally than others. For these people, fewer tools are needed. However, I am not one of these people, so the advice I will give now is somewhat hard-won. A drum can be your best friend for practices that involve invoking spirits, and if working with one, then employing the aid of a magical stave is a perfect way to bring together two aspects of Icelandic magic.

As well as the drum and these staves, one stave is worked to "open hills." This stave is called *hólastafur*, and it is worked by being carved into a staff of rowan wood that is used to "knock" on mounds before they open to you. Traditionally, the rowan stick is whittled down into a wand, but it works just as well on a staff and makes our staff a multi-purpose tool.

It makes a worthy inclusion in this sort of spirit work, though it should come with a word of caution. Thinking from an animistic perspective, spirits are their own entities with thoughts and feelings. If someone you don't know came to your home, opened the door, and started causing a disturbance, how would you feel? How might you react? Working the following stave without first establishing some contact with the residents of said hill might result in a lot of potentially dangerous anger coming your way. So, think carefully and establish connections before you go intruding.

Plenty of herbs and flowers make excellent offerings to leave before holding útiseta and, indeed, any ceremony in spaces. This is a good very first step for those who might be a little nervous to sit outside all night long. Another good thing to do before you sit out anywhere is to do some research about the land and even the specific mound you're sitting on. If you're in the UK, it's very likely that local archaeological records of the area exist and should be available somewhere. Local libraries often have these. In the US, be mindful of the lands' previous inhabitants and their spirits before doing any further damage in the eyes of these spirits. Always ask, wait, and be honest with yourself if the answer you receive is not one you hoped for.

The basic ceremony we follow around útiseta starts with finding a suitable space. Leave offerings and speak aloud to the spirits that you intend to come back to and commune with them later. If you feel a clear desire that they are open to this, once dusk comes, return to the spot. Set up a small fire and bring a fireproof dish with you. I bring a small charcoal disc to burn incense on in the space first to clear any negative or harmful spirits away before I invite others to be present and commune with me. The point of this technique is to sit, listen, and receive. So, sit out for as long as you feel called to. Use the fire as a meditative tool to get into a relaxed state of mind. Some may drum for a while to call up the spirits, then put the drum down and listen. Keep in mind that the drum is not used in the older traditional methods. Listen and absorb until you meld into the land. If needed, I'll repeat this a few times throughout the night. Sometimes, I bring a notebook to make notes of whatever I am receiving, though it can be hard to put these experiences into words.

The most traditional—as well as fantastical—method is detailed by Jón Árnason in *Þjóðsögur og Ævfíntýri*. If you want to do things by the book, then you must find yourself a grey sheepskin (sometimes described as just a grey cloak); there is also mention of sitting with cats or working cat skins. Heading out to a four-way crossroads at night, one with a road or, ideally, two roads that lead to a church. Prepare your space and lay down wrapped in your grey skin or cloak. You should then lay still all night and remain awake while the elves pass you by, sometimes offering gifts and knowledge. If you move or speak or go to take these gifts, they will all vanish. This perfectly details the breaking of trance-state, ending the útiseta. If one can successfully endure the night and all the temptations that have been put before them, they are then said to be able to contact the hidden people, spirits, and more, calling on them to access secret knowledge and more. The spirits of the dead are also said to be at one's beck and call after a successful útiseta, though in contemporary practice, this is often dependant on the spirits we call up, how long they have been dead, and whether we would class them as unclean or not. We draw a line between the spirits called up depending on whether we are working uppvakningar and invoking anything during an útiseta.

Útiseta can be used to call on the dead sometimes. When this is an active focus, I wouldn't call this útiseta, though; rather, we fall into the realm of intentional *andasæring:* necromancy. *Andasæring* literally translates to "spirit conjuring." The dead who show up during útiseta are often the long dead, assimilated into the land often over hundreds of years, whereas we can work specific necromancy on spirits that we can identify, most often calling them up from a Christian grave as opposed to a Pagan burial mound or cairn. Do you want the spirit of a Viking-age chieftain to be at your disposal? Or that of a local farmer? Each has their own areas of expertise and knowledge to offer, so choose wisely, and depending on the method we choose to communicate with them, we will have vastly different results. This sort of spirit communication has played a role in Nordic magic for a long time. We can look to Grógaldur, for instance, to see examples of spirits called up from beyond the grave for their knowledge.

Our understanding of the spirit world, as well as that of the spirit themselves, can often affect how we work with them. Pre-Christian Icelanders, and indeed many long after Kristnitakan, would have still acknowledged that upon death, spirits entered the mounds and hills. Helgafell á Snæfellsnesi was long regarded as the place where souls travelled after death, even after Christianity came to Iceland. If we plan to raise a spirit that both acknowledges that it lives on in the mound and doesn't look at the veil between the living and the dead as so strict, we may have more success calling it up. Simply knocking may be good enough. On the other hand, if you plan to call up a more recently deceased spirit from the pure and holy afterlife of the Christian heaven, it may have a little more resistance to being woken up.

4

TRÖLLIN Í FJÖLLUNUM: THE TROLLS IN THE HILLS

Some areas of the land in Iceland, and indeed other countries, are out of bounds. Our ancestors knew this, refusing to settle them and not seeing these places as dead land ready for new real estate. Sadly, however, in many countries, some of these areas have been built on, causing confusion about the spirits of the land and, in some cases, intense hauntings and negative spiritual activity. In Iceland, the land is in charge, whether that refers to life being at the whim of the weather or when elf stones stand in the way of new roadworks. Some areas are home to trolls; these are usually more desolate and isolated places that are no place for man.

One story from Jón Árnason's *Þjóðsögur og Ævfintýri* tells us of two men camping in one such tröll place. During the middle of the night, one of the two awoke to the sight of the other slipping out of the tent. Upon following his sleepwalking companion, he saw a huge troll sitting on a nearby hilltop, beckoning to the sleepwalking man. She was calling out to him. The sleepwalker sped up, so much so that the second man couldn't catch up, and the sleepwalker was lost to the troll. Sometime later the following summer, the sleepwalker was spotted again by some foragers picking herbs in the area. He looked dead-eyed and weary. They asked him if he still believed in God. He replied that he did, then wandered away. The following year, he was seen at the same time by the same group, but his appearance had grown more trollish. They asked again, and this made the man angry, so the foragers left the area quickly to avoid him.

The next year, they returned and were greeted by the man. He had now become a fearsome troll: his features were warped, and he had a terrifying aura about him. When one of the foragers plucked up the courage to ask if he still believed in God, he proclaimed he belonged to "Trunt and the trolls in the knolls." The poor man had completely forgotten the "word of God," moving from Christian to Heathen, which would have made him a dangerous and troll-like outsider to the audience of the time. The foragers ran away, fleeing in terror from this Heathen tröll, and the story mentions that the area was left well alone for many years after. This is a stark contrast from the tröll of pre-Christian times. In modern Iceland, the saying *tryggur sem tröll*, meaning "loyal as a troll," leans in favour of the devolution of the noble and respected Jötnar to the ugly and dangerous troll.

The stories serve as warnings that we shouldn't forget. These troll areas are usually known either by folklore or by the darker and scarier feeling one gets when wandering near them. Of course, identifying troll areas takes a certain level of discernment on your part, working out which energy and feeling is coming from the place. These troll areas, just like in the folk story, should not be foraged in. Everything here belongs to the trolls. Sometimes, these areas are populated with certain "troll-plants." These trölljurtir should be avoided and never picked or removed. Taking these troll-plants is likely to incur the wrath of the spirits of the place, and trolls have a talent for creating bad weather, which in Iceland can be potentially life-threatening. So, it's best to leave things be if you feel at all like the area belongs to trolls.

Some areas don't just belong to trolls. As we learned earlier, elves have their own spaces, as do the dead in certain graveyards. Sea spirits sometimes live both in the sea as well as venturing into marshland, so it pays to do a little research before you dive straight into a new area. Icelandic sea spirits are tricky and often dangerous; many stories warn us to be wary of the sea and marshland. If you work more with gods and deities, I recommend giving offerings to Rán and Ægir before venturing into their realm, always bearing in mind that Rán keeps the souls of those drowned or lost at sea in her underwater realm. An incense that may be burned at beaches to honour Rán can be found later.

Marshes are wonderful places to find special magical herbs, plants like hófsóley (*Caltha palustris*), hrafnaklukka (*Cardamine pratensis*), and hrafnafífa (*Eriophorum scheuchzeri*) grow abundantly here, all with their own magic. The marsh, however, has always been a potentially dangerous place for humans. Deep sinkholes can open beneath you, maybe leading right into the lair of the nykur, a fearsome water horse with backward hooves. The will-o'-the-wisp doesn't make an appearance in Icelandic folklore, but other dangerous creatures and ghosts stalk the marshlands, mires, and more.

The basic rule to follow when foraging or disturbing any land in Iceland is to be respectful, listen to the land, and leave some offering to show that you mean no harm. Speak aloud to the spirits and let the land know your intentions before preparing to perform any sort of ceremony or working.

BECOMING TROLLISH

Within the other Nordic countries, trolldom is used to refer to magic, the realm of trolls, otherness, and witchcraft. In Iceland, this is not exactly the same perspective. In Iceland, the word *tröll* refers only to the spirits of trolls as well as those spirits, people, and other life forms that have become trollish. Tröll is both a mantle and a description. Tröll are often night-walking beings, often those who were once human, though some have always belonged to nature. Upon moving from life to spirit, some people, or the shades of these people, may remain—now aspects of their once questionable character.

Within an animistic framework, this is one way we can break down what happens after life, with the threefold soul (or further divisions of this) separating once more: one part returns to the ether, one to nature, and one joining the courts of those closest to us in life, both blood relatives and spiritual relatives gained through initiations, tribes, or other non-blood connections, and those attached to us from previous incarnations. The process of a spirit becoming trollish likely begins during their lifetime. One who holds grudges or is unhelpful, abusive, angry, and otherwise not someone many would like to be around may well be on this path. We can look at older Norse sources such as the Hávamál for guides on how to avoid this process, which could be argued to be very tied into aspects of Viking age expectations of hospitality and generally being a good person. This is, of course, my opinion on the subject, and indeed, a mishmash of many ideas around this subject mixed into my own animistic take on things.

To become a troll, one needs to be selfish, dark-natured, antagonistic, and, maybe worst of all, remorseless. Many aspects of this character are said to be shared by sorcerers. We see folk practice the world over talk of dead magicians and witches whose spirits live on as vengeful dead or guardians of graves, treasure, and areas of land, as well as common folk who exhibit these behaviours. Within Icelandic folklore and culture, it wouldn't have paid to hoard resources and wealth, though, of course, we see plenty of examples of this being exactly what happened. In a country of limited resources, we find stories of hoarders, criminals, and even cannibals becoming trollish.

We'll start first with hoarders. One story regarding Bárður, the legendary half-troll guardian spirit of the Snæfellsnes peninsula, tells us of a couple hated by many in the area for their vile behaviour and selfish actions. Bárður's likeness can be seen made of stone in the town of Árnarstapi, overlooking the dramatic sea cliffs below. The couple in question were selfish, often hoarding food in harsh winters and not doing their part to ensure the survival of the town. One day, a whale was beached at Þúfubjarg, a rocky cliff beach down the coast. The town was made aware of its presence, and in this time of need, the whale served as an unexpected gift of food for the town. Bárður forbid anyone to go near it until the following morning when all the residents would be together and could all take their fair share. The couple, ignoring this, went alone in the night. Bárður suspected this and was waiting for them to arrive. Once they arrived and began taking the meat, he made his presence known and fought the couple. After a short struggle, he defeated them, crushing them both with large boulders and his legendary strength. The beach has since been known as a dangerous place, one that surrounds itself with stories of trolls, elf church, and the devil. Were the spirits of these trollish people left behind after death?

Criminals have been said to become trolls in death. Hengill, a mountain near Reykjavík, is home to geothermal springs and tales of trolls. The legendary Jóra was said to have lived here once she had become a troll. Other stories tell us of criminals who lived in caves on the mountain, surviving harsh winters by robbing passersby and stealing cattle. The stories say that these thieves were taking greater amounts of sheep than was possible for their number. Warnings that they had become trolls endowed with preternatural strength grew, and the area was avoided more often. Even today, the area has a trollish feel to it, with plenty of spooky rock formations and spirits roaming the land.

Being trollish within the folklore of Iceland also involves unsavoury acts like cannibalism. In a land of bleak winters, stories of cannibal outlaws during especially hard times are not so outlandish. One story tells of a group of outlaws holed up in an abandoned cabin. They manage to capture a passerby who is, in turn, rescued, and the cannibals are slain. Tales of cannibalism in harsh times echo the North American tales of the wendigo: a human transformed by this horrible act into another creature entirely.

Many trolls are known to be man-eaters. Most famously of all is Grýla, who straddles the fence between troll and winter spirit. She and her giant Yule cat wander the countryside, awaiting unfortunate travellers to ambush, as well as purposefully catching misbehaving children. Grýla is said to have a fondness for eating children, all of which she cooks in the giant cauldron in her cave. Many troll stories warn of the danger of being eaten by trolls. Could it stem from that cannibalism or some ancient memory related to becoming trollish? Where this is not something we will likely ever explore, it is interesting to note that what makes one trollish in nature is the same words one would use to describe cannibals.

One can become trollish, both in life and death, without resorting to cannibalism; we have seen a few stories now of how this can happen. As mentioned previously, we can even see how one becomes trollish from simply being in the wrong place at the wrong time and unable to counter the influence of dangerous spirits. Maybe this danger, or perceived danger, is one reason for so much exorcism and banishment work within Icelandic practice. We see trolls and travellers using words as weapons, trying to outsmart each other with their choice of rhymes, the loser often losing more than just a rap battle. At the end of the day, it pays to not be trollish, whether you live within Icelandic society or anywhere else in the world. These warnings are even taken at face value as cautionary tales and teach us it never pays to be a troll.

5

Viðvörun Egils: The Warning of Egill

Egill Skalla-Grímsson, the skaldic poet and anti-hero of *Egil's Saga, Skallagrímssonar*, delivers a famous warning to those who work with staves and runes. During the saga, he examines a sick woman who was the victim of what was supposed to be love magic. The charm, which had been carved and left under the woman's bed, was carved incorrectly, resulting in her sickness. Egill fixes the runes on the charm, and the girl instantly recovers. He then gives the warning that one should never work with runes and, further, should never carve runes or staves that one does not fully understand:

> *"Skalat maðr rúnar rísta,*
> *nema ráða vel kunni.*

> "A man must not carve runes unless
> he knows well how to interpret them.

> *Þat verðr mörgum manni,*
> *es of myrkvan staf villisk.*

> It happens to many men that the dark
> stave goes wrong.

> *Sák á telgðu talkni tíu*
> *launstafi ristna.*

> I saw on the hewn whalebone ten
> secret letters carved.

> *Þat hefr lauka lindi langs*
> *ofrtrega fengit."*

> That has brought long suffering to
> the linden-of-leeks."

This warning should be held in high regard, as working with these forces and powers can and occasionally does take a grave toll. Some stories have mentioned the deterioration of mental and physical health because of angering spirits and powers that weren't shown the proper respect. What I take from this warning is to be as informed as one can be, read often, and practice critical thinking. Don't jump the gun and dive right into things that you don't understand, at least somewhat thoroughly. Plant spirits are sometimes more forgiving, but other spirits may not be.

One should not expect or assume that the spirits will simply bend to their will. We aren't ceremonial magicians conjuring and controlling demons; we are folk practitioners working with the land. The strong emphasis should always be on the "with," and it pays to never forget this. Setting aside personal disappointment when the spirits discourage a working or you from being in an area will save you a lot of trouble.

There are also workings that one should never take lightly. To birth a tilberi that then runs rampant and wreaks havoc—and that can even follow families for generations—is more of a common occurrence than one would believe. Working with plants such as holtasóley (*Dryas octopetula*) and the spirits of the dead can lead to all sorts of problems with parasitic spirits. These "magical ticks" are often harder to remove than they are to invite. Necromancy in Icelandic folk magic shouldn't be taken lightly, either.

Working a níðstöng (a cursing pole) is something that might sound cool or flashy to newcomers to Northern traditions, but without an understanding of the mechanics of this magic, one can cause a whole boatload of issues that might then make the landvættir turn from all practitioners in the area. We see examples of this sort of damaging seiður in Buslubæn, which I discuss in more detail later. Working sendingar is also risky business for those not well versed in this sort of magic. It pays to listen first, learn second, and practice third. Find teachers and practitioners who live within the land you wish to learn from before looking for those who live elsewhere. Read as much folklore as you can, if not at least for the warnings many stories carry.

As mentioned in the previous chapter, certain plants and areas belong to trolls in Iceland. In contemporary folk magic, certain plants are considered trölljurtir (troll herbs); these troll plants should be avoided. They are not simply a list of species. Any plant can belong to the trolls, and it is up to the foraging practitioner to deduce which plants are not for us. Like trolls, some areas and plants also belong to the hidden people. This also extends to stones known as álfsteinar (elf stones) and larger groups of stones or small hills, which we call *álfaborgir* (elf settlements). This is why the practice of asking permission to enter the places in which we forage and gather materia is so important.

We must also take the law into consideration. Some Icelandic folk magic involves the use of endangered and protected species of orchid. These we don't forage. On the same theme, certain spells call for staves to be carved into various materials, some of which may not be legal to acquire in your area, such as human bone. Some are less savoury, such as fresh animal skins. Others may be impractical to many. Lignite (*surtarbrandur* in Icelandic) may be found in areas protected by law, and the removal of this is a crime; even entering these spots can be illegal without a ranger or guide.

Angry spirits and the unclean dead are often warned about in Icelandic folklore, and we would do well to heed warnings about these spirits. Certain spirits have been known to follow and cause all sorts of trouble. It would be incredibly unwise for us in Iceland to begin working in an area that is known to belong to an unfriendly spirit, much less spend time there. Folktales echo the fate of those who mess with certain spaces. Even children have been known to be punished by spirits for their innocent and unintentional upsetting of peace within these spaces. We would do well to avoid working magic or creating ripples of unrest in the lonely and often desolate spaces we know to be inhabited by trolls. Keep in mind the boundaries of these areas can be hard to define, though sometimes working magic is permitted not one hundred metres away in the next valley. These spaces don't often follow rules that seem logical to us material humans. We are also forbidden to disturb certain areas where spirits have been laid lest we incur the wrath of whatever lays trapped within the earth or, worse, set it free.

I also wanted to mention two other points. The first is about the use of blood in empowering staves. As mentioned elsewhere, we don't always need to use blood. We can work the lifeblood of plant materia, as well as mixtures involving blends of this materia with ground dragon's blood. This potent resin has been worked in many aspects of magic in various traditions. We can work it as incense, but working it into this "false blood" creates a potent mix of different plant materia suitable for the empowering of many staves. As we know, blood is life—specifically, our own magical signature of that life—and, when worked into spells, creates very personal magic. By adding spittle to these blends of materia, we create a link to ourselves that is suitable enough for many staves and workings. For the squeamish, this opens doorways and creates opportunities for powerful magic without the use of blood. The over-use of blood is also a danger, so I suggest working a mix of these two methods for the best effect.

The last point is about human hubris. Putting our own perceived needs above the land and its spirits is a product of both Western individualism as well as capitalism. Sadly, for many, our wishes do not supersede those of the land. And as magical—especially animistic-focused—practitioners, we must recognise this in all we do. This can be a hard lesson to learn, but one that, without constant work, leaves us to fall victim to our own hubris. Remember, simply, that if a working doesn't feel good, and our confirmational divination gives us further proof, we do not do it. While we all have our own varying amounts of personal power, the majority of the energy and magic we access belongs to the land and its spirits. Should we anger them, they may well deny us this access. It is a poor spiritual practice to ignore the land, and as we can see from many folk stories, those who do don't tend to fare well.

6

DRAUGAR, VÆTTIR, OG GOÐ: GHOSTS, SPIRITS, AND THE GODS

In Iceland, the word *landvættir* may refer to the spirits of the land that are natural, human, animal, and all things in between. Local landvættir may be called on for protection, fertility, or aid and should be given suitable offerings as compensation. This practice is a good first step to working with local spirits of all kinds. Many Neo-Pagan practices emphasise working with deities. Within contemporary Icelandic folk magic, this is not as common as one would think. We do work with the gods, but we do so within an animistic framework, understanding that the big "high-ups" are occasionally less likely to work with us than the local spirits around us.

Often, Norse Pagan deity work emphasizes Freyr and Freyja as the lord and lady. This may well be the most accurate for much of the pre-Christian faith in Scandinavia and Northern Europe. Though we often see Óðinn as both a high king of the Æsir and a figure one could associate with a folk devil and witch father, as Snorri paints him, it is unlikely that Óðinn would have been regarded in the way most modern Neo-Pagan traditions see him. It pays to remember that Snorri was writing (and possibly reshaping) Norse mythology to best fit his audience of rich Norwegian kings, who he stood to make the most money from and gain political favour through. As Terry Gunnell lays out in his chapter of *Theorizing Old Norse Myth*, Óðinn was "little known" or, at the very least, less revered in Iceland based on the prominence of Freyr and Þór in Landnámabók (105).

This doesn't mean that we shouldn't be working with Óðinn. We should just keep this information in mind for historical accuracy. In fact, due to the more modern (or at least twentieth-century) perceptions of Óðinn, I argue that we would do better working with him as the witch father figure. Within contemporary witchcraft and Pagan circles, his wide-brimmed hat and Mercurial image conjure a much more devilish (or at least folk-devilish) depiction of the god of mead, poetry, and magic. And the othering of this figure who practices traditionally "female" magical arts makes him much more aligned to the contemporary figure of the witch father.

Personally, I don't think it matters where Óðinn or any of the gods came from or if they ever came from anywhere other than the minds of their followers. What matters is how we interact with these spirits and beings now. Óðinn's practice of seiður is important, as it transgresses gender norms and enters firmly into the realm of queerness in Norse mythology and literature. This makes Óðinn very much an entity on his own, able to share knowledge and teach those he wishes. This magic—much of which was taught to him by his sometimes wife, sometimes fellow god, Freyja—shows us Óðinn as patron of all sorcerers, regardless of gender, sex, or much else. He seems to play a special role for those who are comfortable in the role of the other and are often queer.

We see Freyja as the witch mother and Great Goddess figure. Through her, the gods learned seiður. Half of Óðinn's great power comes from the knowledge she shared with him. Would Óðinn have acquired all he knows without her help? Surely not. She holds a special place in her heathen form, as well as in her assimilated guise as María-Freyja. Her role as the highest female figure is mostly based on what we see in the poem "Grímnismál," which tells us that while half the slain goes to Valhöll, the remaining half goes to Sessrúmnir, a hall belonging to Freyja.

Early Christians in Iceland seem to have realised her importance, assimilating and quickly associating her more gentle aspects with the Holy Virgin. However, this guise of the "gentle mother" is not so black and white. In her MA thesis, *A New Kind of Feminine: The Effects of the Icelandic Conversion on Female Religious Participation and the Image of the Feminine*, Ólöf Bjarnadóttir shows us the first written source found, in which Mary was noted as being called upon to aid in sparing ships from wrecking at some point between 1050 and 1200. In contemporary practice, we also find ways to ask for her help in somewhat darker work. After all, what mother wouldn't go to lengths to protect and care for her children? It is also through this mother aspect that we see her and Frigg as one and the same, something that is now somewhat more accepted by scholars and academics as likely true.

Other gods are called upon, but not often in the same way as Neo-Pagan practices like Wicca. The gods do appear in the folklore of the island, and many locations and rock formations are given heathen associations, some even long into the Christian era. These mythical origins for features in the landscape, in particular, give us good focal points to utilise and include in our practices, such as Ásbyrgi canyon, the hoof print of Sleipnir, and one proposed capital city of the Huldufólk. The gods often return, popping up in spells and stories, but generally, these forces are less influential to the day-to-day goings-on of practitioners who choose to focus on an animism-heavy practice.

Óðinn, Jesus, Freyr, Satan, and more tend to make appearances all together in spells found in galdrabækur, usually due to these being recorded by priests and other learned folk who also would have been responsible for penning and copying the ancient stories. Over the centuries, religious thought has added layer after layer to the overall spiritual consciousness of the land, leading to the assimilation of many influences and spirits. The modern-day Ásatrú religion in Iceland has placed more significance on the gods, much like those who romanticise Iceland as a non-Christian nation. However, sadly for the "true Pagan" Viking enthusiast, this is far from the reality of Icelandic folk practice.

Jesus is very much a friend to the Icelandic wizards of the last thousand years. The influence of Christianity has certainly bled into folk magic. We see this in spells ending "Í Jesus nafni" (in Jesus' name), as well as the focus on Maríu-Freyja. Many places that may have once been sacred to Freyja have been renamed after María. One cave just on the outskirts of the Reykjavík area is named *Maríuhellar;* some suspect this was once a sacred place to Freyja, although this connection is tenuous at best. There are also a few natural springs around the country attributed now to María that may have previously been held as places sacred to Freyja. We know that many bishops throughout Iceland's history blessed Pagan places in the name of God to help convert the population.

As the attributed spiritual overseers of places changed, the belief in elves held fast. Just the same as the fae in other parts of Europe, the álfar or Huldufólk are a source of hope and terror. They may be bargained with, but just as with their continental counterparts, extreme care and a large amount of common sense are essential. Álfasteinar are found dotted all over the country. These serve as focal points for all dealings with the elves. As mentioned earlier, these stones have been known to halt construction work around them, with tools mysteriously breaking and electronics not working at all. Due to this, many stones can be found in residential places that haven't been moved during the construction that took place around them. Offerings for local álfar may be left at these to appease them or ask for their protection. Some older burial mounds are also known as homes of local elves and spirits. These, too, are a great point for leaving offerings, especially if the local dead of the mound or the surrounding area are known. The elves have often been called the "ancient dead," or older human spirits who have assimilated into the land and become landvættir. They may live within mounds and be called on for all sorts of help.

The álfar are not the only spirits called on within Icelandic folk magic. The spirits of long-dead Christian priests also play a role in our workings. Most famously, the priests of Skálholt and Hólar have been known to be called on for a few reasons. Working relationships can be formed with these spirits, but be warned, some of them were disreputable in life for good reason, and none take offense lightly. The highest and most dangerous of these long-dead priests I mentioned earlier. Grimmi, Gottskálk Nikulásson (1469–1520) was the former bishop of Hólar and the supposed author of the infamous grimoire *Rauðskinna*. His nickname, *Grimmi*, means "cruel," and Gottskálk has been called on by many throughout history, with results ranging from the unsettling to the spine-chilling.

The general dead play an important part in our spirit ecology. Churchyards and graveyards are places of power in Icelandic folk magic. Great respect must be paid to the dead as we move through their spaces. It is also here where we contact them. Some follow certain rules of leaving a coin at the church gate, knocking three times on the gate, and stating why you are visiting. The more frequently talked about theory—that the first body buried in the graveyard becomes the head spirit and guardian of that space—is something we modern Icelandic practitioners believe to be true. This spirit is known here as *vökukona* or *vökumaður* (though we could now also use the term *vökukvár*). Its role caused fear for the living, a job of much responsibility, as common people were often scared to be the first buried and have to perform this role. Vökukona should be consulted, and all workings undertaken in the graveyard should only happen after they have given permission.

Gravestones, in particular, are, of course, a focal point for Icelandic necromancy. Many workings require you to be close to the body of the spirit you are calling up. Knowing the location of the body of a spirit or dead person that you work with gives you a huge advantage. Icelanders love keeping records, so the name of any ancestor or human spirit that might be worked with in most graveyards will be recorded somewhere and is usually fairly easy to find. While the organised or "clean" dead have a heightened importance in Icelandic folk magic, the "unclean" also play their part.

Ghosts and the "unclean" dead in Iceland are known to behave in a very specific way here. We have a few theories as to why. Icelandic ghosts are unique in that they are forced to follow rules. It is common knowledge that they are supposedly forced to comply if told to leave. They may return later but can then be told to leave again. Exorcism and the banishing of spirits and entities plays a prominent role in Icelandic folklore, more often for spirits that have become something more than just human dead. One theory within our working group as to why human dead take longer to assimilate into the nature around them in Iceland is because people remember names for generations on the island. You could visit a supposedly haunted farm and have a close encounter with Gunnsi, the farmer's ghost who died hundreds of years ago.

While many ghosts, according to our theory, don't hang about for longer than one hundred years, the ones that tend to are those whose names are remembered and, more importantly, spoken. Does knowing, speaking, and remembering a human spirit's name anchor it to this plane for longer than those forgotten? We believe so. Iceland has memories of names since the original settlers, and many ghosts in folklore are known by name, regardless of their time of death being fifty or five hundred years prior. Many ghosts who remain, in our theory, are aspects of the middle soul, more commonly called "the shade." That part of our spirit remains as a memory with varying levels of coherency. The shades who still linger on farmhouses in the countryside, for example, may just be repeating the tasks of their daily lives for hundreds of years, remembered but unnoticed by those around them, until a sensitive relative visits the family land and sees them at some liminal time going about their business. This sort of happening is as common in daily life in modern Iceland as it is in folklore, often becoming an important part of the very same positive feedback mechanism that anchors these spirits to place.

There are many ways to categorise Icelandic ghosts and spirits. Within this book, for the sake of ease and to not overload the reader on hard-to-pronounce words, we will categorise them by the behaviors they display. (Keep in mind that this categorization is from the perspective of a contemporary practitioner and not a scholar.) To begin with, *afturgöngur* or "following ghosts" are the easiest to deduce simply because they follow. (This is a category of all spirits, not just human dead.) Many spirits have the potential to become afturgöngur. It may be a sendingur that follows a family for generations, or maybe an ancestor of yours played a part in the tragic accidental death of a farmer, and now his spirit pops up every generation to cause trouble.

Some afturgöngur may be skotta or móri. These classes of spirits verge more towards the dangerous and harmful side. Many are known for being able to mentally torment their victims to the point of suicide, as well as one skotta, Móhúsa-skotta, who strangles its victims to death. Some afturgöngur may simply be vofa (specters) or aspects of shades that follow, seen only by those more sensitive to spirits. *Vofa* is the word we would use for a spirit that lacks the power to make itself apparent within the world easily. They are seen more at liminal times when it is easier for spirits to be perceived, like while driving a road at dusk or in the moments before sleep. Vofa and skuggi would often be catagorised as the same thing. I would personally say the difference is that skuggi is used more to describe apparitions of shapeless darkness or shadow without the more solid shape or appearance of something recognisable.

Afturgöngur aren't the only spirits that follow. Usually, the word *afturganga* is used to refer to something that follows with negative aspects. Móri, skotta, and vofa tend to fall into the category of afturgöngur more often. Móri are most often male ghosts, sometimes (but not always) sent by a sorcerer, and skotta are the female equivalent. These two words are used to describe the spirit's gender, or at least their guise. More importantly, the way we tend to classify these spirits is typically based on whether or not they can cause physical harm to people. Sendingar and uppvakningar are capable of direct attack and death. Móri and skotta tend to be unable to harm directly, scaring or shocking people, and occasionally leeching a person's sanity until they take their own life, but most often only capable of causing fear, unease, and panic.

Folklore tells us that occasionally, a spirit will be sent that is not able to cause direct harm, either due to the sorcerer's lack of power or discipline or because of any protections in place when the spirit arrives. Occasionally, sendingar may be trapped within a place, depleting their strength enough to make them less harmful, if not harmless. If these spirits are directly attacked by a sorcerer, they may be weakened to the status of some other afturganga. Staves intended to trap and weaken sendingar exist. We will go into these and other practical methods of laying and banishing sent spirits later.

Some spirits that follow aren't inherently negative in and of themselves. In the case of Þórgeirs Boli and other birthed fylgjur, these spirits can take on the role of the families' fylgja and follow families for generations. Fylgjur are both a part of and apart from us; our own fylgja is the doppelgänger which, if seen by us in our own image, is most often a portent of our own death. We will discuss them and their overlaps with familiar spirits, as well as being their own aspect of a person's or beings' soul, later.

Other harmful spirits that can do real damage are uppvakningar. The methods that surround the resurrection and commanding of spirits within Icelandic folklore are quite grim. Waking the dead is one of the most dangerous things one can do within Icelandic folk magic. The caster is always at risk, even with the help of other living (and maybe even dead) allies. Folklore tells us that the longer the body of the spirit you're trying to wake up has been dead, the stronger they will be. It is for this reason that many spirits we know about from folklore were likely the ghosts of children sent to harm the sorcerers' enemies.

Some uppvakningar are raised completely accidentally. One such story from Villingarholt tells of the ghost of a Dutch sailor buried in the kirkjugarði, accidently raised by Icelanders who then failed to communicate with him as neither of them spoke Dutch. Some spirits wake up in cycles. One example is a ghost in Stokkseyri. This spirit needs to be bound every seven to nine years, lest it rise and cause havoc among the townspeople. Opening a floodgate by commanding a spirit to cause the death of an individual is not done lightly, and should the spirit fail, folklore tells us that it may come back years or generations later with all the descendants of the original target on its hit list.

It is worth mentioning that it is taboo to call your own ancestors "draugar." This word has negative connotations and should be reserved for spirits that have been woken up or are "stuck" in a place. Óhreinn andi and dólgur are two other words used to describe negative spirits and ghosts in Iceland. Dólgur is darker: these spirits can occasionally be tröll, and the word is used to describe spirits with harmful intent.

Andar is the general word for spirits. This can be a catchall or umbrella term for any and all spirits, with *andi* meaning, in general, the concept of the spirit and ethereal spirit. *Illur andi* (ill or malevolent spirits) can also be used to refer to all negative energies and entities. The word *vættur* (plural *vættir*) also means "spirits," though as with landvættir, these are often spirits of places, the English equivalent coming from Anglo-Saxon England being the landwights, or simply, wights. *Vættur* is almost the same as the Swedish väsen, meaning either a supernatural entity or the inner nature of someone or something.

The word náttúra is the most fitting to describe something's magical nature or virtue; magical stones, for example, are known as nátturusteinar. Spirits of the house are generally referred to as húsandi, a literal translation, and occasionally húsálfur, more like the typical European house spirit. The term "góður andi hússins" is used, to this day, to refer to a home's good feeling, as well as the good spirit of the house itself. There isn't the same exact tradition in Iceland as the British house brownie or Slavic domovoi, but just as with any spirit of the home, one can create a relationship with it.

Dvergar (dwarves) might give a very Tolkien image to some, but in Iceland, the dvergar can sometimes come across as malevolent spirits living deep in their caves and holes. Descriptions of these spirits often overlapped with dökkálfar (dark elves). Dvergar live in deep, dark caves and don't often come to the surface if folklore is to be believed. Sometimes they are known as *bergbúi, bjargbúi,* or *steinbúi.* All of these terms mean "rock dwellers," or those who live within the stones and mountains. These spirits are not always dwarves; it's just a name for anything living within a stone or mountain. Occasionally, these terms are also used to describe elves that live within stones. Dvergar are deep and dark and are often only felt within caves or in the dead of winter when the sun doesn't grace the sky. Tröll are the trolls, though these beings are sometimes assimilated with jötnar (giants). There are different types of tröll in Iceland, and humans can themselves become trollish through their actions in life and death. The *nátttröll,* or "night troll," is the more fairytale-type troll. These trolls can't walk about when the sun is up, and if they do, they turn to stone. Folklore tells us of times they sat outside the windows of houses, tempting the inhabitants to come outside or engage in their riddles. These trolls are also known to walk about during bad weather and lure people out into the hills. Other trolls can be reasoned with, tricked, or bargained with, but the nátttröll seem to be the least willing to control their trollish nature.

Named trolls in folklore are often more reasonable, but some, such as Grýla, move into darker territory. Bergþurs, or bergrisi, are the rock giants. These beings are wise, usually benevolent, and occasionally help people by giving them prophecies. Bergrisi, also known as "Járngrímur," the giant of the South, is one such rock giant. The sagas tell us that he was often called upon to give advice and counsel in Iceland's past. He lives in the rock Lómagnúpur, one of Iceland's highest standberg (rock faces).

Two darker spirits within Icelandic folklore worth mentioning are útburður and tilberi. Útburður, sometimes referred to as a type of changeling, are spirits created out of tragic circumstances. Often, these are the spirits of babies left outside to die in nature. Due to whatever circumstances, these tragic spirits played an important role within folklore, discouraging childbirth between any unmarried or otherwise complicated pair. As a cautionary tale, they are tragic, but as a spiritual entity, they are terrifying. They have been seen following their mothers through life, just as their guilt and grief may do. Apparitions of these spirits have been seen crawling on their elbows and knees, often moaning, unable to speak as they were never taught how.

Tilberi are a type of familiar, similar to other familiars of European witchcraft lore, such as the Swedish milk hares and British imps. The tilberi can be birthed in a number of ways and may well serve as a faithful familiar—if not one that is somewhat needy. They tend to treat their creators as mothers. Born of wool, bone, and blood, they most often act as thieves and spies but can serve many purposes. This sort of spirit birthing is not something I recommend doing without much thought or planning, as tilberi can be hard to dispose of. A woman in Hafrafell was once foiled in her attempts to birth a tilberi. She had removed a bone from a grave in the churchyard, bound it in wool, and was about to have it covertly blessed at the altar during Sunday mass when it fell from her dress in front of the whole church. She was taken away and burned for this.

Another servitor spirit in Icelandic tradition is the púki, also known as *drýsildjöfull*. In English, this is simply translated as "imp." Púkar (plural) may have been human spirits at some point, or they may have been a nature spirit or an animal, insect, or anything else living. A púki exists to serve, fulfilling an often simple role, such as being employed as a thief, spy, or messenger. One practitioner may have many púkar within their lifetime, and like the imps and familiars of British and continental witches, one may pass their púki on upon death. This can also be done within one's life. Púkar should be housed and cared for like any other familiar, though they often don't need as much as spirits you have more formal or contractual relationships with.

Púkar can be "handled" just as we would plant spirit familiars. If we wish, we can create vessels for them, though this is not always necessary. We find púkar in a few stories, although two tales from Jón Arnason's work mention them specifically as púkar. We see one púki watching a church service from the rafters while sewing discord between two women squabbling away during mass. This púki is only seen by one man, likely one who had the sight. Another tale tells us of a púki sent to a farmer who swore and cursed too much. The imp would torment him until he stopped swearing; unbeknownst to him, this led the imp to shrivel away until one day, he had enough of the torment and let out a stream of foul words, upon which the imp fed and grew back to its original strength. We can see how púkar were (and still are) assigned tasks to torment others and sew discord. We may also work púkar to spy on others and bring us knowledge. If we want, we can assign our púkar sigils and symbols; this just helps us to give the creatures more of a focus. For example, a simple sigil for a púki carved into a candle gives us a focal point to burn and concentrate on when assigning our púkar tasks.

Another interesting spirit that might be an entity in its own category is the Icelandic equivalent of the will-o'-the-wisp. This specter isn't the same as its continental relative. There aren't many records of swamp lights in Icelandic folklore, which is interesting considering that the country contains a large proportion of mýri (mire). However, one saga in particular gives us one explanation for these mysterious lights. The urðarmáni, mentioned in *Eyrbyggja saga*, is a floating orb said to be made of fire. I remind the reader that those alive in the thirteenth and fourteenth centuries wouldn't have referred to a glowing orb of light as anything reminiscent of electricity, which is where the softer glow that we tend to visualize comes from when imagining these whisps nowadays. This ineffability is likely why it is named after the soft light of the moon in one sentence and a small ball of fire in the next.

Either way, seeing these orbs is an omen of misfortune. In the case of *Eyrbyggja saga*, it was to be the beginning of a series of deaths and problems, appearing the night of a funeral when the deceased woman returned from her fresh grave. The appearance of the orb was followed by a mysterious disease that killed six. I recommend reading the saga as it gives a great insight into the role that the restless dead play in saga literature and very much aligns with our persistent animistic view of the spirit and its posthumous parts. The orb in the saga could well have been one part of the soul of the deceased woman and not some otherwise natural wisp at all.

It is always good to be aware of the specific rules and guidelines when exploring a new place and its spirits. This is important in mundane aspects, such as tourism in Iceland, which sadly does incredible damage to the land when warnings go ignored. As animistic practitioners, it is always good to be aware of who or what makes its home in the land we are walking. The nuanced spirits of every land are important and should not be forgotten or assimilated with others, something I touch on later. In reading about these spirits from other lands, we may recognise similar behaviours in the spirits of our own lands and, as such, learn methods of connection or, indeed, avoidance. It behooves us to behave with respect wherever we find ourselves, and being aware of things that won't cause the land or ourselves harm when travelling is something we should remind ourselves of just as much as we do when we are at home connecting with our own landscapes.

7
Hamingju, Fylgjur, and the Multi-Faceted Soul

The concept of hamingja can be hard for some to grasp. This isn't the same idea surrounding luck and prosperity as Eastern karma. Where one may obtain "bad ill" or hamingju resulting from dishonourable actions, these actions need not necessarily be those that harm others. This is quite different from the Western New Age approach to karma. For example, revenge killing could be seen to bring good hamingju if the cause was believed justified by the community. It pays to remember that Iceland was and, in some ways, still is an island of limited resources. Due to this, the act of righting a wrong may well have been the difference between life and death.

Icelandic magic pays a lot of attention to identifying thieves for a reason. Early and medieval Iceland was somewhat forgiving of violent crimes, although there were rules which governed violence and how it could be lawfully conducted. This moral viewpoint may be part of what gives us the unique cursing staves we find in Icelandic grimoires around workings such as causing the death of livestock and people and laming horses. Keep in mind, though, that committing violence through witchcraft was often seen as less acceptable than physically performing it yourself. For example, murder was only considered unlawful if conducted in secrecy and then discovered later. Murder for revenge was much more permissible, even bringing good hamingju to the one committing the crime. Hamingju may also come from an animistic view of the luck and well-being of a person being attached to a spiritual entity that is both a part of and apart from one's soul.

Hamingja, like the fylgja, is seen by some as an aspect of oneself that dictates one's well-being, affecting wealth, social status, and more. The word also denotes aspects of shapeshifting: the changing of the hamur (the guise, skin, or form). From this, we get the words *hamfari* (the act of travelling in a guise or altered form or state) and to *hamhleypa* (shapeshift). We will cover more on these later. The many animistic aspects of the soul can be a bit confusing and overwhelming for some, given that Western society's idea of the soul is of a singular, untouchable entity. Throw in Christian influence and pop culture, and it can become quite hard to unlearn the single soul concept enough to understand the fluidity (and sometimes ineffability) of the multifaceted "moving parts" of the soul from a Nordic animistic perspective. For this reason, I like to divide the soul into three categories. Each can be dissected further, but for the most part, three parts cover the main concepts we will discuss.

This threefold soul fits many spiritual worldviews. We begin with the upper soul or the divine spark. This is the spark of life, the closest to the Christian concept and the Buddhist view of the divine soul, which comes and goes from physical forms over lifetimes. It returns after death to the beyond before returning in the cycle of reincarnation. This is also referred to as the "spark of divine inspiration," and it is through it that we feel unity with the whole of humanity.

The second part, the middle soul, is what we refer to as the shade and sometimes the *vard*. It is that part of us that may remain, joining spiritual courts and watching over, though it may also be that part that can get stuck and remain within a space, such as one that was special to us in life. This middle soul may take on the role of a guardian spirit, standing over one's shoulder, watching, and gently helping.

The third aspect is the lower soul. In Icelandic tradition, this is the *fylgja*, sometimes called the "fetch" by others. It is part of us which we send forth in animal form, both a part of and apart from us, our vehicles for spirit flight, hamfari, and more. This part of the soul—to us, at least—is believed to remain in the world, often assimilating over time into nature and its spirits. Though sometimes it may remain and change its roles, maybe as a púki (an imp) able to perform tasks for us or an afturganga (a ghost returned from the dead). The Icelandic view on these spirits and how we can categorise them depends on one's understanding of the soul not being a singular entity.

I'll discuss further how we can work with the middle souls of ancestors, both blood and spiritual, and how it dictates our graveyard etiquette, based on the previously discussed fact that Icelanders have a detailed record of the names (and sometimes facts) about their ancestors, dating all the way back to the settlement of the land. We will also discuss work with the fylgja, how we may know the forms it takes, how we work with it, sending it out, and how we can understand the nature of this part of our soul that is able to act independently of us. The souls' aspects are many, and I hope that, through some of the exercises offered later, one can begin to grasp how our soul(s) always interact with the magical landscape around us.

While the three main aspects of the soul give us a simplified overview of what makes an individual themselves within Icelandic folk magic and tradition, the external parts of ourselves can be harder to explain. As with the hamingja, the fylgja (or plural *fylgjur*) is both a part of us and apart from us. The fylgja both follows and travels ahead, announcing us before we arrive. A perfect example of this in saga literature comes from *Njáls saga*. Gunnar dreams of animals, which represent the attackers coming his way, a very clear example of one way that fylgjur interact with each other and the world around us. The fylgja may even do so in animal form in the natural world before someone receives a text or call from us, such as seeing the animals you know your friends' fylgjur to commonly take. It may announce itself, along with mutual thoughts about each other, as it appears in our mind's eyes throughout the day before such a call or some form of contact later.

Like hamingju, fylgjur may be passed on through families. Family hamingju is something still recognised in Iceland. Old families with honour and pride in trustworthy ancestors benefit from this. Whether this is through spiritual power or by good old-fashioned Icelandic nepotism in the workplace, it is still a part of society. Descendants of those families with good hamingju benefit but also bear the responsibility of continuing this hamingju and remaining honourable and of good morals in their actions should they wish it to pass to their children. These parts of the spirit that are both a part and apart from us could be compared to Jötunheimar and the way that this world exists as a branch of Yggdrasil, as all worlds do. Though it is a part of the world tree, this world exists in its own space apart from the other realms in Norse mythology, influencing it from afar yet remaining close enough to spring into action.

Fylgia exists in the physical world as (and is the modern Icelandic word for) the placenta, an ingredient in a few spells and magical techniques recorded in Icelandic tradition. The fylgja grew with you in the womb and will be with you always until you choose to pass it on to your progenitors, or after death when it may naturally assimilate into the land or move on to fulfil a separate role, possibly as a púki or other spirit just as part of your own self may do.

The last thing to mention is that one's own fylgia may appear in different guises. Animal form guides are often fylgjur, whether these are the family fylgjur or those of living or passed relatives, both spiritual and physical. However, we may also see others' fylgjur in the form of their human appearance. When we see others, this is often not something to be concerned about. However, when we see our fylgjur appearing as our own form (like a doppelgänger), this is most often a portent of death and is not something we would be happy to see.

8

Draumagaldur: Dream Magic

The magic of dreams makes up a large part of Icelandic folk magic. This may cross over with spirit flight and shapeshifting, as both these experiences can take place nocturnally. Much of the lore we have around dream magic and its practice involves staves, herbs, and specific times. I would argue that this sort of magic can include the likes of forspár and fjarsýni if taken place during sleep; these two are discussed later.

Dreams were revered in ancient times, and until recently, dreams have been heeded in Iceland to tell of the coming of visitors, events, and deaths. The sagas tell us how important these dreams and prophecies were and how those gifted with this power were revered. This type of *forspár*, or foreseeing, is a skill that can be learned, though, for some, it may take longer than others. The following staves, herbs, and exercises may help build this skill.

When we talk about dreams and dream magic in Iceland, we need to include the use of certain Icelandic terms. *Draumvitjanir*, or "dream visitors," play a part in Iceland's folklore; whether they be human, animal, elf, or otherwise, these spirits can bring important information, visions, and warnings. Folk tales here are full of dream visitors foretelling danger or informing people that they have died and where to find their body. One such tale involves two friends who were travelling from one town to another when an ash storm arose.

The two friends were separated, and only one reached the village that night. The other appeared in the dream of a girl who lived nearby, telling her where to find his body. The following morning, she told the townsfolk, and sure enough, the man's body was found almost exactly where the spirit had told the girl in her dream. We see ghosts appear to people in dreams, asking for specific things. One night, the sheriff of Strandasýslu in the Westfjords died. His ghost then appeared to Jón, the coffin maker assigned to him, in a dream. The ghost told Jón not to use many iron nails in his coffin, and that was that. A simple message, but spirits in Iceland seem to appear to any and all in dreams, rather than just those who practice some form of magic as in many other places.

9

FORSPÁR OG FJARSÝNI: FORESEEING AND FAR·SEEING

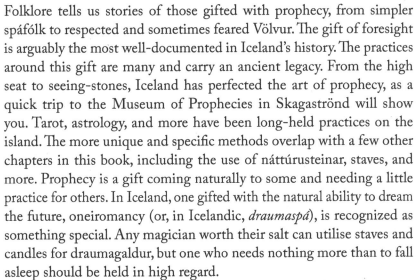

Folklore tells us stories of those gifted with prophecy, from simpler spáfólk to respected and sometimes feared Völvur. The gift of foresight is arguably the most well-documented in Iceland's history. The practices around this gift are many and carry an ancient legacy. From the high seat to seeing-stones, Iceland has perfected the art of prophecy, as a quick trip to the Museum of Prophecies in Skagaströnd will show you. Tarot, astrology, and more have been long-held practices on the island. The more unique and specific methods overlap with a few other chapters in this book, including the use of náttúrusteinar, staves, and more. Prophecy is a gift coming naturally to some and needing a little practice for others. In Iceland, one gifted with the natural ability to dream the future, oneiromancy (or, in Icelandic, *draumaspá*), is recognized as something special. Any magician worth their salt can utilise staves and candles for draumagaldur, but one who needs nothing more than to fall asleep should be held in high regard.

For those of us not gifted with this natural ability, we need the aid of various *materia magica*. Plants are, of course, the easiest to find and work. Draumagras (*Equisetum arvense*) is one plant utilised to aid in forspá. The plant is gathered during summer, ideally under a full moon or an otherwise Lunar hour and day. It should be dried within a Bible or otherwise holy book, then placed within or underneath the pillow of the one who wishes to dream of the future. Other elements of forspár involving plants include burning plant materia as incense, leaving things under the church altar to acquire power via transference or association, and acquiring plants seemingly at random when out walking in nature.

Everyone has their own natural flavour of divination. For the dreamers, it may come easy, and for some of us, we may see signs or understand the language of the birds (*fuglamál* in Icelandic). We may see the future in candle flames or wax dripped into water, in stones or the reflections on moonlit water, or in smoke, beans, or the yolks of eggs. I personally think that it is every practitioner's duty to try as many forms of divination as possible until one discovers where their natural talents lie.

For some, especially according to Icelandic folklore, the future may come in moments of lucidity on long journeys across the country. For some historical figures in Iceland, the future comes in flashes or glimpses seen as they traverse the landscape. Priests are said to have perceived events before they arrived during long journeys on horseback. Reverend Þorlákur Þórarinsson was said to receive glimpses of the future as he travelled throughout his parish. We know this tradition of walking prophecy was, and still is, evident in Sweden and Iceland. The *ársgangur*, or "year walk," is a tradition that occurs in Sweden and is practiced by us here in Iceland much in the same way: wandering, encountering spirits, happenings, and more, foretelling the year ahead. Time isn't a linear being, and, as such, we may see events unfolding long before they occur for us. Taking a year walk is something I recommend greatly. Traditionally, this is done between Christmas and New Year's Eve. As always, when moving through times and places where the veil is thin, protections should be worn.

Sometimes, forspár can signal the knowing of one's own time of death. Omens of death are another common element of folklore, and in Iceland, these are sometimes connected to sights of huldufólk or other mysterious occurrences. The sound of ringing bells at night is said to be a bad omen, referred to sometimes as *líkhringingin*, the corpse bell ring, or a death toll. This occurrence, although more of a happening, can be perceived by those with forspá, and sometimes, the one who is to die is seen wandering the landscape at night following the tolling bell. Those who see the future may also see the shades of those to die wandering into the hills. It has long been known in Iceland that many of the dead end up entering the hills. With Kristnitakan came a change in the way the souls of the dead move about, but those who could see the shades of the soon-to-be-dead moving about the landscape still noticed them moving between new graveyards, mountains, and spaces they favoured in life.

Some stories of prophets are sad. Besides seeing their own deaths or the deaths of their loved ones, sometimes the stories tell of those gifted with foresight going blind. One story tells of the nanny of a prominent family who told one of the children that they would soon be moving abroad, which came to pass. She then told him that once he set out into the world, she would never see him again. When he returned some years later, she had gone blind a few days prior to his arrival. The ability to see spirits of the dead or most other spirits is called *skyggni* in Icelandic; sometimes, scrying or seeing other things is referred to as *sýnir*.

Another sad example of this sort of sjón (vision) comes from a student in the Latin school of Reykjavík in 1869. Björn Jónsson, the student in question, saw an apparition of his mother's face, clear as day before him, looking sullen and tearful the same moment his mother had died in the West. We know of the warnings of going too far with prophecy, as well as the dangers of not heeding the warnings that prophets give us. This balance, like many other aspects of the occult, is the juggling act one needs to constantly play to avoid going "off the deep end." That being said, a simple exercise follows for those who wish to engage with and practice their ability to see the future.

A SIMPLE EXERCISE TO AID IN PROPHETIC WORK

We can increase our proficiency in forspár in a few ways. Simple meditative techniques can help us get clearer pictures when in trance, helping us to focus on what it is we're seeing. Learning symbols and gaining a deeper understanding of the symbolic way we can receive information about what is to come is also very helpful. Finally, we can work with herbs and tools to aid our latent talents with this skill. Working with herbs is the easiest way for someone with little to no experience to begin building up this skill.

Herbs in Iceland that help improve our prophetic skills include maríustakkur (*Alchemilla mollis*), hvönn (*Angelica archangelica*), and maðjurt (*Filipendula ulmaria*). Making a hot infusion of these three herbs and drinking it before we engage in the following exercise can be very helpful, as can burning incense, especially that of bláberjalyng (*Vaccinium myrtillus*) and hófífill (*Tussilago farfara*), though I encourage you to work with your own plant allies and appropriate materia wherever in the world you are. Once the space has been set and you've worked with some plant allies' help, sit down and begin to relax into a calm and meditative state.

Remember, the goal of this meditative state is not a clear and blissful focus. This is rarely achievable for those beginning, and still difficult for those with years of experience. Relax your mind and focus on your own breath, your heartbeat, or, better yet, some gentle nature sounds played in a way that won't be interrupted by adverts or track changes for the full duration of the exercise. The sound of flowing water can be helpful for this, as well as having nice correspondences with the Moon and the subconscious, however tenuous.

Relax your body and mind, bringing awareness to your breath and any sounds. Once you've finished your tea or burned your incense, visualize yourself sitting at the base of a tree in a great forest. Look around and take time to notice the plants, the light, and any sounds within this landscape. After a while, stand up and walk through the forest until you find yourself at a well. You may encounter spirits on your journey but remain focused. Once you reach the well, make a cup with your hands and drink from it. Cast your mind forward and receive whatever vision or visions come to you, making a mental note of what happens.

Allow whatever comes to reveal itself to you; don't try to lead what happens. Also, remember that anything you see can be (and most likely will be) symbolic, so don't be discouraged if nothing makes sense initially. It may well do when you think back to it later. Once you've had your visions, thank the well and return to sitting beneath a tree. Focus again on your breath and bring awareness slowly back to your physical body, feeling out your fingers and toes, and slowly, once you feel grounded within yourself again, open your eyes.

Dissecting these visions can take time and practice. Even getting to the point of having more coherent experiences at the well can take time, so don't be discouraged. Ask for the aid of the plant spirits you are working with, or even utilise a stave if you wish. Also, keep in mind that this is not something that everyone can do well. I have struggled with it for a long time, only feeling more confident in this practice a few years after I started. There are other ways to work forspár, so if after a good many tries it still doesn't stick, focus instead on these.

Fjarsýni (far-seeing) is another ability that pops up in Icelandic folklore. This type of clairvoyance is evident in much of world folklore. In Iceland, this type of seeing was mostly noted around times of storms and bad weather, often a natural talent of the women of the house. If a member of the household had not yet returned before the bad weather set in, it was a useful gift for checking on them. As one story goes, a storm rolled in, and the woman of the house knew one of the family members had yet to return. Using her gifts, she remotely located him within a lava field, knowing that he had taken shelter there from the storm and was alive and well.

He later arrived when the storm had passed, and his story matched what the woman had seen and knew to be true. Like draumaspá, this sort of gift is much more a natural talent, but with time and practice, some may be able to get the hang of it. This sort of remote viewing overlaps with spirit flight and sometimes with seeing through the eyes of animals. Ravens have been used by those with this gift, a habit which aligns well with Norse myth and stories of Óðinn's ravens who travel the world for him, bringing him information. Making special bonds with certain animals is not something all of us get to experience, especially with animals that aren't tame or domestic in any way. This power of seeing through the eyes of animals occurs in sagas and old oral stories, so we in Iceland know this to be a power that some possess and a power that, as humanity grows further away from the natural world, will likely go unnoticed by many who possess it.

Another story tells us of the mistress of a house far-seeing the events of a shipwreck unfold one night. Three men died in this wreck and were never found. In her vision, she saw the mast of the ship snapping in two and the men being thrown overboard. Later, upon discovering the shipwreck exactly where her vision had shown it occurring, it was reported back that the mast had indeed snapped in two as she said it had been. Another story, this time from Skagaströnd, tells us of a sick woman, bed-bound and ailing. A man named Benedikt was sent to fetch her medicine from a doctor in the next town. While he was travelling, the sick woman saw an unkindness of ravens begin to gather in the churchyard. "They have taken his eyes," she said to the nurse beside her. Sadly enough, poor Benedikt had fallen on his journey and drowned in the mire. He was discovered with eyes gouged out by ravens. Not all stories of far-seeing are so bleak, but the landscape of Iceland, with all its natural danger, can be an unkind place.

Some use stones to see far and wide; these stones are discussed later, but possessing a stone that helps one acquire or facilitates this power is a useful tool and ally to hold. Scrying via stones, water, or fire also occurs the world over and is indeed a manifestation of a practitioner's divinatory gift. Scrying overlaps prophecy and far-seeing, with the main difference being the time one is aiming to look at. For us, the definition goes that as soon as we move out of the realm of the present, it becomes divination. I encourage you to attempt to develop these gifts or discover latent talents for them, as they can become extremely useful gifts that aid in all sorts of other magic, especially spirit communication.

There are many types of forspár that don't involve psychic gifts. For example, passing comets (vígahnettir) were held as heralds of major events about to unfold. In 1756, such a fiery globe was seen in the sky and noted by Eggert Ólafsson. According to Jón Árnason, the name comes from Vígabrandur, a warrior who won many battles. He had a most excellent sword, and when he was finally defeated in combat, he commanded his shining sword be thrown into the river Tiber. The shining sword, therefore, became the name for these shining lights slowly crossing the sky.

The Moon can also reveal the future to us. On nights when there is a rosabaugur (a ring around the Moon), we know that bad weather is soon to follow; the bigger the ring, the worse the weather. When the Moon is a red colour, this foretells tragedy and even war. And when we see the Moon just as a sliver but can also see its dark shadow, this foretells storms and gales. The Sun can also foretell ill happenings. When we see a sun dog on only the side of the Sun that moves ahead of its course, ill tidings are sure to follow.

Árnason also tells us that the biblical pair Adam and Eve's faces are reflected in the Sun and the Moon, respectively. I remind the reader that this Christian view of the Sun as man and the Moon as woman is contrary to the Old Norse view of the Sun as Sunna and the Moon as Máni. Personally, I don't recommend assigning a firm gender to any celestial body, recognizing that our human experience of gender is beneath planetary spirits, and instead, working off the attributes that any and all may possess to varying levels within themselves.

Another type of for-seeing is *hrafnamál*, or the language of ravens. More on these birds, heavily associated with omens and prophecy, can be found within the bestiary on page 158. Hrafnamál can be a learned skill as an example of augury, reading the future in the flight of the birds, as well as an innate talent for communicating with and having special bonds with ravens. Learned augury is an acquired skill, but true hrafnamál is a rare gift known within Icelandic tradition. This gift is said to allow one to communicate with ravens, receive information from them, and seemingly be able to speak to and with them. This gift echoes that of Óðinn's power of communication with Huginn and Munin within Norse mythology. While innate hrafnamál can't be taught, we do see it featured in a few folk stories, mainly those foretelling death and disaster.

10

Hamfari og Sálarflug: Shapeshifting and Spirit Flight

The act of shapeshifting and sending one's spirit out has always been a part of Nordic magic. If the sagas and stories are to be believed, then this vehicle for performing magic may have been part of the practice of more than a few people in the pre-Christian world. This practice also relates to what we know and believe to fall under the umbrella of seiður. Many methods are recorded that aid in spirit flight and shape-changing, including staves, brews, and spoken galdur. I will break a few of these down and give folkloric evidence and inspiration, as well as my own practical advice and anecdotal experiences. Shapeshifting, or the changing of one's hamur, can include physical elements in the form of the berserkur, or, as is more spiritually common, by taking the form of or occasionally seeing through the eyes of some animal or animal spirit. We have examples of Freyja's valsham, her falcon feathered cloak, which gives her the ability to shapeshift into a falcon. Other such feathered cloaks that give this ability are named in Norse mythology.

The first is a method I don't recommend expecting immediate results from. It takes time, practice, and, ideally, large open areas where one would be undisturbed for long periods of time. This method can also involve the ritual imbibing of highly toxic and dangerous materia such as baneful herbs, belladonna or henbane-infused wine, or other psychoactive chemicals and alkaloids, which I strongly recommend against doing.

The ancient world would have been just as aware of the dangers and complications of this as we are. However, the main difference is legality.

Flying ointments sit within this gray area for now, and the ointments themselves are not a big part of Icelandic folk magic. If we look at the Oracle of Delphi and her supposed inhalation of dangerous volcanic fumes, there is the vague potential to assume this could have taken place in similar volcanic areas of Iceland, though there is no evidence of this anywhere. Of course, I don't recommend experimentation in this area, having felt firsthand the choking feeling that volcanic gas offered those of us who hiked to the eruption at Fagradalsfjall in 2021. Physical shapeshifting, like many forms of ritual is, in essence, a type of performance art, one that you don't necessarily need to imbibe anything dangerous to experience.

The spiritual practice of shapeshifting could fill a whole book. Every tradition and working group has its own methods. We work predominantly with enchanted objects, skins, staves, plants, and spoken galdur. This practice is sometimes classed under gandur. Most countries in Europe have their own spirit flight lore and stories, and Iceland, although somewhat different from the typical sabbath, is no exception. In place of the witches' mountains of Blåkulla and Brocken, Iceland has spirit flight gatherings in small houses, flown to by practitioners via the methods I'll discuss.

Usually, these houses act as meeting places for spirits and magical folk under the watchful eye of the devil. One main difference is that, within Icelandic folklore, the man in black doesn't often appear as more than a large hairy hand reaching from the dark to grab those who try to flee from these meetings (usually uninvited tagalongs). Icelandic spirit flight folklore speaks more of unsuspecting victims being swept up in the flight, often nosy farm hands curious as to what the master or mistress of the house is doing by night. This is similar to the wild hunt, though the stories don't tell of seeing others or animals while flying. Maybe we would know of all number of spirits in flight if the stories were told from the perspective of the witch rather than the nosy farmhand.

These stories of flight, depending on the version, often involve gandreið, sometimes described as a bridle used to ride others as if they were a horse, and sometimes as a stave engraved on another tool, a short staff, a stone, and other objects. Throughout these differing versions, the consistent use of a tool is the most important aspect we can draw from in our craft. The inclusion of the most likely early modern-era galdrastafur, appearing in a few collections and manuscripts, is the second most important focus to aid in our spirit flight for many of us.

While other staves also work to aid in getting our feet off the ground, gandreið carries the weight of these folklore stories. By simply looking at it, one can feel the depth of its magic. It may be inscribed or engraved on any number of tools, and I recommend you experiment to see which tools feel and work best for you. For simply flying, the stave can be embroidered onto a cape or cloak worn while in flight. It may be engraved or burned into a short staff, along with other protective symbols. The stave is, in our experience, most effective when inscribed on the skin of an animal, though this is more specifically for shapeshifting than simple flight. Folklore also tells us of shoes used to fly, and the stave can be inscribed onto the bones of various animals to utilise the virtues they held in life.

Gandreið itself has a lot of complicated lore, being a stave, a tool, and somewhat of a horror story. It is said one can make the tool from human skin, human bones, and different animal skins. If one makes it from the skin of a long-dead animal, it can only travel via land and cannot cross large bodies of water. If it is made fresh, it will give the wearer more agility and make them able to travel in the air. Supposedly, the best belts are of fresh human skin, though it is also said that the skins of domestic dogs and cats were used, and tame dog skin allows for faster travel than cats. All fresh animal skins were said to be able to cross anything except the sea.

The idea of flight being limited to the land is interesting, as is the theory of one being unable to fly to different land masses from an animistic perspective. Each region has its own gathering point for the witches' sabbath, and many places in Europe have their own variants of the wild hunt. Local big hills were often the places flown to in European witch lore, and each practitioner went to their own local hill when engaging in this sabbatic flight. There aren't so many commonalities between continental witches' sabbaths and the gatherings that might be considered sabbaths in Iceland.

Jón Árnason records that Ingólfsfjall above Selfoss was once a gathering place for witches and magicians at a place on the mountain called *Valakirkja*. One story surrounding gandreið gives us something somewhat more similar to European witch lore. Supposedly, the wife of a priest who was using a gandreið tool had been studying at the devil's black school for twelve years and only needed one more to complete her education. This use of thirteen around a sabbatic gathering invokes continental witchcraft lore, as well as her supposed payment to the devil being menstrual blood.

For aids in simple flight (that is, flight that involves one leaving the body in human form and travelling from your own human perspective and perception), I recommend the following stave.

This stave above, designed to be carved into tools or tattooed on one's own body, is a contemporary stave of my own making. It has seen me up and down the world tree safely. It is "built" from runes and cypher alphabet letters and is simple to carve into most tools. Work it into broomsticks, short staffs, stangur, wands, or any tool one would use or carry while in spirit flight.

If the flight is to take place in your dreams or sleep, the following draumagaldur could easily be used along with various staves to help you achieve this flight. Spirit shapeshifting is the more commonly worked method of shifting one's form or perception while in flight. Working within an animistic framework, we need to consider that it is most often the lower soul, or the animal fylgja, that we are sending forth. Understanding fylgjur and the various forms these spirits take is something that becomes invaluable to us as we walk further down the Northern paths. I highly recommend putting aside a few months to try to focus on connecting with your fylgja every so often. It is, of course, a part of you, so it is always there. We can connect with it in many ways.

Some find meditative practices enough to establish a deeper connection with the various forms their fylgja can take. Some see it as more of an external entity, which, in my opinion, creates an unnecessary barrier one then needs to work past to heighten their bond with it. (The fylgja, while apart from us in some respects, is not removed from us.) Some find it helpful to visualise the animal fylgja in their everyday life, seeing it as an animal walking beside them, sitting on their shoulder, or flying above them. I would suggest not getting too caught up in doing this, as we may be creating limits that we don't realise and potentially ignoring other fylgjur and guide spirits that wish to communicate with us in forms we would reject.

LISTENING TO SPIRIT GUIDES

This simple meditative exercise is a good starting point when beginning to work with the various fylgjur and guides that appear to us. Find a quiet, comfortable spot where you won't be disturbed for about an hour or so. Use incense, music, or whatever you wish to help you reach a calm state. Once you've found a good state and rhythm of breath, begin to visualise yourself sitting at the base of a great tree. Observe the tree and see how it appears to you. I personally see it as a great tree trunk that stretches out in front of me, too wide and tall for me to see fully.

Imagine a doorway opening in the tree. Sometimes, I see this as the tree trunk with a natural cave inside of it. Walk through the doorway and through the darkness until you see yourself emerge into a forest. I see the forest often full of ponds; this is usually the in-between place I visit before journeying. Look around and, if you wish, call out to whatever spirit that wishes to guide you to make itself known to you. Then, wait and see what animal or other form appears. Do remember that the animal you see may not be one you particularly like; this is something that we all must come to terms with. Fylgjur and guides can appear as any animal, and while it is often something we have some level of familiarity with, this is not always the case.

The animal it appears as often has some anthropomorphic likeness to our current state, and recognising these traits in the animal form we see is a clear lesson to where we are and how we feel. Seeing a deer or other skittish animal, for example, may indicate some amount of anxiety in ourselves. A wolf could indicate some level of headstrong independence, or it may represent the need for community and pack. These spirits can teach us plenty about ourselves just by how they appear. Discernment and intuition—two skills we would all do well to develop thoroughly—are key here. You may see yourself as a bear, then have your guide appear as a squirrel with a valuable lesson in needing to focus on aspects of yourself

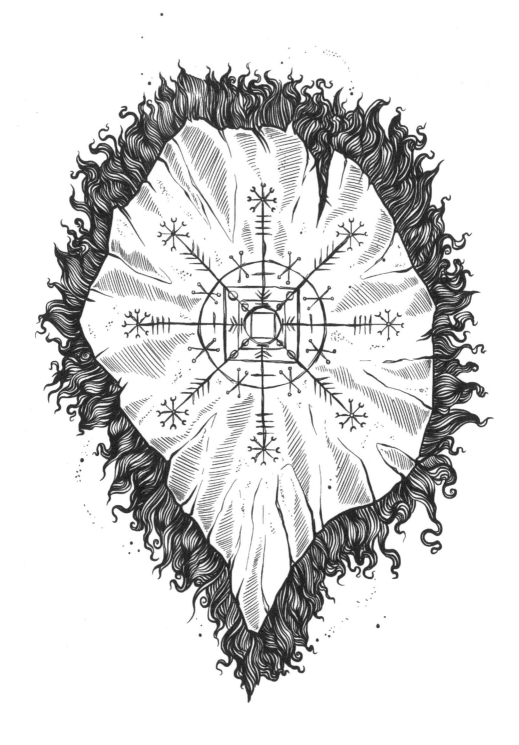

you may have thought useless. There is a lot about the inner worlds that fylgjur and guides can help us learn. As a means for venturing forth in spirit form, this animal form can serve as both a guide and vehicle itself. So, sit with whatever form appears to you, and when you feel you've taken in what needs to be learned, visualise being sat back at the base of that tree (maybe with your animal fylgja or guide sat beside you) before you return to yourself and go about your day.

Physical or conscious shapeshifting—moving about within the physical body within altered states of consciousness—or ritual is an experience I'd suggest every practitioner tries at some point in life. This sort of performance of moving the body as if it were in another shape can help us gain deeper understandings of animals and serve to aid in our spirit flight, too. Having moved through the woods as a hare, a favorite of Sussex witches, I saw the landscape from a new perspective, moving close to the ground, observing what my hands and feet touched, and how much sound a woodland makes when you don't lift your head more than a metre off the ground. Of course, one will never know what it's actually like to fly through the treetops or sail along the ground with the speed of four swift legs, but this sort of performative ritual can give us insights we otherwise would have never imagined. If you plan to go ahead with some form of physical shapeshifting, I recommend following this sort of formula.

"Physical" Hamfari

Find a space and length of time (I recommend one full night if you dare) to be undisturbed in a place. Keep safety in mind, and if planning to be outside for a long period of time, make sure a friend knows your whereabouts and avoid dangerous places. I appreciate that Iceland is a uniquely safe country with ample olpen space, so this may take more effort for those elsewhere. The rituals we can build around this sort of practice have a lot of folklore to draw from. We can observe the use of staves and herbs from Icelandic folk magic, skins from Sweden and Norway, and animal remains and footprints from German and continental witchcraft. A belt made from animal skin, for example, engraved or embroidered with a stave such as gandreið becomes a useful tool for both spirit and physical forms of shapeshifting. The method one chooses to follow could, for example, be taken from German folklore, drinking the water from the footprint of an animal. It could involve the Swedish trolldom practice of moving three times through the skin belt, or it could follow the Icelandic folklore of working with a pair of shoes, likely inscribed with staves such as gandreið.

Of all these methods, I have had the most successful ritual experiences working with a skin belt and sometimes simply a pelt inscribed with gandreið and reddened with a drop of blood. I then pass the belt or skin over my body three times while inside a simple circle in the woods. The circle need not be complicated; a simple circle such as the one included on page 133 has worked very well for me. One should undress, not necessarily going fully nude, though if space and safety allows, then this is ideal. Leave your clothes and all your belongings in the circle. I would then suggest lighting some incense and suffumigating yourself with it. The body is then passed under or through the skin or belt three times. Each time, I recite the following Icelandic galdur:

"Upp og fram, en hvörgi niður, í krafti þessari orði."

I first visualize my head changing, then my torso, then my legs. Once this has been done, I am free to venture out of the circle and explore my surroundings, moving through the woods and performing the role of the animal I've chosen. While this experience can be initially hard to engage with for those who have trouble placing themselves in other roles, once one moves past this, it can be quite an exhilarating experience, best when uninterrupted by dog walkers and other uninvolved parties. Once I feel the energy of this experience begin to dwindle, I return back to the circle and, in that safe space, go backwards three times under the skin or through the belt, returning to myself more with each passing.

If you wish to experience this sort of ritual shapeshifting, then I highly recommend taking things slow and emphasising safety and caution the first time. Make sure you create a space where you can be both ritually and mentally vulnerable. Also, it could be wise to make use of some paint mixed with powdered herbs to draw staves and symbols on the body. Always remember how this sort of thing may look to any mundane hiker you may come across, as well as avoiding this sort of practice during hunting seasons. As with all things in your craft, take time, care, and consideration for your own well-being before engaging in anything. If you want to make a pair of simple leather shoes to wear for this sort of practice, take the time to sew or emboss symbols into them, too.

Spiritual Hamfari

Physical shapeshifting may not be something you wish to engage in or something simply unreasonable due to season or location. In this case, you may make good use of most calm outdoor spaces to experience spiritual shapeshifting. Find a space where you will be able to comfortably sit for a good length of time. (Make sure to check on the weather forecast before this.) Create a small circle for yourself using the same method as before. If comfortable, wear a vest or some other clothing that allows you to feel the sun, wind, or moonlight on your skin. This sort of physical feeling on one's skin while engaging in shapeshifting can be very helpful.

Choose the timing of this exercise well, as liminal acts work best in liminal times; sunrise and sunset would be wise choices to utilise while beginning to explore this work. If you wish to work staves, choose a few to draw on your body and the tools you use. I suggest working a drum with a stave, or you could well work the skin method earlier while going forth only in spirit. Choose some incense that might help you access these deeper states as well. Once you feel the mood is set, take your drum, or, if lacking a drum, some sort of shaker, or maybe even an improvised packet of dried beans or nuts if that is all you have at hand. Begin to beat a steady rhythm, letting it slowly build as you feel yourself shift into the form of the animal you wish to become.

Let the drumming or shaking build and build, faster and faster, until you are ready to exhale your spirit out in one final breath. Do so, sloping back into a comfortable position, and let your spirit roam the landscape around you until you feel ready to return. Once you are ready, find your path back to your physical body. Some experience the silver tether, a sort of spiritual umbilical cord that connects your spirit and your physical body. This is sometimes also felt more than seen, so reach out for it if you can't see it. Follow this back to your body before you simply open your eyes.

While starting out at these practices, it can be tempting to simply feel our own bodies again and open our eyes. This doesn't help in making this practice as grounded as it needs to be. We are moving as spirits, exploring the world around us, so jolting our eyes open and pulling ourselves back can be a bit of a jarring experience that has left some quite disoriented, like the feeling of ascending too quickly while scuba diving. So, take time to return, and if needed, once back next to your body, slowly start to come back to yourself physically by bringing awareness to your breath, fingers, toes, and so on, moving up the body until you feel grounded and ready to open your eyes. Practice this again and again; it will help with general spirit flight, and once you have a good level of experience with one, the other usually follows.

SÁLARFLUG

Much of spirit flight is nowadays focused on the quite New Age idea of it being a psychological tool for personal development. Personally, I see it as much more than this. Though one can use it to discover inner worlds, these outer worlds exist and can be seen and explored through spirit flight. The modern notion that magic is about personal development alone is short-sighted. Our ancestors knew of spirits, entities that act like you and I, of their own accord. Yes, we are all connected, and yes, much of what we experience in life is seen through our own lenses. But Jung's archetypes, the idea that we contain the "all" within ourselves, washes away the nuance and perspective of other entities. The villains and heroes we see in stories can serve as mirrors to ourselves, yes, but we exist in a universe teeming with life and perspectives so vastly different from our own that approaching spirit flight solely from the mindset of inner meditation does you and your craft a disservice.

As animists, we understand fundamentally that all things have their own agency. Through this lens, we can't simply dismiss spirits and entities as aspects of our own psyche. We feel them, know their names, and recognise to varying extents the personhood of these non-human spirits. Good spirit flight takes you out of your body into the spirit realm (in whatever context you view it) and facilitates conversations with beings we would otherwise not often be able to hold coherent conversations with. We must, of course, be discerning and understand that, though we see these spirits, we see them as they appear to us, which may be vastly different to how they appear to others. It is with corroboration of experiences with others who speak to them that we can find commonality with many of these spirits.

Take the invocations of Goetic spirits, for example. We know the names and most common forms of these spirits through the corroborating experiences of ceremonial magicians over long periods of time. Of course, our individual experiences will contain individual differences, but common themes remain. These beings are real, and we must acknowledge them as such, both out of respect and for our own safety. This is why we work staves to protect us while venturing out in spirit: without these, we may be leaving ourselves vulnerable and practicing poor spiritual hygiene. If local folklore the world over is anything to go by, we know that some spirits are not so fond of humans (or, indeed, too fond), and we must do well to avoid danger. Once we acknowledge these dangers and the personhood of these entities, the fun can begin. Deep trance and long sessions of spirit flight can bring experiences many only have in dreams. From a Norse and Northern-based practice, we may find ourselves exploring the lush forests of Vanaheimur or the deep cold of Niflheimur, all with their inherent dangers and treasures.

Taking Flight

Spirit flight is begun in many ways, and just like with shapeshifting, you should take time to practice this skill. It is a lot easier for some than others, but don't let failure the first time put you off. I recommend following the same method of finding a suitable space and time and creating a circle you can comfortably lay back in, with space enough for your tools. Burn a suitable incense. Use staves, tools, and whatever feels most appropriate for you; the tools mentioned earlier suffice. A consecrated, stave-inscribed short staff or broomstick is an excellent start for those who don't have a drum. Sometimes, in-ear headphones with multiple hours of ad-free drum tracks make excellent aides, though I recommend getting yourself to a place where you can do this without the use of electronic tools over time. Once you've set up a suitable space, at a suitable time, with your tools and supplies inside the circle, take a few breaths to centre yourself. If you have a drum to use, I recommend following a similar drum beat to the previous example. If you wish, speak aloud the Icelandic words mentioned earlier:

"Upp og fram, en hvörgi niður, í krafti þessari orði."

Use this to mark what you are about to do. Start slowly and watch your breath, breathing slowly and deeply at first. Then, as you feel ready, increase the drum beat and speed of your breathing. Once you feel it build, work it faster and faster, following the growing energy within your body. At the point your breathing and drumming are fast enough, exhale and release your spirit. Guide yourself onwards. Whether you wish to visit a spirit in your area, explore a mound or hill inhabited by them, or fly to the sabbath, this technique is a good jumping-off point for many traditions and practices. As before, if you find yourself lost before you return to your body, feel for that cord and follow it back. Take time, as always, to ground yourself into your body before opening your eyes and rejoining the physical world. Some more guided experiences may be useful to try, such as exhaling one's spirit to begin a journey at the base of the world tree or within a forest of ponds and trees. Work with a few different examples and see what fits best for you over time. Just as with shapeshifting and útiseta, this technique takes time, but once you get the hang of it, the other two will be a lot easier to work with.

A Map for Flight

Some occultists and Pagans map the world tree overlapping the Kabbalistic tree of life. Sometimes, this overlapping of esoteric paths can be helpful, but the focus should be on testing and trying various examples of these overlaps if needed rather than getting lost at the new hurdle of trying to merge these theologies and traditions. Keep it simple and keep it practical. The world tree, Yggdrasil, can be seen as one tree among a forest of various worlds and lands from all paths around the Earth and beyond. The *axis mundi* can be experienced in many ways, but we tend to see Miðgarður as the world of physical form, bound and contained. Other realms outside of this exist in spirit as the other world(s). We can look at a map of the world tree to help us navigate our journeys, knowing which directions we should be heading and what they should feel like while remaining open to how they show themselves to us.

We know from myth that Niflheimur is cold, more aligned with ice and death. Múspellsheimur, in contrast, is hot, full of fire, and, again, death, echoing somewhat the infernal concept of the Christian hell in appearance. Hel is the land or lands of the dead. Within Hel, we find several areas where various types of spirits live. If we look at this from the animist perspective, it is where we might find some of the shades of our ancestors. The goddess Hel, sometimes called *Helja*, rules this realm, and it is not one I would recommend visiting or attempting to visit without need. Spirit flight to these sorts of underworlds can be dangerous, and more than one folk story and myth from around the world has carried the warning of what one might inadvertently bring back by mistake or get lost there entirely.

Other realms like Vanaheimur are much more gentle and safer to travel. In these realms, those of us who work with verdant spirits and occult herbalism may find a lot of knowledge. Much of this is, of course, the UPG of myself and my group, as well as others connected to these places that I've had the pleasure to talk with. Where that does not make it a solid fact, it does lend itself to the discerned commonalities between these realms. For those interested in this sort of exploration of the green realm, I suggest reading the work of Daniel A. Schulke and his descriptions of these verdant landscapes. Getting there from a Norse path perspective is easy. We can follow the spirits of plants we work with out in the field, asking them to take us there, or we can simply enter the reflection of the garden that dwells in Vanaheimur. Vanaheimur is the home of all the plant spirits of the world. This realm is green and lush, as myth dictates. We see it as the verdant realm itself, seen through many lenses by many people.

There are other realms one can visit, and the danger of doing so is up to the witch to weigh up. Within the Norse focus, we know that not all souls go to Hel or Óðinn; some go to Rán, the giant of the sea and wife of Ægir. The souls of those lost at sea are said to dwell in Rán's halls. The world of Jötunheimar, home to the jötun or þurs (giants), is somewhat of an isolated realm, and if the stories of Norse myth are much to go on, it is full of danger, considering that giants are forces of chaos. I encourage you to explore moving up and down the world tree as much as exploring your local area in spirit form.

For those of us who follow more traditional witchcraft-oriented paths, explore the sabbath, maybe in animal form if you wish. It would serve the traveller well to not get caught up in how the otherworld makes sense. This world is not bound by logic and matter like Miðgarður. It is free from these constraints, and it may well be that this land has no difference, but our lenses and perspectives influence how it appears to us. So, the Nordic ancestors who saw the green realm as Vanaheimur may have seen the same green realm experienced by all other peoples and faiths. Maybe the zeitgeist or volksgeist of where and when we are dictates how the otherworld appears to us.

11

Hɛlgidagar: Spɛ(ial Days

The Wheel of the Year in Icelandic practices looks a bit different from that of the UK and other British seasonally-inspired Wiccan wheels. Summer and winter in Iceland each take up half of the year, with a local joke being that spring and autumn last for two weeks each. Winter is long, and in the old days, it would have been a struggle. Both winter and summer consist of twenty-six weeks, with the first day of summer coming in April. This may seem odd to a lot of people, I'm sure, but spend any time in this landscape, and you'll see how all-encompassing the seasons are. The middle of winter is dark, cold, and usually stormy, and without modern comforts, it would not have been so fun to endure. During these darker times, people gathered (usually in family groups and small villages), coming together to share resources, housing, and stories. While no longer officially used by anyone, the old Icelandic calendar does give the Year Wheel of our practice. The old months were Lunar-based, and each month had its own feeling.

Þorri, for example, begins towards the end of January. During this time in the ancient past, there would have been a large midwinter feast. This tradition was revived in Iceland in the form of Þorrablót. We hold our own Þorrablót, with a ceremony and shared meal. I'll break down each festival around our year, along with the blóts we hold to honour the calendar months. We begin on January 6, the last night of Jól (Christmas).

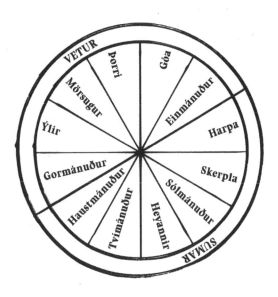

ᛒᚱᛖᛏᛏᚨᚾᛞᛁᚾᚾ PRETTÁNDINN

TWELFTH NIGHT, THE LAST NIGHT OF CHRISTMAS; JANUARY 6

The Álfar move house on this day and return from venturing into the human world. Nowadays, it is more associated with the Yule Lads returning to their mother Grýla one by one. Bonfires are lit in towns up and down the country to honour this day. In the past, townspeople dressed in costumes and masks so the elves could come and dance with humans around the bonfires without anyone knowing who was who. The acknowledgment of this tradition supposedly resulted in the town then being safe from the trickery and mischief of the hidden people for the following year. Herbs can be burned for the elves as an offering; this is the time that juniper would have been burned and used to smoke out the home and farm to prevent the elves from moving house and setting up shop in your home.

This dark time is perfect for divination, and often, people would come together for this. In a more modern context, it is the time of year when people come together to read tarot cards and runes and ask questions. In the old days, however, this would likely have been the time that the local spákona or travelling völva would have made an appearance, divining the future and usually sitting on her high seat sharing prophecies, visions, and thoughts on the coming year. It is also one of the nights that animals were supposed to be able to speak and communicate with humans. There is plenty of folklore around this, telling us stories of sneaky farm hands hiding in stables to hear the cows speak at midnight. This is also one of the nights when the selfólk (seal people) would come to shore and dance. We see this happen later on Jónsmessunótt as well. When planning our own practices on Þrettándinn, we have tools such as bonfires and divination aids to use. We can work our own blóts of thanks over the past Jól season and perform divinations for the year ahead.

THE START OF ÞORRI
JANUARY (FRIDAY BETWEEN JANUARY 19 AND 25)

The old calendar month of Þorri and its surrounding feasting may well come from an ancient midwinter feast that dates back to before the settlement of Iceland. In Iceland, this is the halfway point of winter. We mark this day with a blót followed by a feast. Within Icelandic folklore, the month of Þorri is personified as a misanthropic old man, often seen as a figure who needs to be invited in for the meal despite his unsavoury personality, lest ill befall the family. In later centuries, and as nationalism and romanticism of the Viking-age past crept in, poets often described him as a valiant figure in full armor, riding a horse with a spear in hand.

We see him mostly through the somewhat darker lens that reflects his season: a grumpy, gloomy guest, as dark and cold as the season he carries, who must be invited in as a means of appeasement more than a courtesy. He wears a cloak of bleak midwinter snow, as grey as the midday sky of Icelandic winter. His sullen face is often blue as the cold, and his hungry spirit should be fed as though he is one of the family so as to spare the worst of his season's weather. He was often sweetened by the tradition of the woman of the house inviting him in with a warm welcome; the modern marker for the beginning of Þorri is Bóndudagur (men's day). This is a day when women are supposed to be especially attentive to their husbands, echoing the woman of the home welcoming this spirit. This is reversed later when the man of the house invites Þorri's wife, the gentler Góa, into the home at the start of the following old calendar month. For blóts on Þorri, we can include feasts, small fires of thanks offered to this winter spirit, as well as gatherings of family. This season has become much more of a feast day since its resurgence in the last hundred years.

PÁLSMESSA
THE FEAST OF THE CONVERSION OF ST. PAUL; JANUARY 25

This Christian day is little celebrated by those who practice the folk magic and traditions in Iceland nowadays, save for the small piece of weather lore that comes from it. Supposedly:

"If Paul's day is fine and clear,
For the farmer it bodes a peaceful year.
But should a fog be on the land,
Death it brings for beast and man."

KYNDILMESSA
CANDLEMAS; FEBRUARY 2

This is the Icelandic name for Brighid's festival of Imbolc, or Candlemas to the Christians. On this day, the special kyndilmessa candle, which was made around Christmas, would have been burned. Within a historical context, this act would have been in keeping with Christian traditions. I, however, suggest that, as candles may be utilised by any spiritual practice, our local tradition of creating a candle around Christmas—involving herbs, oils and any other such magic you wish—may be burned this day for the protection of the home and family. The candle itself can be dipped, adding layer upon layer, with essential oils added to the melted wax, or crushed herbs rolled into it while still soft. This candle, once created at Christmas, could be blessed in any way one sees fit. Upon lighting the candle at Kyndilmessa, it would be wise to ask that it extend its protection over the family as winter wanes. The whole candle should be burned down within the day. Some weather lore surrounds this day, with the phrase going:

"Ef í heiði sólin sést,
á sjálfa kyndilmessu
snjóa vænta máttu mest
maður upp frá þessu."

"If the sun shines in a
clear sky on Candlemas,
you can expect snow
to come along next."

This foretells that good weather on this day will often give way to more snow and frost in the coming weeks.

THE START OF GÓA

Góa is the name of Þorri's wife. She is a much more welcome spirit than her husband, bringing with her the promise of gentler weather. Should the first three days of her season be fair, then the following months will remain harsh and cold. If these three days are full of snow, storms, and rain, then the worst of winter has passed and will give way to good weather. There is some suggestion that Góiblót, another (albeit smaller) midwinter feast, was held on this day, but this is not something that has much supporting evidence. We hold a small blót to mark the start of this season, though not a feast afterwards. As mentioned earlier, Góa is welcomed into the home and farm by the man of the house. This tradition has now become Kónudagur (women's or wives' day), a day where women are celebrated, especially by their partners. For our own Góiblót, we could centre it around celebrating and honouring the women in our lives.

GVENDARDAGUR
MARCH 16

This day is dedicated to a saint who never was: bishop Guðmundur Arason, known as "Gvendur the good." He amassed a large following of Icelanders in the 1200s and was very popular. His exploits tell of how he blessed many places within Iceland but eventually stopped when attempting to bless Drangey, an island off the coast. While swinging over the cliff on a rope, a voice could be heard telling him to stop as "the wicked must have somewhere to rest." The island was later known as Heiðnaberg (heathen's rock). This day can be utilised by those who wish to include his blessings on protective talismans and amulets. As what could be argued as a folk saint within Iceland, he falls into the category of holy men that it is not considered proper to include in worship, though we as practitioners may call upon his aid when blessing and purifying spaces and things.

THE START OF EINMÁNUÐUR
MARCH (SUNDAY BETWEEN MARCH 20 AND 26)

The next month in the Old Icelandic calendar often translates to "lone month." This day would likely have been marked with some monthly blót of some kind. Our group works the day as not only time for blót but also work relating to the beginning of spring and new starts. It's even better for this purpose if the time coincides exactly with the new moon. The spirit of this day may well have been the son of Þorri. If we follow the logic of the last two months giving way to days for men and women, this day this month gives way to what was known as *Yngismannadagur* (young men's day). We don't have a name for this young man, but this energy coincides with the reawakening of spring, an easy parallel to draw with puberty and the awakening of this new chapter in the lives of young adults.

Perhaps the reason we don't have a name for this spirit is due to the repressive views of Christianity towards the "spring awakening." Either way, this month may be welcomed with a blót that focuses on the beginning of spring and the welcoming of new growth and beginnings. A little modern folklore we associate with this month is the welcoming of Einmánuður with offerings to Freyr and other such spirits of fertility and traditionally masculine aspects of growth. Weather lore tells us that should this month be wet, then a good and fertile spring will be on the way, providing even more associations to the fertility imagery surrounding this month.

PÁSKAR
EASTER; THE FIRST SUNDAY AFTER
THE FULL MOON FOLLOWING THE SPRING EQUINOX

Icelandic Easter traditions are many. Of course, as one of the holiest days for Christians, the theme of birth and rebirth flows throughout from Pagan days to modern times. In Iceland (and elsewhere), the Easter fire played an important role. This fire had to be blessed by the priest, although for us who practice, we may bless our own Easter fires not for Christ but in the name of the rebirth of the Earth and the return of plant and animal life. Easter morning in Icelandic folklore is a perfect day to search for óskastienar (wishing stones). Along with Whitsunday, Easter morning is a day so holy that trolls and spirits are said to sleep all day, making it safe to venture out to find various magical stones and objects. We may use this in our practices to find various magical stones usually protected by trolls and unclean spirits. It is also a day used to consecrate tools, especially those baring staves such as the stave of Móses, Aaron, and María. The sun is said to "dance" on Easter. This is likely the natural phenomenon of the sun shining through ice crystals in the sky. This shining sky is also part of Irish and Scottish traditions and folklore and may well have traveled to Iceland with Scottish and Irish slaves.

THE START OF HARPA
April (Thursday between April 19 and 25)

The start of Harpa, the next old calendar month, also marks the official beginning of summer in Iceland. Harpa is the daughter of Þorri and Gói, sister to the spirit of Einmánuður. She is the innocent and youthful energy of summer, full of hope and freedom, and ready to start frolicking around the awakening meadows and forests. We celebrate the beginning of this season with a blót to Harpa, as well as to Freyja, asking her to share in her abundance and bring us all the fruits of Summer. Don't be fooled: this day isn't usually a warm summer's day. She marks the beginning when lots of plants are still just beginning to grow. This is a time for sowing seeds that we wish to bear fruit in the coming few months, a time for putting energy into projects and socialising. Nowadays, the energy of this season is reflected in *Yngismeyjardagur* (young women's day). Like the previous young men's, women's, and men's days, this day was intended for young people to court each other or otherwise show interest in marriage and romance, very much fitting with the vibe of the season.

VALBORG
Valpurgisnacht, May's Eve; May 1

Known to those in Sweden and Germany for bonfires and celebrations, this day is also observed by some practitioners in Iceland. The origins of this day are obviously Pagan, but Valborg is named after a Christian saint whose cult developed in the Middle Ages. Valborg, in the past, was a time to light protective fires. In modern practice, this day can be celebrated in the same way. It's a perfect time for all works of protection, as well as foraging for early sprouting protective herbs and creating protective powders and oils. The week between May 1 and May 8 is revered for good foraging in Northern Europe. In Iceland, the land is waking up, and summer has begun, but not all the plants one would want are fully grown or large enough to really be of use. We celebrate this night by working any magic regarding spirit flight, protection, and work connected to the Sabbath of the mainland. This day is also now focused on workers' rights. It was marked by marches for fair labour laws and union establishment and is now marked as a public holiday in celebration of workers' rights.

HVITSUNNA
WHITSUN OR WHITSUNDAY; SEVENTH SUNDAY AFTER EASTER, BETWEEN MAY 10 AND JUNE 14

In Iceland and abroad, this is a holy day. It's so holy, in fact, that all trolls and creatures are said to sleep this day. Along with Easter, this makes it a great day for finding náttúrusteinar and vanquishing trolls. One story tells us how the King of Norway helped advise in the slaying of the tröllkona Jóra. He instructed Icelanders to wait until Whitsun, then seek out a troll, as she would be sleeping on this holy day. The Icelanders then struck her in the back with an axe, and she leaped up, running down to Þingvallavatn where she drowned. Folklore says that an indicator of illness and evil on this day is sleep, and anyone who falls asleep during the day should be watched carefully for trollish behavior. Of course, to us in the twenty-first century, this may sound a little ableist, but should you suspect someone of working sorcery against you, you could work a spell to put them to sleep on this day if they have worked against you. If it works, you can deduce how best to proceed.

THE START OF SKERPLA
MAY (SATURDAY BETWEEN MAY 19 AND 25)

Not a lot is known of this month besides its mention in the sagas as Eggtíð and Stekktíð. We mark it as the beginning of the month of Skerpla, in keeping with the old Lunar calendar. A small blót is held around this time. This season usually has good weather before the height of summer, so the spirits and deities you wish to venerate with this blót are up to you. It is a good time for focusing on growth and perseverance, in keeping with the sun gaining power each day.

THE START OF SÓLMÁNUÐUR

June (Monday between June 18 and 24)

This month is the height of Icelandic summer. In the old days, it was a time for foraging herbs, grazing sheep and cattle, and castrating lambs. This month occasionally coincides with Jónsmessu, and usually, instead of holding two blóts within the space of a week, we focus on marking Jónsmessu and the start of Sólmánuður at the same time with one big midsummer blót and celebration, including the traditions found below. This is supposedly the best month for harvesting angelica.

JÓNSMESSUNÓTT

June 24

Jónsmessunótt takes place the night before the Catholic feast of Saint John. In Icelandic folklore and magic, this is the most important night of the magical year. It is a night for collecting certain herbs and rolling naked in the morning dew—as well as collecting it for making magical waters. Many specific oils and brews are made on this day. It is also a prime night for collecting náttúrusteinar and other magical objects, as well as another day that animals are supposed to be able to speak. Jónsmessunótt is also used for divination, with many magical herbs being used to divine the names and faces of thieves, future lovers, and more. We can't really call this night a true night in Iceland, as the sun only barely dips below the horizon. However, from dusk to dawn (usually a period of only a few hours), we should be out picking, foraging, and finding, ready to roll naked in the morning dew when dawn arrives. It is said that this dew should be left to dry naturally on the skin. Jónsmessunótt is also associated with selkie lore as the night that the seal folk would come ashore and shed their seal skins to dance in their human form.

JÓNSMESSU

The Old Summer Solstice; June 25

After a night of gathering and rolling naked in the dew at dawn, we light bonfires and hold blóts during the day to honour the fullness of summer and all the joy it brings. This day is also another house-moving day for the hidden people, and bonfires were held in the past to commemorate this. It is also the best time to cleanse and bless tools for the coming year. One such cleansing ritual can be found later on pages 121-122 involving forget-me-nots, other plants, and spring water gathered on Jónsmessa. Jónsmessa clearly became a Christian stand-in for older summer solstice traditions, but no matter what you call this day, the energy remains the same. Gatherings for this day aren't as commonplace nowadays, but plenty of magical folk organise gatherings for this day and sometimes the night before. This liminal time is a day when many spirits and entities are said to be seen much more clearly.

THE START OF HEYANNIR
JULY (SUNDAY BETWEEN JULY 23 AND 30)

As the name suggests, this month focuses on gathering hay and fodder for storage over winter. A blót may be held as the first of many small harvest gatherings, utilising the fruits of early summer, such as rhubarb jam in Iceland. This is a good time for beginning to give thanks and offerings to the landvættir. It is the time of year when söl (dulse seaweed) is collected, as well as certain herbs like caraway and alpine bistort.

MARIUMESSA
AUGUST 15

The day of Mary in spring is March 25, and the day of Mary in summer is August 15. These two days are the most appropriate for harvesting herbs for working with the Christian Mary as they are specifically Christian holy days. Magical workings for all things that Mary rules over are best performed on these days. All workings of motherhood, childbirth, chastity, fidelity, and faith are all most appropriate for these days.

THE START OF TVÍMÁNUÐUR
AUGUST (TUESDAY BETWEEN AUGUST 22 AND 28)

Another month with a focus on the harvest. This month in Snorri's *Edda* is called "kornskurðarmánuður" (the month of corn harvest). In general, this is the time for harvesting all of the grains and grasses in Iceland before the cold of September begins to creep in. The sun's power is beginning to wane, and so we focus our blóts deeper into giving thanks and acknowledging that the seasons are soon to shift from summer back to winter. We prepare ourselves for the return of darker spirits and ready offerings to appease them, sometimes creating wreaths and sun crosses of corn and barley to be burned once the sun returns after winter. Blóts often honour Freyr, who begins to mourn the loss of his love, Gerður, and, with her, the passing of summer.

MARY'S BIRTHDAY
September 8

The date of the birth of Mary is a day to focus specifically on workings of motherhood and nurturing. As you will have seen by now, Iceland was not entirely immune to religious syncretism, and for many people, Mary replaced Freyja as the patron of women, which makes this a day to also work with Freyja.

THE FINAL DAY OF MARY
September 15

This is the last day of Mary within the year, held as the last day to forage certain herbs specifically for working with receptive, motherly energies. This is also the last best day to gather maríustakkur (*Alchemilla vulgaris*) for winter supplies.

THE START OF HAUSTMÁNUÐUR
September (Thursday between September 21 and 27)

This month, literally called "harvest month," marks the final moments for harvest before the frost sets in. This time is about beginning to say goodbye to the lighter aspects of the land and releasing summer and its spirits. A blót can be held with a focus on the importance of grain and corn, with a focus on Freyr and Gerður and their combined effect on the year's harvest, feasting on bread and other baked goods, as well as any of summer's bounties that won't be stored for winter feasts. Freyr and Freyja can be bid farewell, as well as gerður and other summer figures, at the end of the blót. The beginning of winter is one month later.

THE START OF GORMÁNUÐUR
OCTOBER (SATURDAY BETWEEN OCTOBER 21 AND 27)

This month begins with the first day of winter. Typically, this was a time for the slaughter of animals after summer. For us, this marks the last of the harvest festivals, and we hold a blót that marks the change from the spirits and season of summer to the spirits and season of winter. The coin flips, and this date marks the day that the darker spirits (or aspects of spirits) regain their hold over the land. It's not a dismal or "evil" time, just the natural turning of the year and the handing over of nature to the less gentle, harsher, and more dangerous spirits of the lands. We hold the first winter fire on at this blót. Usually, the air is already cold, and bad weather may have already come.

Skaði and other winter figures begin to be venerated and have their stories told. We focus on the importance of taking stock, beginning to slow down, and consolidating for winter. Offerings at blót include tobacco, spirits, blood, and bread. The herbs of last summer that have gone unused this year should be burned to appease approaching winter spirits. This is the time for Álfarblót, dedicated to the elves, but we also honour Freyja and Óðinn. A blót to all these forces is appropriate at this time, and offerings can be made to the mounds, hills, and stones we know the hidden people inhabit.

THE START OF ÝLIR
NOVEMBER (MONDAY BETWEEN NOVEMBER 20 AND 27)

This is the second winter month. The name *Ýlir* is of unclear origin, though some think it relates to *Jólnir*, one of the names of Óðinn. November can be a harsh month in Iceland, with plenty of storms and unstable weather. During this time, we give offerings to the spirits of the land and sky that hold sway over the weather. This would be a good time to hold a smaller blót and last harvest, giving thanks to the land spirits before the last of the summer spirits fall dormant. I recommend burning dried angelica leaves as incense for this blót, honouring the spirits falling to sleep before turning to the coming winter spirits, and asking for a gentle winter that all will survive through.

SAINT LUCY'S DAY

DECEMBER 13

Saint Lucia (or Lucy) of Syracuse was a Christian martyr. Her symbol is the crown of candles, which is familiar to many in Scandinavia. This day is not such a big part of Icelandic practice, but some local practitioners do hold this day sacred. She is patron of the return of the light in the darkness of winter, and due to this, some witches have mixed Christian traditions with their own and call on her to bless herbal blends, candles, oils, and more with her energy of light in the dark nights. I personally incorporate her into my work around this time, bringing her light into the depths of Icelandic winter to empower blends against seasonal affective disorder, if only by bringing that much-needed light to the home for a moment.

THE START OF MÖRSUGUR

DECEMBER (WEDNESDAY BETWEEN THE 20 AND 27)

The third month of winter brings the solstice as well as Jól and all its thirteen days, looping us back around to Þorri. The name *mörsugur* means "fat-sucking," with *mör* being the word for the hard fat that surrounds the organs of animals, an important food source in the old days during this month. Now, we luckily don't need to rely on the fat of animals to help get us through winter. It can be a time that we give thanks to the animals whose lives help sustain those who consume them. A small blót can be held during this month, though we use solstice for the monthly festival. It is a time of great activity for the huldufólk, who are said to move homes around the solstice and again at New Year's, as well as one of the months we utilise the crossroads for útiseta and more.

YULE

VETRARSÓLSTÖÐUR, MÓÐURNÓTTIN;
DECEMBER (BETWEEN DECEMBER 21 AND 23)

The winter solstice is the darkest point of the year when almost all plants are buried in snow or deeply asleep. The energy in Iceland shifts to something darker, and Grýla and many other troll figures roam the land. We call on our foraged reserves of herbs to work with now that they are unavailable in nature. Winter solstice is a perfect time for any workings of prophecy, such as burning certain herbal blends and scrying with dried herbs. The solstice is also a time for many divinations and herbal workings, as the thin veil between the realms is felt and Huldufólkið make more mischief.

This also means it is a time for inner work and protections. I try to use this time to make small torches from any mullein (*Verbascum thapsus*) that I have collected on travels throughout the year or have been lucky enough to grow myself. This non-native plant is a powerful plant ally in many workings, and I'm sure many readers in the rest of Europe will be familiar with it. My group holds a bonfire and blót ceremony on this night, usually honouring and appeasing the darker forces of the land and comforting the god Freyr now that the giantess Gerður has turned her back to him, bringing winter. Skaði and Grýla rule and forces, such as the terrible Angurboða, make their influence on the world known. Usually, we would have a small feast on this night as well, and as a tradition, it has grown into something we all look forward to each winter.

JÓL, CHRISTMAS
DECEMBER 25

Though now a massive Christian festival, in the old days, just as with midsummer, this time would have marked midwinter. This shifted later to Þorri, which we now use to mark the middle of winter, but for many of those not in Iceland, this time already marks the shift of darkness back towards the light. Jól in Iceland has a lot of associated folklore. Many will know of the "Thirteen Santas," the children of Grýla and her less-mentioned second husband, Leppalúði. Grýla has only been associated with Christmas since around the seventeenth century, but her name is mentioned much earlier in Snorri's *Edda*, along with other troll women:

"Skal ek trollkvenna
telja heiti:
Gríðr ok Gnissa,
Grýla, Brýja,
Glumra, Geitla,
Gríma ok Bakrauf,
Guma Gestilja,
Grottintanna."

Grýla has been a popular boogeyman for children in Iceland for a long time. At this time of year, it is said that she spends her days and nights searching the countryside for children to catch, cook, and eat. If you want, you could hold a specific Jólblót for Óðinn under his name, Jólnir, offering seasonal things such as food and beer. These dark months are also an excellent time of year to practice draumagaldur and forspár, as well as all forms of divination. New Year's, especially in modern Iceland, has become an occasion for those of us who practice gathering for annual divination for the year ahead. This is based on the ancient tradition of the völva travelling from town to town to perform this for the townspeople.

PLANNING BLÓT AND CEREMONY

Actually, planning and preparing blóts and ceremonies should have been made a little simpler now that we know which days are traditionally worked on and a little of what might be involved in ceremonies held on these days. For example, we know we can focus on harvest during the autumn, as many witchcraft traditions do, or that we can work with bonfires on þrettándinn based on this long-standing tradition in Iceland. We should always remember that blót means sacrifice, and, as such, our blóts should always include some aspect of this.

Whether it be food offered up, blood, burned herbs, burned paper covered in words of gratitude, or whatever fits your blót, it is good to remember that the focus should be on sacrifice and offering. What we do this for varies, but especially in the often-harsh landscape of Iceland, we recognise that blóts are more often worked to appease forces beyond our control. We can, of course, create blóts of thanks and offering to different deities and spirits, but there should always be an element of sacrifice within them.

When planning blóts outside of Iceland that are intended to correspond with seasonal milestones, such as the solstices and equinoxes, it is always a good idea to relate these changes to those within your own land. Marking the first night of winter during late October in a more temperate climate wouldn't be the most appropriate. Instead, work with the seasonal calendar of your own land and its spirits. If you follow Ásatrú a little deeper, work offerings to the gods around the most appropriate times within your own environment. This might sound intuitive, but many people outside of Iceland get stuck on this, stating it as inaccurate to mark these occasions on days other than those named in Iceland. This is counterproductive and ultimately works towards unalignment with the very natural forces you may be trying to appease or honour.

We can work with Jól as more of a static happening, placing it before or between the winter solstice and Christmas day, based on its modern assimilation with Christmas. However, to hold a blót to the álfar or mention the jólasvienarnir (the yule lads) in lands whose spirits are not these entities should not be the focus. We can take the regional aspects out of these ceremonies, blóts, and traditions and still find enrichment within them. We don't need to worry about things being authentic to the tradition when we are in a land foreign to the concepts and spirits we are trying to venerate.

This is part of how traditions change as humans migrate, but as animists, we must always acknowledge the nuances and differences between spirits wherever we are. Ignoring native spirits of the land in the US, for example, and placing imported gods above them in hopes of authenticity should not be the focus. We should be doing our best to honour the land, especially in the US with all its history. Of course, we can pray to our gods from wherever we may be, but to conduct a ceremony in the US the same way one would in Iceland would not be in alignment with the land.

As we learned, in Iceland, we open our blóts and ceremonies by acknowledging the four dwarves who hold up the sky. This is fine to do wherever you are within the world, the sky of which these dwarves hold up. However, to take it a step further and try to acknowledge native spirits of lands outside of Northern Europe as elves and trolls is where we begin to run into problems. Some may argue that as people migrated, so did the spirits of their land. This may be the case in some instances, but we need to remember that the real world doesn't work like the plot of *American Gods*, and we would often do our best to acknowledge the land spirits by their own names, forms, and nuanced beings.

This is not intended to discourage anyone from working with the material in this book, nor is it to undermine anyone's practice. But when specifically referring to the land, we would do best not to copy and paste ideas from one culture's understanding over those of the one that first inhabited the land and understood its spirits. Nowadays, things such as land acknowledgement in the US and Australia have become part of many ceremonies, meetings, and gatherings.

This is exactly the mindset that we, as animists, should be working with. Ignoring the difference in the spirits of the land is not a practice we want to perpetuate. I feel a distinct difference between the landvættir of Iceland and the landwights of the UK. The way hills and mounds feel in Sussex, England, is completely different from those of Australia and Iceland. When holding ceremonies in places outside of Iceland, I focus on giving thanks to these land spirits, whether we know their names or not. Burning certain herbs, as long as local folklore and knowledge say this is inoffensive to the land, is a great action to build ceremonies of thanks around.

Working simple magic circles is also a method we can use to create our own bubble for ceremony that then won't leak into the realms of local land spirits we don't want to offend. Two of the circles I work with for this can be found on page 133, and creating sacred spaces is expanded upon on page 130 and again on page 304. We can work out our own small sacred spaces—both circles and vé—anywhere as long as this won't offend the land we are working on. A simple blót, then, may consist of the creation of a sacred space in land that we know to be suitable.

A small fire can be made within this space, and offerings can be burned while we sing, pray, chant, or otherwise express our thanks and devotion to certain spirits and deities. The simple form of this is easy enough to tweak to whatever specifications we may have, and we can work all sorts of elements into it: sacred wine drinking, the burning of woods like juniper with its protective virtues, and even magical staves traced in the sand or soil.

A final word on creating spaces for ceremony outside: we should always do our best to leave the land the way we found it—or better. So clear away after yourselves and do your best to make sure the land is in good shape. For those who wish to work with more Neo-Pagan and Ásatrú style rituals and blóts and want to include prayers and chants in your work, I suggest a book like Eirik Westcoat's *Viking Poetry for Heathen Rites* for some good inspiration.

12

Kyngiveður: Weather Working Magic

Weather magic has always played a role in the folk magic of the Nordic countries. From the tales of storm summoning seiður in the sagas to contemporary and folkloric works to bend the sky to our will, nornir all over the Nordics have used this magic to harm or help. Within our practices in Iceland, we find prayers for good weather, contemporary work with herbs and staves to summon or repel the rain, and, most notably, the summoning of storms. From our animistic perspective, weather work is hard. We approach the spirits of these forces, the loftandi and giants who shepherd the sky, with care and respect.

Changing the weather is difficult. These spirits move of their own accord and don't often tend to listen to us way down here. Summoning storms, for instance, is hard work used in the sagas in times of dire need, working not only the spirits of the Air but also those of the sea. For us, the sea spirits are more easily swayed, and with the addition of offerings, changes in the weather of coastal areas usually receive positive results faster. Offerings to sea spirits to calm the wind seem to also work well for us.

This relationship between spirits that inhabit the sky and sea might not be as complicated as one would imagine. Sacrifice plays a large part in the success of weather work, whether this is our own sacrifice or the promise of the lives lost at sea, which the weather work in the sagas may have gained success from. Now, of course, this sort of storm rising with the promise of loss of life is incomprehensible. However, we can use alternatives to try and sway the land and sea to our cause.

As with all things in animism, personal relationships with these spirits may be the easiest way to work these. We could befriend or pact with a spirit somewhere along this chain of command and hope their influence with higher powers pays off. For example, making pacts with the spirit of a lake or water source that governs the groundwater in your area could, in turn, provide us with a route to asking the spirits of the sky above this place to bring about rain. Making pacts with a land spirit of a large area of forest could mean we can ask it to ask the loftandi above to calm the wind or stop the rain.

Human motives for wanting to change the weather rarely work. Spirits won't care that we ants don't like the rain and want to use our day for something trivial. They may, however, care if there is a real need for less or more rain, such as during a drought or time of flooding. Rain is the easiest to call on, and the slight wind is also simple. Calming and stopping these is often less effective. Some contemporary staves exist for calling rain and wind, which can be worked alongside plenty of techniques from various parts of Europe and Iceland. The use of heather, for example, plucked and sprinkled with a little galdur and a stave works well, especially when performed out on a heath. Whistling the wind is found in a few countries and works well for summoning up light gusts, such as needed for fishermen's sails. According to anecdotes, this sort of work is made even more fruitful in the future if an offering of some of the fish caught is offered to the sea and wind spirits after the work succeeds.

The loftandi who shepherd the sky are elusive and often unreachable in our experience. Though we have seen them in trance, they could be imagined as giants made of wind with long staffs who stir the sky. This interpretation is entirely our own UPG and not based on any folklore visualisations of what sky spirits look like. However they may look, these spirits are the ones you need to appeal to if you wish your weather work to work in Iceland (or to a higher spirit that has some sway over them). Workings such as the contemporary stave to encourage rain have worked well in my experience, though I would suggest that, as the weather spirits of various regions of the world may differ, it would be wise to try out how it works and tweak it should it be needed. In contemporary practice within Iceland, we can also ask the four landvættir for help with the weather and hope they deem it appropriate to help.

Other spirits that we might classify as Airy or sky spirits include all eagles, bird spirits, and creatures such as the dragons birthed in the following folk tale. In Icelandic folklore, dragons are born from the eggs of eagles. All one needs to do is find an eagle's nest and place some gold beneath one of the eggs. This egg will then hatch into a dragon, which, within a short time, may cause a lot of trouble. The folklore tells us that this happened once in Borgarfjörður. A man named Jón knowingly placed gold under an eagle's egg, trying to produce a dragon. This is said to have worked, and many of the townspeople claimed to have seen the dragon fly over town and south across Leirárvogur. They tasked Jón with killing the creature, which he said he was only able to do by making bullets from the silver of his shirt buttons.

Dragons in nineteenth-century Icelandic folklore are much closer to the ideas of four-legged, winged dragons flying about mountain tops, such as Drekki, the landvættur of the East, though spirits appearing as subterranean dragons, closer to the mythological Níðhöggur, as well as sea serpents, also pop up in stories around the country. Gammur, the great eagle of the North, is said to rule over a whole host of bird and bird-like spirits. These may well include some of the spirits which influence the weather.

Some Icelandic weather magic involves conjuring storms. This sort of magic, at least in the Viking age, would have likely been classed as seiður. One method for working foul weather involves the use of niðstöng. This action of stirring up and enraging the spirits of the land would very likely result in a violent storm. Where niðstöng topped with the head of a horse or land animal enraged land spirits, niðstöng topped with a fish head may well have been worked to enrage the sea spirits. I don't recommend this sort of work. When working in an animistic framework, the discord it can create is damaging to relationships with spirits of place. We would do better to try to work various staves and other less offensive workings.

One weather-related stave from stave collections stands out. Named a stave "to call Northern weather," it may be worked to bring about snow, storms, and more. In Iceland, snow and storms can come at any time of year, so working it outside of Iceland may have a different feel. Keep in mind the damage a storm can do, as well as the ethics of this sort of work.

This stave comes with no specific instructions other than to be wristed and reddened as usual. I suggest working it into treebark to be thrown to the sea or worked into a stang, thrust into the ground in the direction one wishes to conjure this Northern weather.

Other staves of this nature can be found later, on page 206 of the grimoire, as well as other workings of weather magic. Remember that, often, weather work is fickle and needs to be worked at just the right moment to take effect.

13

Sjónhverfing:
Butter to Rocks and
Rams to Mice

The Icelandic art of casting an illusion, or *sjónhverfing*, has been well-documented throughout folklore. Both humans and magical creatures make use of it. Sjónhvefing can take many forms, from the previously mentioned green ointment of the álfar to the following story of human deception.

In the early fifteenth century, there lived a woman named Halla on the trading island of Straumfjörður. When a merchant ship docked in Hraunshöfn on the nearby Snæfellsnes peninsula, she decided to go meet the merchants to purchase household necessities. She went with a caravan of horses and twelve old rams to trade with the merchants. She traded them a good amount of butter and tallow, as well as the rams, for all that she needed. She packed her horses again and went to leave. But just as she was leaving, someone looked over the goods she had traded and saw that the butter and tallow had turned to rocks and the rams to mice.

The merchants were shocked and left to peruse her. When she noticed their pursuit, a fog descended so that none could see their own hands before their faces. Still, they pursued and, once out of the fog, chased again. When crossing a river, they caught up to her. Again, she deceived their eyes so that they only saw sods of grass and strewn boulders where the horses were. She escaped without being seen and returned home with her new goods.

This nineteenth-century folk story gives us examples of both sjónhverfing and weather work. Practically, these techniques are both useful and potentially lifesaving to the Icelandic conjurors and wizard priests of the fifteenth century and beyond. In Icelandic folklore and stories, illusion work tends to be used mostly either in escape or defence, deceiving humans or dangerous trolls, as well as the álfar working illusions and invisibility as part of their being. A few staves have been worked throughout Iceland's history for illusions and invisibility; the instructions for some are like other invisibility spells found around Europe. (You can read more about this in Chapter Twenty-Seven.)

Some illusionary herbs worked in Iceland, backed up by use elsewhere, are the seeds of *Aconitum napellus* (known in Iceland as *Venusvagn* and *Bláhjálmur*), Venus's wagon, and blue helmet. On the mainland of Europe, the seeds are said to make one invisible when worked into a pouch of lizard or sheep skin. In Iceland, they are to be worked along with berries of *Cornus suecica* (the dwarf cornel or *skollaber* in Icelandic), as well as *Bartsia alpina* (alpine bartsia or smjörgras).

These three are to be gathered in a pouch made of the skin of either a fish or an Arctic fox. The fox skin makes sense, as this animal is a cunning and elusive one (more on the properties of the fox later). As for fish skins, many kinds of fish skins will work for this, as the theory is that the reflective properties of the scales, as well as their ability to "melt" from perception into the water, make skin a useful tool for going unseen. Making a fish or fox skin charm bag for this sort of magic would be best done under the day and hour of Saturn.

The fox is a wonderfully elusive creature, aspects of which can be used perfectly for this sort of sjónhverfing. Working with the spirits of foxes as both familiars and servitors may help, but utilising the remains of these animals makes for potent works of deception and trickery. Bones and remains worked into vessels for birthed or otherwise acquired fox-like spirit servitors are a useful tool for the særingarmaður who wishes for themself or their spirits to pass unseen. Working a fox skull as a vessel or tool, or parts of fox bones as amulets to acquire the fox's sneaky abilities, is also an option. A small fox bone inscribed with a stave or two and reddened with blood under the auspices of Saturnine spirits and herbs also makes for a potent tool. A stave such as this would work well.

Halla of Straumfjörður and her sorcery, while recorded, is sadly not expanded on. For all we know, her methods weren't written down or recorded. As for sjónhverfing, fox bones and assorted seeds are just the beginning. It wouldn't be Icelandic magic without a healthy number of magical staves thrown in. There aren't many older staves that work specifically with illusion and deception, so many contemporary staves that we work with are used for these. However, there are plenty of staves that simply work to grant your wishes and requests. The innovative witch would do well to work these to their advantage with small illusions and tricks. While no one can truly go completely unseen—besides our hidden neighbours—plenty of plants and staves have been used by many of us in living (and recent living) practice.

As mentioned before, *Bartsia alpina*, *Cornus suecica*, and *Aconitum napellus* are three perfect plants to work with for this. I would also add the seeds of most *Papaver* species to workings intended to hide. As with the previously mentioned working of invisibility, bring these all together within a pouch of some skin. Rabbit skin is also a good animal remain to add in the virtues of cunning and ability to elude. This pouch can be inscribed inside and out with various staves. The Icelandic invisibility stave that most people know is Hulinhjálmur.

There are few recorded original instructions. The most intensive is, of course, both very difficult and ethically questionable (though you can still read about it in Chapter Twenty-Seven). As a hjálmur (helmet or helm), this stave is ideal to work with either on one's brow or placed about the head. I would personally suggest that the stave be carved into either a small piece of wood, written on fresh parchment, or drawn on a small piece of leather. The stave should then be reddened with blood. If you can manage to take it from all of these spots, then feel free; otherwise, go with Saturnine points such as the hands, legs, and middle fingers. Then, anoint it with an oil of the flowers of another hjálmur, the bláhjálmur (*Aconitum napellus*).

Do this with extreme care, especially around any open cuts, as this plant is toxic. This should be undertaken within a Saturnine day and hour, ideally also on a dark moon, just to get as much shadow and secrecy involved. Read galdur over the talisman, especially if it's something mentioning how the stave will hide you from sight. If you wish to work in the names of Óðinn as the concealer and mask, then call on him under the names *Gímnir*, *Blindi*, and *Fjölnir*. Touch the finished talisman to your brow, then either place it within your hat or wear it in a secured and enclosed pendant around your neck.

Black cat bones have been worked as talismans for secrecy in many parts of the world. These, too, would make useful talismans for turning sight. As the black cat melts into the darkness of night, this contemporary stave is designed to cloak one in darkness to go unseen. It's specifically designed to work with a feline feeling rather than the previous staves, which worked with fox remains.

Cats have been a part of Icelandic folklore and culture since the settlement of Iceland, inspiring legends of mythical offspring such as the Skoffinn and Skuggabaldur, as well as, more recently, Jólakötturinn, the Christmas cat and pet to the giantess Grýla. Feral cats can occasionally be found in Iceland. I was fortunate enough to receive some remains of a feral cat, which I have since put to very good use in a few workings. The fur of black cats especially can be worked into charm bags for illusions and blekkingar (deception). Certain náttúrur (stones) and objects can be worked to protect and turn sight. These powerful talismans can be engraved or inscribed and reddened with staves for aiding in deceit and turning sight. Maybe Halla employed some of her own náttúrur to turn mice into rams or make her horses appear as large tufts of grass. Some náttúrur work disguises on their own, without staves, but these powerful talismans are only found by the individual and should be kept secret in case their magic vanishes once mentioned.

As mentioned before, we now live in a global world with apps like Instagram influencing our practices with those of others from all over the world. This influence is no new thing. Occult tomes and grimoires have been passed about from all over Europe and beyond for centuries. Iceland is no exception, with much of the magical thinking of the Christian priests being aligned with that of Paracelsus and later Agrippa, perhaps due to what they learned studying abroad. The influence of twelfth-century grimoires like *Le Petit Albert*, for example, can be found in Icelandic folklore, where one spell utilises substituted ingredients due to the originals being unavailable in Iceland.

14

TÖFRAVERKFÆÐI: WORKING TOOLS OF ICELANDIC FOLK MAGIC

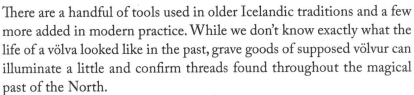

There are a handful of tools used in older Icelandic traditions and a few more added in modern practice. While we don't know exactly what the life of a völva looked like in the past, grave goods of supposed völvur can illuminate a little and confirm threads found throughout the magical past of the North.

Roots, plants, wood, charm bags, and things coming from or easily made from the natural world were extensively utilised. The askur (bowl), hnífur (knife), and the stangur (staff) were the most commonly used tools. It wouldn't be out of the question to suggest these tools have been the same tools used for magic in the interconnected Nordic landscape since the Viking age. One burial at Fyrkat in Denmark suggests a völva was buried at this site; her charm bag filled with henbane seeds, stangur, askur, and hnífur was buried alongside her (National Museum of Denmark). We know that these tools are found worked in more modern sources.

Notably, Jón Árnason states the use of the bowl for divination in *Þjóðsögur og Ævfintýri*. (The staves worked in various manuscripts confirm this.) We also know of less common tools, like a copper bowl used in some divinations. Iron staffs might well have been used by völvur throughout Iceland's history; they are, at least, worked by those who earn the title of Völva these days, though many use wooden staffs. Cursing poles have been worked throughout history as well, though they are less of a tool and more of a specific working; they at least would have utilised things found about the natural landscape. Root fetishes might well have been worked in the past also. We know that other natural objects, such as horse bones and animal teeth, were used as both toys and magical tools, so to suggest interestingly shaped roots may have held a magical purpose isn't that outlandish.

Wands weren't utilised in Iceland in the same way as other European magical practices. Sticks and shorter staffs engraved with magical symbols most likely worked the same function as wands, but in contemporary practice, a synthesized wand or engraved short stick can be worked as a powerful tool. Knives are found, but one more contemporary working I will mention later is known as a Vindhnífur, a wind knife worked to cut the wind and break storm weather.

It is not my intention to standardise a set of tools by detailing them in this book. If you feel drawn to add in one or two of your own, I encourage that experimentation. The staves worked with the tools I give are also not a standard. Everyone should feel free to create their own should they feel moved to. The ones I use have worked well for me and others, but, as always, take what works well for you and cultivate it. We'll start with the stangur, a tool many who practice traditional witchcraft paths will no doubt be familiar with.

STANGUR: THE STAFF

The stangur pops up in a few places in Icelandic lore. The root word, *stang*, is used in many forms of traditional witchcraft. Notoriously, a stangur can be used to create a niðstöng (a cursing staff). These are created with vicious intent and left on the property of their intended victims. This sort of bannfæring (cursing) is touched on later. For the most part, however, the stangur is used to walk spaces, establish boundaries, and is also worked with to anchor and aid in sálarflug (spirit flight). The stangur should be made from a strong wood or iron. I suggest the source of this wood have some protective virtue or enhance travel between the realms. Reynir (rowan), stafafúra or greni (pine), and askur (ash) all make excellent woods for the stangur, as do yllir (yew) and alaskaösp (black cottonwood). The stangur should also be inscribed with relevant symbols, sigils, and staves for its purpose. My personal stangur is made of reynir and inscribed with the following staves.

Salómans insigli, found in the Huld manuscript, works as a wonderful and simple protective stave, making it ideal for working with the stangur. Its power, reputed for exorcism, makes your stangur an even more powerful ally. I also work it into broomsticks for the same purpose. In Icelandic folk magic, broomsticks don't make a historical appearance. However, I have worked them into contemporary practice as a useful tool with a slightly different function than the stangur. More on that can be found in my previous work, *Icelandic Plant Magic*.

Like most tools, before it is worked, it must be consecrated and blessed for its future as your ally and guide. Consecrating tools in Icelandic tradition reflects the often-simple nature of much of the magic on the island. A good, clean, flowing stream should be used for many of the consecrations in this book. Failing that, saltwater from the sea works as a great substitute. The basic method of the consecration of tools involves water, occasionally plant materia, and sometimes specific days, times, and staves.

For the stangur, I recommend finding a stream or some fresh and flowing waterway. Ideally, you will have engraved, burned, or carved any symbols into the stangur beforehand so that all is complete besides the cleansing. Bring a bowl with you: maybe your askur, but if not, any bowl will do. I recommend working with the planetary virtues of Sunday as well as the specific Icelandic virtues of Sunday as a day of victory and righteousness. Use these times to bless your stangur with virtues of protection and Solar power in all its future workings (so, on a Sunday, ideally within the hour of the Sun).

Bring your staff and bowl to your chosen waterway and fill the bowl with its water. At this point, I might work in some herbs, such as hvönn (*Angelica archangelica*), maðjurt (*Filipendula ulmaria*), and einir (*Juniperus communis*). I recommend letting them sit in the bowl for a while as you mentally bring yourself to a calm place, ready for working. Once you are ready, take the bowl of herbs and water and, with it, anoint the stangur. While doing so, speak any galdur you wish. For example, one could say:

"I bless you, my stangur,
With these magical herbs.
May you hold fast, guide my way, and
Steer me onwards down the path.
Heill."

Once you've spoken your galdur, the staff should be submerged in the waterway. Then, upon raising it out of the water, hold it above your head and say something along the lines of:

"Blessed, cleansed, and empowered
With your water, o' flowing spring,
As I raise the stangur, I bring it anew into this realm,
May it guide me, steady me, and speed me along my path."

The stangur is now cleansed and ready to be worked as your tool.

HNÍFAR: KNIVES

Magical knives appear in traditions worldwide, and Iceland is no exception. Hnífar, sometimes called *galdrahnífur* or *jurtahnífur,* are practical tools both physically and magically. In the past, the practitioner would have likely only had one knife and used it for all things. It would have needed to be constantly sharpened, which may be why we find specific whetstone staves for sharpening in some manuscripts. I recommend acquiring a small whetstone for sharpening your magical knives and inscribing the base or wooden casing of this stone with this stave.

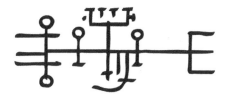

When sharpening magical knives, I recommend feeding the blade with a suitable oil. Many plants make good oils for this task, but I personally prefer to use *Aconitum napellus* and *Artemisia vulgaris* oils for feeding magical blades. One can sing or speak some galdur over them while sharpening to put as much power and focus into our tools as possible. Something like this will suffice:

"I conjure you, spirits of aconite/artemisia,
Impart your potent virtues upon this blade,
That it may serve me as tool and ally,
And protect and aid me as I walk along my path.

Brynslustafur, sharpen and rend this knife potent in all ways.
By the reddening of my blood and this magical oil,
May this knife be a tool for potent harvest and magic."

I recommend repeating this process at least once a year, alongside the following small cleansing of magical knives. Gleym-mér-ej (*Myosotis arvensis* or *scorpioides*) can be used as a wash for knives. Gather some of the plant, let it soak in water for a good while, then use the water to wash the knife while asking the plant to clean and empower it. Use any galdur you wish. I personally use:

"Forget-me-not, sweetest of flowers,
Your virtues of reinvigoration, I ask you impart,
Bless this, my working knife,
Retain its potency and re-enliven its spirit.
I ask of thee, fair Myosotis,
As I ask, so shall it be."

The knives themselves can be adorned with staves and consecrated for magical and specific use. As with the consecration of the stangur, the knives should be taken to a flowing waterway. The knives or their sheaths may be engraved or carved with any staves and symbols you wish prior to this. For a knife that is specifically used in herbalism (a *jurtahnífur*), feel free to use any of these staves that I have worked for this knife in the past, found in my previous book, *Icelandic Plant Magic*.

The second stave is from the text *JS 375 8vo*, known as *Ægishjálmur stóri*, or the large ægishjálmur. This stave can be utilised in magical tools as well as many protective workings, giving its protective powers of inspiring awe and terror.

Go again with your askur and fill it with water from a stream or river. If you wish to work in herbs, add the same as were worked with for the consecration of the stangur. Anoint the knives with water from the bowl while speaking something like: .

"I bless you, my askur,
With these magical herbs,
May you hold fast, guide my way, and
Steer me onwards down the path.
Heill."

Then submerge the knife in the water for a moment, raise it out above your head, and say:

"With this, your cleansing water,
O'flowing stream, bless my working bowl,
Enliven it and empower it,
Cleansed and pure to work my magic."

The knife is now ready. Do this for each knife if you have a separate knife for herbal magic and ritual.

BRÚÐA: POPPETS

Poppets and dúkka (dolls) have been worked all over Europe for the magical and the mundane. While they didn't play a huge role in the folk magic of Iceland in the past, the use of dolls and poppets made from all materials work wonderful magic. Iceland has a few areas of good clay soil perfect for making clay poppets. A great example of a crossover in practices from nearby Orkney, magical poppets for sleep are stuffed with bog cotton and placed beneath the bed. I often work them for healing using green linen cloth stuffed with healing herbs and inscribed with runes and staves to aid swift healing. These can be the most intricate or simple of workings. Wax poppets can be moulded, with a little time and skill, into figures that resemble individuals for focused healing or harming.

RÓTBLÆTI: ROOT FETISHES OR VESSELS

The specific use of roots as spirit homes and fetishes made its way to Iceland at some point between the sixteenth and early twentieth century, and we see this in the way that European mandrake lore is mirrored nearly entirely by the lore of the national flower of Iceland, holtasóley (*Dryas octopetala*). Certain roots found in Iceland can be worked into excellent vessels for spirits. Hvönn (*Angelica archangelica*), in particular, is a perfect example of this. These roots are most often carved with the visage of some human likeness and worked alongside various staves to empower them. Much more of this specific plant magic can be found in my previous book, *Icelandic Plant Magic*.

HEILLAPYNGJA: CHARM BAGS

While a charm bag might seem like a more modern aspect of witchcraft, carrying small pieces of plant and animal materia within a pouch has been a long-held practice all over the world. Take the example of the burial of the völva at Fykat in Denmark, found with a small pouch containing seeds of black henbane (*Hyoscyamus niger*). Small pouches containing various blessed or magically acquired animal remains also make up a big portion of Scandinavian and British folk magic. We can work with Agrippa's breakdown of planetary correspondences to further utilise charm bags, using his method to dictate their colour, material, and, most importantly, the timing of their creation. When making charm bags, I find that it's always best to work with natural materials such as jute, linen, or cotton, and, of course, when adding some Icelandic flair to your charm bag, we can blend plenty of stave work with these practices.

MÁTTARGRIPUR: TALISMANS

Talisman is a word that means many different things depending on whom you ask. Within Icelandic folk magic, this could be a heillapyngja, a small root charm, a metal or wood trinket carved with staves, or any other number of items and objects that hold some magical significance. I refer to almost any item that has been magically enchanted as a *máttargripur*. Certain powerful ingredients may be used to create a máttargripur, such as materia obtained with difficulty or highly specific things like blood for the body parts of animals. Some grimoires call for the blood of a black-haired dog, and nearby Scandinavian magic gives us items such as stones from the inside of toads and birds. I would classify items made from these and other specific magical ingredients as máttagripur.

GALDRABÆKUR: GRIMOIRES

The galdrabækur of Iceland are legendary. Some existed for certain, being passed down, copied from, and torn apart throughout history. Some may or may not have existed, such as the infamous *Rauðskinna*. All of them contain the history of Icelandic magic and big chunks of the history of the magic of continental Europe. It is recommended that the budding seiðkona or galdramaður obtain their own journals and notebooks to collect all the magical information they may need. I highly recommend Owen Davies' wonderful book *Grimoires* for both accurate information on these magical tomes as well as inspiration for creating your own grimoire. I've been lucky enough to purchase an authentic-looking galdrabók to use as my own grimoire, and while aesthetic isn't always the most important, recording your own workings and staves is, so anything you can use for this will work. If you want to spend a little more money, find a journal that feels right for you, and if you feel compelled to, spice it up with calligraphy, pictures, sketches, dried plants, and anything else you wish. This will eventually be your personal book of magic. Grimoires can even take on a life of their own over time and can be ensouled by some familiar spirit or other entity if you wish.

GALDRAKERTIÐ: THE MAGICAL CANDLE

Candle magic is another aspect of magic that has been worked globally. The origins of the more commonly used methods today may come from American Hoodoo, though many authors have disputed this, confused it, or given their own opinions. Lots of people like to claim candle magic in this form is ancient, but besides providing light, coloured, carved, and anointed candles don't appear all that much in folklore outside of later Christian-influenced magical practices, especially in Iceland. Candles would have been reserved for lighting the home during winter and not used for magic specifically, although one candle would have been made over Jól and reserved for Kyndilmessa (Candlemas) on February 2. Candle magic became more common in Iceland only with the introduction of the New Age movement in the last forty years.

Within my personal practice, I tend to work with beeswax, often creating small torches from plants like mullein (*Verbascum Thapsus*). Mullein isn't native to Iceland, though it is known in Danish, Norwegian, and Swedish as "King's Light," reflecting its likely use as a tar-dipped torch in the old days. These torches have been worked for many types of magic within Northern folklore, especially necromancy, and I recommend looking into this if it interests you. Along with mullein, græðisúra (*Plantago major*) can work well as small candles or torches. I recommend creating these torches at some point with beeswax and herbs or powders rolled into them. Otherwise, feel free to utilise candles as many magical practitioners do now with various sigils and staves (and more) carved into them, oils anointing them, or anything else you wish. Plenty of examples of this can be found later on.

TÖFRASPROTAR: WANDS

As I mentioned previously, wands don't make as much of an appearance in Icelandic lore as they do elsewhere (though short sticks inscribed with runes and staves do). These sprotar (plural) or sproti (singular) can be worked as tools for channelling, as with the modern athame and other such tools. They can also be worked specifically for marking out working spaces if carved with only protective and banishing runes and staves. Any protective staves may be carved into them. However, I recommend these few from my own personal experience.

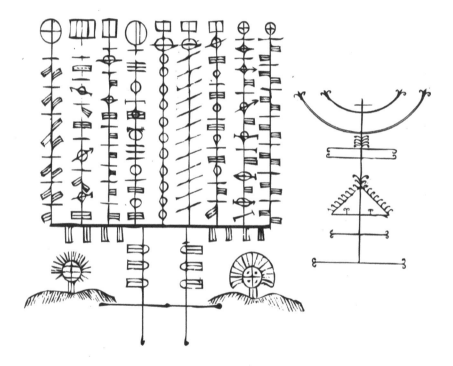

This tool isn't used for much more than creating magical spaces, circles, and drawing out staves in snow, sand, or soil, but it can become a useful aid if you're suddenly in need of a protective circle around your property or working area. This can be the size of the fantasy wizard's magic wand, but to work more in a folkloric way, we use a short staff. This should be made from a protective wood—ideally rowan—as opposed to the wooden staffs of völvur, which most likely would have been beech, birch, or ash when not made of iron. The sproti should be big enough, either at the base or throughout, to decorate with protective staves and symbols, some of which have meanings or origins known to the bearer. Once carved, the tool is ready to be consecrated with water and oil, like other tools. Find a fresh flowing stream, ideally far from people. Within a Martial or Solar day and hour, take the sproti to the stream. Hold it under the water and say:

> *"I consecrate you, sproti/wand of mine,*
> *by this water, I wash you clean.*
> *By this water, I bring you into a new purpose."*

Hold the wand above your head again and say:

> *"I consecrate you that you will protect me from all forces,*
> *as deep as this river and as high as the sky."*

The next step might not be for everyone. You can work with some Solar or Martial oil blend, a drop of your own blood, or maybe even both. If using blood, be sure, as always, to sterilise the needle used to draw the drop. Take the drop of blood or oil and rub it into the staves carved into the hilt of the sproti. Once this is done, say:

> *"Sproti/wand of mine, consecrated by air and water,*
> *I claim you as my tool, with (my blood/this oil),*
> *Empowered to protect me and my space,*
> *To carve the circle of protection,*
> *To carve staves empowered with your protective virtues."*

The sproti is then your tool. It should be wrapped in black cloth or in fresh white linen with protective staves embroidered on it. Use it for its specific purpose and, when it feels in need of a refresh, reconsecrate it. You can also wash it with an infusion of bláhjálmur (*Aconitum napellus*) and gleym-mér-ei (*Myosotis arvensis*).

SPITTING

Spittle has long been regarded as a technique for apotropaic (protective) magic. Within Icelandic folk magic, this is no different, with spitting once to your left, front, and right being a common practice of protection. We can take this further, involving materia—especially herbal materia—by chewing and spitting cleansing herbs to add a little herbal magic to this technique. Spitting for protection is one side of the coin, and the other is spitting a curse. Working sympathetic magic by spitting down on something is one way we can use physicality to aid in spellwork. Fasting spittle, specifically when the reason for the fast is religious or part of some ritual, is worked to draw a stave on one's own body. We see this spittle being used to draw staves of luck and love.

LÆKNINGASTÖNG: HEALING STAFFS

Nordic healing charms from outside of Iceland have inspired the use of certain tools and charms. One such tool is a healing staff, modelled on the Ribe healing stick or staff. Found in Ribe, Denmark, it is dated to the fourteenth century and is a clear example of magic using Christian aspects for healing. The stick is carved with a poem in runes, used to call on God and Mary to heal. We have worked this same blueprint into a tool used for healing. The main idea is that the staff or stick is carved with a healing poem or song (in runes if you wish) and used to direct healing energy and the power of your galdur at the intended. The staff or stick may be charged, suffumigated, or otherwise empowered in any other way to add layers to its power. It is then usually moved slowly over the one who needs healing while using herbs and plant allies' assistance.

For the most appropriate planetary virtues, I recommend creating this tool in Lunar or Venusian time. The tool can be consecrated using seven herbs, as seven is a number of Venus, or nine if working with the Moon. You could use several different methods of herbal preparation, suffumigating it with a seven-herb incense of Venus or the smoke of four burning Venusian herbs after washing it with an infusion of three others, for example. You could repeat the charm of healing you inscribe onto the staff or stick seven times. Or, you could bless it seven times by Freyja, Mary, Maríu-Freyja, the goddess Eir, any other appropriate deity, spirit, or even the planetary intelligence of Venus.

The idea here is to create a tool that is both practical and unique to you and your practice. You could even inscribe other healing staves, runes, other sigils, and symbols onto it: whatever you wish to make it something personal to you. As with all galdrastafir and wristed runes, a drop of blood is really needed to get them going.

As an example of the type of consecration ritual one could perform after creating this tool, gather together seven herbs of Venus, a charcoal disc for burning loose incense, and a glass of freshly boiled water. Take a handful of sea salt and dilute it in a little of the water. Sprinkle the staff or stick while you say something along the lines of:

> *"Lækningastöng of mine.*
> *I cleanse you with salt.*
> *May you be pure and clean,*
> *Ready to work my will."*

Then, take a little of each of the seven herbs and add them to the remaining water, letting it sit and infuse for a moment before moving on. Dip your fingers into the water and sprinkle the infusion over your staff. Then, take some of the herbs and place them on the charcoal. Suffumigate the staff or stick while saying something along the lines of:

> *"By this water, pure,*
> *And these herbs of Venus,*
> *I consecrate this tool to bring good health.*
> *By Venus' gentle virtues,*
> *And by the power of (*),*
> *I consecrate and empower this lækningastöng,*
> *May it always heal,*
> *As I say it, so it is."*

Here (*) is where you should be inserting the name of any deities or spirits you work with or under and wish to include in your healing work from now on. An example might be Eir, one of the suggested handmaidens of Freyja and Frigg, who has been identified with healing arts and herbalism. Calling on Freyja, Mary, or Maríu-Freyja is also very much appropriate. Try to complete this working within the hour of Venus for the best effect.

BÆNIR OG SÁLMAR: PRAYERS AND PSALMS

As Icelandic folk magic falls firmly into the category of a dual-faith tradition, we see the use of many Christian texts, prayers, and names alongside those of the old gods. As with many other folk magic traditions, psalms and prayers—often those mentioning God, Jesus, the Virgin Mary, or one of their monikers—are involved. In particular, Catholic prayers, sometimes even recited in Latin, were held in high regard after the Reformation in 1550 CE. Regardless of the hostility towards Catholicism in Iceland, prayers and psalms are still worked in many practices today. Once one can separate religious trauma from folk Catholic practices, this opens a whole extra layer of Christian magic from Iceland's past.

The most worked psalms tend to be the same as those utilised in modern Catholic folk magic elsewhere. Psalm 3 for healing, 91 for protection, 4 for luck, 72 for success, and 10 for deliverance (exorcism) pop up most in modern Catholic-influenced folk magic practices. Some other Catholic prayers are utilised in Icelandic folk magic—the *Ave Maria* and *Pater Noster*—as well as prayers to local and Nordic saints. These tend to go hand in hand with prayers to Pagan deities (most commonly Þór, Óðinn, Freyja, and Frey). Other prayers worked are those of exorcism and banishing of ghosts and spirits, a long-running practice in Iceland with hundreds of these prayers recorded and used by priests and lay folk alike.

HEILÖG RÝMI: SACRED SPACES

Within Icelandic tradition, based on whether you want to work with a more traditional Norse framework, a Christian-influenced one, or a more traditional witchcraft aesthetic, there are many types of töfrahringur (magic circle) or heilagt rými (sacred space) one can work with.

Starting with the Norse influence, we have the vé. This is the sacred space of modern heathens, used for blóts and all sorts of ceremonies. The vé isn't a circle but a triangle. Three is a sacred number utilised to create order from chaos in Ásatrú and heathenry. This is due to Óðinn and his two brothers, Vilji and Vé, being the three gods to rise and conquer the giants, who were the agents of the primordial chaos. Each corner of this sacred space is marked with a post or stick, which can be carved with a sacred stave intended to further hallow the space.

Offerings of tobacco, often blown at each corner while the space is being consecrated, are used to honour the spirits and deities. A central fire is then often used as the focal point of any sacrifice or work. Once the vé has been established, like the magic circles of high and low magic alike, it is prohibited for one to step outside. Once the work or ceremony is done, we disassemble the space, thanking and releasing the spirits and deities we have called upon. Creating a vé is a nice and fairly simple alternative to some of the more complicated spaces worked in traditional witchcraft and Icelandic traditions. An example of the layout of the vé follows below. However, as with all things, giving it your own flair or element that incorporates your own styles and favourite herbs, for example, is always preferred.

Secondly, circles that resemble or contain influences from ceremonial (high) magic are sometimes used in Icelandic tradition. More contemporary work that includes Goetic influences can utilise more symbolism and, sometimes, many complicated staves and symbols within and outside of the circle, depending on whatever one may be calling upon.

Solomonic influence is also clear in many magical staves. A few examples of more complicated circles created on linen clothes laid out on the floor or drawn with sanctified chalk follow. These are contemporary circles; however, we know that the importance of a circle was noted post-1500s in Icelandic magical texts and traditions.

The last type of circle is the simplest to utilise and works best in alignment with an animistic framework, especially one in which we recognise the multitude of spirits and entities floating about the world. We create these simple circles for workings, meditation, and otherwise just to have a small and safe bubble to be in while working out in nature. Simple staves or protective symbols drawn within the circle are enough to fortify them. A simple circle—sometimes a double circle—containing a stave for each direction is usually the best way to go.

These simple circles are mostly used when we want a stronger boundary between ourselves and any unclean spirits that might be lingering in a space, especially those who need more than a simple burning of herbs to exorcise. Circles such as this are also useful when working in graveyards or along other highways of the dead or spirits. To create this space, draw out one of the simple diagrams below. Do this while chanting, humming, or singing a protective chant, spell, or other galdur. (A few examples are given in the appendices.) The space should then be suffumigated with appropriate materia, such as burning dried einir (*Juniperus communis*), or a resin such as frankincense or copal. Dried leaves of hvönn (*Angelica archangelica*) or hóffífíll (*Tussilago farfara*) also work perfectly and should be a part of one's herb stores.

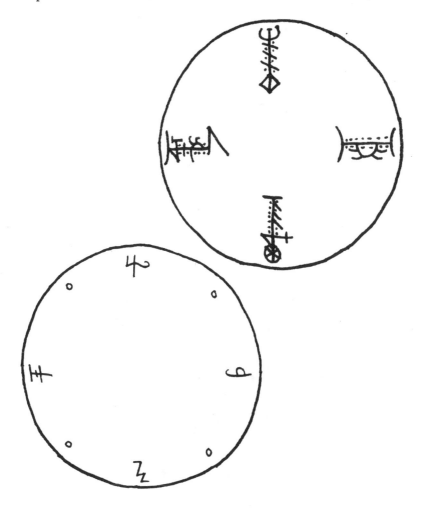

BEINAKAST: BONE THROWING

Sheep knuckle bones have been long used in Iceland as both children's toys and divinatory tools. You only need one for this type of simple "yes or no" divination. The knucklebone is to be asked a question, then blown on three times or have the sign of the cross made over it three times. One then recites this rhyme over the bone before it is rolled:

"Spávala mín, ég spyr þig að,
Ég skal þig með gullinn gleðja
og silfur seðja
ef þú segir mér satt.
En í eldinum brenna
ef þú skrökvar að mér."

"My bone of fortune, I ask you,
I'll make you happy with gold
And gratify you with silver
If you tell me the truth.
But in the fire you'll burn
If you tell me lies."

If the bone lands on one of the two flat sides, the answer is unknown or the question should be reworded. If the bone lands with the hollow indent facing up, the answer is a no. If it lands with the rounded hump facing up, the answer is yes. If you have a few bones, you can ask questions with a wider answer than just a "yes" or a "no." Work out the likelihood of your answer from the number of yeses or noes you receive. The bone should be kept safe in a small pouch or bag. This can be inscribed with a few staves, but the one I suggest comes from *Lbs 977*. It doesn't have a name, but it is noted as *"stafur til að detta margt í hug,"* or a "stave to think of many things."

The bones should be kept in here. You could also try engraving them with small staves or symbols. I inscribed mine with letters of Saturn from an Icelandic grimoire, but any other symbols that you think work best would do. I would also recommend working in Lunar and Saturnine virtues and methods of empowering and cleansing these bones, such as working in Moon water with Lunar and Saturnine colours and times. Place them with divinatory stones, such as obsidian and moonstone, if you work with these. Happy throwing!

15

Herbarium

Within my previous work, *Icelandic Plant Magic,* you can find a whole collection of magical plants suited to all sorts of workings. I felt, however, that I should include a little on a selection of plants that are freely found in the countryside (and even within cities in the rest of Europe and North America) in this book as well. I include some information and suggest uses for plants not covered within my previous book as well, due to this book being more of a guide for many outside of Iceland rather than a guide to plants that grow within Iceland.

Yllir (*Sambucus sp.*), Ýviður or Ýr (*Taxus baccata*), and kóngsljós (*Verbascum Thapsus*) can be paired wonderfully with old and contemporary stave work, something that you won't find in work concerning only Icelandic flora. I'll also expand upon Völvuauga (*Atropa belladonna*) and a few other baneful herbs. These should be used with extreme care and not taken lightly. The bitter but caring spirit of wormwood (*Artemisia absinthium*) is also discussed; she is worked for a variety of spells and can partner brilliantly with some staves. Other naturalised species within Iceland that can be found in North America that is also naturalised in other parts of Europe include alaskaösp (*Populus trichocarpa*), a strong and sturdy plant ally that will also be discussed in more depth here. Other smaller but equally useful species, such as viper's bugloss (*Echium vulgare*), are also wonderful when partnered with stave work, in my experience, and will be elaborated on later. I also include methods of utilising the plants that

I didn't include in my previous work, such as the ancient and continued use of charm bag necklaces full of herbs, many of which are mentioned in Icelandic literature. Here, I will also discuss uses for these plants from other threads of Nordic magic, both older and contemporary. Swedish and Norwegian trolldom overlaps a great deal with Icelandic plant galdur. The list later in this chapter is an ideal herb cabinet for any practicing sorcerer, magician, or seiðberi.

On the planetary rulership of these plants, I would remind the reader that where the overall feel of the plant may express virtues more aligned to one planet, we must do our best to discover the virtues of each individual plant we find. A small group of field gentian, typically ruled by Mars, found growing in a dry, well-drained patch of soil in full sun may express more Solar virtues than normal. We can then utilise this plant best for areas where Solar and Martial work overlap. Or, we may come across Saturnine alpine bartsia, growing close to the water in the shade of larger plants; this plant may express more Lunar virtues that make it useful for areas where Saturnine and Lunar virtues overlap, such as necromancy by dreams.

The location of the plant is important, as is its proximity to other plant species, sacred rocks, and spaces, including ruling trees of areas of woodland. The part of the plant we work with may also express virtues different from its typical ruler. The roots of many plants can be worked for their more Saturnine and Mercurial nature, moving between the terrestrial and the subterranean realms. Fruits and berries, as well as flowers, designed to allure and aid in spreading pollen and seed, can typically be worked in areas where the plant's typical ruler and Venusian magic overlap. Learn to communicate with the green realm and discern which plant spirits express which virtues so as to best utilise *materia magica*.

One final note: Jón Árnason gives us the warning that, when gathering herbs in Iceland, we must bear venerisjurt (Venus's herb) on our person. Although this could mean a great many herbs, we have found the greatest success when the Venus plant we carry is maríustakkur (*Alchemilla potentilla*). Carry enough to keep some on your person, as well as leave a little to say thank you once you've finished foraging. Of course, one can forage and gather without carrying a Venus herb, but this "rule" is more for those who wish to follow the folklore closely. This, as well as the following guidelines for foraging in Iceland, follows similar animistic-focused practices as other spheres (mainly not putting our desire to gather herbs above the desire of the land and its spirits).

When gathering benefic herbs and materia, we should do so with our right or dominant hand, and when gathering malefic materia, we should do so with the left or passive hand. A lot of practices, especially those that equate the fae to all spirits of the land, dictate that we must never harvest herbs with an iron blade. In Iceland, however, these blades were the only blades available, so we have no qualms about using them.

Besides the issue of cost and availability in the past, the threat of iron to the álfar is not commented on as much in neighbouring Ireland and Scotland. The comparison of iron representing the human industrialisation that eventually led to the separation of science and magic, therefore being of harm to the fae, the land, and the old ways, is not really present in Iceland. Where Iceland did industrialise, it did so later (around 1900), and, even now, one can travel thirty minutes outside of Reykjavík and find themselves in a relative wilderness. Respect for and belief in the land never died here.

When using a blade to gather herbs, let it be your consecrated working knife. The last point to consider before one starts to venture out to forage is that we cannot simply take and not give back. We must leave an offering of smoke, food, or other biodegradable materia, and we must verbally present these gifts to the land. Most simply, you can leave a tea of herbs from the landscape gathered at some other time. Incense, even store-bought, burned with reverence for the landvættur also works, but leaving water, some fruit, homemade food, or baked goods is best. Baking bread and leaving it to the land's spirits and animals is the best way to show care and reverence, especially if the bread is filled with local herbs. The rowan berry bread, most often used in devotion to Þór, is also a wise choice for offerings to the land. You can find the recipes in my previous book, *Icelandic Plant Magic*.

A(ONITE
(Venusvagn or Bláhjálmur, *Aconitum napellus*)
Saturn • Mars

This toxic and potent Saturnine plant, aconite, is a common garden plant in Iceland, with many cultivated varieties available. The true blue-purple aconite, also known as "wolfsbane," is most often used in magical work. It is a powerful protective aid as well as a cursing plant. We can work the Martial qualities of wolfsbane into protective charm bags, and the seeds can even be worked into spells of invisibility. As a key ingredient in flying ointment, the plant can work well for spirit flight. Include it in Saturnine incenses and only ever burn it outside. Work it into an oil and use it to anoint magical tools for extra potency.

Angelica

(Hvönn, *Angelica archangelica*)
Sun

Found growing all about the country, hvönn is a quintessentially Icelandic plant used as food, medicine, and for all sorts of magic. It is known as "master-wort" in the English-speaking world, and when looking at its magical properties, we see why this may be the case. Sacred to its Latin namesake, the archangel Michael, hvönn is a devout protector, fierce ally, and troublesome enemy. The spirit has appeared most often with the feeling of a young but capable warrior, much in the likeness of the archangel's imagery. The root is the seat of its power and can be dried, ground, and added to incenses for protection and healing. Burn it alongside frankincense for the archangel's aid. Worked into a rótblæti, hvönn can be a powerful home protector; write out a contract for this spirit, feeding it blood, milk, or honey once a month as payment for its service.

Arctic Thyme

(Blóðberg, *Thymus praecox*)
Venus

Blóðberg is one of the most important magical and medicinal herbs in Iceland. It has long been held in high regard, being worked into medicine to soothe sore throats and promote healing. It is sacred to Freyja and Frigg and can be worked into all sorts of charm bags and offerings to her. Gather it within a Venusian day and hour for the greatest magical potency. Work it alongside honey for wonderful medicine, as well as linking two of the goddess Freyja's sacred things. It may also be worked with for healing, sleep, courage, and love. Work it into purifying ritual baths before work with Freyja is performed. Blóðberg is an herb I go into much more detail about in *Icelandic Plant Magic*.

ASH

(ASKUR, *FRAXINUS ECELSIOR*)
Moon • Mars

The mighty ash tree, seen by many as Yggdrasil, is an important plant in lore and mythology. Within Norse mythology, we see Askur and Embla as the first man and woman, named after the ash and elm. The ash is a strong tree that lends its strength and protection in workings, asking for the safety of homes and families. It works well with all sorts of protective staves. Ash tree branches make good handles for broomsticks, and when combined with birch and willow twigs, the three make an excellent aid in spirit flight. *Askur* is also a name for a bowl, as they were often made from ash wood, a fast-growing useful resource in Iceland. As one of the trees that represents the *axis mundi*, I feel it is harder to place a general planetary ruler on it. However, due to its aid in protective magic, as well as spirit flight, I suggest that the Moon and Mars are its most likely celestial rulers.

ASPEN

(ÖSP, *POPULUS SP.*)
Saturn • Mercury

Aspen is another important plant in the magic of Northern Europe. Some species of aspen grow in Iceland, though not as well as they do in other areas of Northern Europe. The aspen can be worked with to aid in spirit flight. Specifically, the black cottonwood, an aspen tree from the Americas, is perfect for this, though other aspen trees share these virtues. Crowns may be made from the branches they drop; wear them during trance work for potent experiences.

BEECH

(BEYKI, *FAGUS SYLVATICA*)
Saturn • Jupiter

Beech is another species introduced to Iceland in modern times, though it did grow in Iceland in the distant past when the climate allowed. Today, there are only a handful of examples of the species known in the country, with two famous examples in the capital area. (One of them was voted "Tree of the Year" in 2017.) Beechwood works wonders along with dream staves and those to see or get what one wishes. The magical uses of beech elsewhere in Northern Europe include use as a wand wood, which I absolutely agree with. Some people place beech under the rule of Jupiter in areas where it is abundant; however, I am more inclined to put Saturn as its ruler. The bark can be worked as paper for staves and petitions to be drawn upon. I have had good experience working the leaves in blends for foresight and trance work.

Belladonna
(Völvuaugn, *Atropa belladonna*)
Saturn

Belladonna is the witch's plant, queen of poisons, and most revered of Saturnine witchcraft plants. Belladonna has a huge cultural history as a plant of death, spirit flight, and madness. It doesn't come up much within Icelandic folklore due to the plant not growing in Iceland outside of the botanical gardens and some private gardens. I have managed to grow it within my garden in Reykjavík and am always amazed when it survives a hard winter. All parts of the plant are toxic and, if misused, can lead to death. The berries and roots are the most potent parts, then the flowers, and, finally, the leaves. All are worked into ointments at one's own risk. The plant spirit often shows herself as a beautiful woman, terrifying when scorned, and willing to aid us in all sorts of malefic and seductive workings. Take the utmost care with her. If harvesting the root for use as a rótblæti, I recommend doing so delicately, washing her clean before hanging her to dry. Then, a few days later, suffumigate her with frankincense. Working an oil of völvuauga into malefic stave work adds a potency like no other.

Birch
(Birki, *Betula nana*)
Moon • Venus

Birch has played a role in the protective folk magic of all the Nordic countries. Used to "whip the evil out," it is a key component of sauna practices. Both objects and people may be struck with birch branches for this purificatory magic. The plant may be used for exorcism work in the form of incense as well, used to clear spirits from places. You can also craft these branches into brooms and adorn them with staves and sigils for spirit flight, cleansing, healing, and more. Birch makes a good wood for protective staffs and stangs.

Powder the leaves and bark and add to necromancy blends to burn when calling or clearing the dead. In Scandinavia and Eastern Europe, birch bark is also used to write petitions to the local spirits of the land. One can very well adopt this practice as a method of communing with the landvættur of almost any region. Leave these with offerings in the woods around where you live.

Black Cottonwood
(Alaskaösp, *Populus trichocarpa*)
Saturn • Mercury

Like the aspen, black cottonwood branches can be gathered after storms and worked into crowns to aid in spirit flight. The buds can be gathered just before opening and worked into an oil that is both beautifully fragrant and magically potent. This oil should be used to anoint all sorts of candles for dream work and spirit flight.

Black Nightshade
(Húmskuggi, *Solanum nigrum*)
Saturn • Venus

This climbing and binding flower is part of the nightshade family. It grows on almost any plant, using it as a support. The small white flowers can be gathered and included in Saturnine incenses and can be added to blends for seduction, enticement, and persuasion. The flowers can be worked with roses for binding unfaithful lovers and binding Venusian desires of love and lust. Work a stave of discontent along with these two plants for the best effect. Black nightshade doesn't grow in Iceland but works well alongside many staves aimed towards malefica. I've had good experience working with this plant and its cousin, bittersweet, with many staves and workings of Nordic folk magic while in the UK and Sweden. Bind the long strands of this plant around photos of those whom you may wish to ensnare and seduce for magical ends.

ELDER

(YLLIR, *SAMBUCUS NIGRA*)
Moon • Venus

Yllir is a magical tree known for its wonderful medicine and flowers elsewhere in Europe. We do find rauðyllir (*Sambucus racemosa*) growing in urban areas in Iceland. Lots of the folklore of the elderberry and wood carries over from mainland Europe. We know not to burn its wood or work the tree into cradles lest the baby sleeping in it be taken by the álfar. The berries are used for medicine, but less often than those of the black elder, as they can cause stomach trouble. The wood makes for good wands, which can be carved with staves and treated with magical oils. The berries and leaves make for good offerings to the land spirits, though never burned. The wood and berries are also good to work alongside dream staves and other aspects of draumagaldur.

HENBANE

(SKOLLARÓT, *HYOSCYAMUS NIGER*)
Saturn

Called *skollarót* in Icelandic, meaning "devil's root," this is a magical and medicinal plant used much more commonly in many places before modern medicine. As a member of the nightshade family, it is poisonous. The seeds were likely used for divinatory magic; as mentioned earlier, a pouch of them was found in the grave of a supposed völva at Fykat in Denmark, as well as findings at the Viking age site at Birka in Sweden. Many suppose that these seeds were at least a part of a recipe used to induce the rage of the berserkur. The seeds and roots were once used as a calmative and sedative for children, though this is, of course, very dangerous and not recommended. A small pouch of the seeds may be carried to aid in divinatory work and help us engage with spirits. The plant, like many others that open the mind to the otherworldly, brings these spirits into our realms of perception.

JUNIPER

(EINIR, *JUNIPERUS COMMUNIS*)

Sun

Juniper is a truly Solar plant, embodying the clearest Solar virtues of protection, power, dominance, and cleansing. Juniper in Iceland is worked to clear the home once a year on New Year's Day. Burning the dried branches is the most effective way to work this plant, and we can utilise plenty of clearing and exorcism chants while burning it. It makes an excellent magical pair with wormwood, especially when the two are burned together during rites of banishing and clearing. Juniper and rowan used together need to be kept in perfect balance. The two are prone to jealousy over each other if one is used more than the other. For this reason, ships used to include an equal amount of each to utilise the protection of both working together. If the balance was disrupted, the ship was said to be prone to capsizing due to the imbalance. Juniper can be worked for anything Solar and is a powerful plant ally to use in Solar oils and brews.

MULLEIN

(KONGSLJÓS, *VERBASCUM THAPSUS*)

Sun • Jupiter • Venus

Kongsljós is a plant that we don't find growing natively in Iceland. Most of the Nordics know this plant as "King's Light." British traditions call it "Hag's Taper" and sometimes even "Death Light" because of its use as a torch of necromancy. It has been worked to call upon the dead likely since the time of the Roman Empire. We work its leaves for healing, as well as in some traditional European smoking blends. When put in garlic oil, the flowers are worked to heal earaches. Magically, these flowers can be added to incense to call in spirits of the dead. I have had great success in burning them on an altar with other herbs of the dead to call in ancestors. They have a much lighter energy than holtasóley; this may be due to their bright and lighter nature, as they flower in summer while still retaining a Saturnine undercurrent.

The dried stalks, best gathered once summer has waned, are worked into torches, either soaked in paraffin or covered in beeswax. I go for the beeswax, rolling other ground and powdered herbs into them before the wax has fully cooled. They may then be burned to call on ancestors. Use smaller stems of flowerheads for small altar candles. The larger torches can be placed in the cardinal directions when working necromantic rites and rituals. Kongsljós acts as a light in the dark for spirits, drawing them in. It is the torch that bears us through the darkness of the underworld. When engaging in darker and deeper realms during spirit flight, it may benefit us to have a torch lit, steadying our path.

The spirit of this plant often appears with the appearance or feeling of an old man. Sometimes, it is hooded, giving further alignment with chthonic figures like Charon, the ferryman of the Greek underworld. In terms of Norse deities, kongsljós has been said to feel aligned with Baldur, the bright and shining god whose death is a significant moment in Norse mythology. I see this clearly during summer, before the plant's nature shifts to the darker half of the year. Baldur is typically associated with mistletoe, another plant that connects us to the underworld. Work mistletoe and mullein together in necromancy.

The overarching spirit of the species of the plant, while being an entity that contains as many virtues and facets as each individual plant, expresses two clear sides. As with many Icelandic plants, this duality is profound and dependent on the season the plant is harvested in. In late summer, once the power of the season and sun has waned, the plant shifts to its darker side. We see this shift in many plants as their power retreats within themselves to the subterranean roots. Stalks harvested once the height of summer has passed are the most potent for use as necromantic torches. During the lighter seasons, the leaves can be harvested best under Solar and Venusian times; the flowers especially are best when harvested under Solar times. A tincture of the flowers can be added to floor washes and sprays for Solar purposes.

Mugwort

(Malurt, *Artemisia vulgaris*)
Moon • Venus

One of the most well-known and frequently worked witching plants in the Northern Hemisphere, mugwort and its cousins, wormwood and southernwood, can be worked as protective plants, dispelling spirits and entities alike when burned. Mugwort and wormwood share divinatory virtues, best extracted via tea or ointment. A tea of mugwort before bed will bring vivid dreams, sometimes those of the future. An ointment of both rubbed into the feet and palms works well to carry us to other realms in sleep; work these plants alongside all staves of draumagaldur and draumaspá.

Likewise, mugwort ointment can be stored in a bottle or jar inscribed with various dream staves. It can also be used to trace these staves upon our bodies before sleep. Mugwort may be burned alongside fjandafæla and coltsfoot leaves to clear spaces; do this while signing staves of protection in the air around you. While mugwort is not native to Iceland, it does pop up in urban waste areas, and I have had successful plants over two metres tall grow in my Reykjavík garden. Known as *malurt* in Icelandic, the plant can help us connect well to the landvættir of our local areas, as well as aiding in our connection to deities and higher spirits.

ᛈᛁᚾᛂ PINE
(STAFAFÚRA, *PINUS SPP.*)
Mars • Saturn

Pine is an excellent plant ally. I see this from a place of bias, of course, as it is one of the primary trees I work with. Pine expresses many virtues, though, by growing habits and some of its uses, we often classify it as a Martial or Saturnine plant. Pine is strong, though elderly; its spirit appears often in the form of an old man, usually mysterious, with a manner often like Óðinn. When used as a building material, it makes strong structures and has been used as the base for many talismans and holder of many staves. The living wood, harvested after offerings have been given, is a potent materia for wands, short staffs, and other tools. It may be worked into talismans of Martial virtue, such as fertility, and large poles of this pine may be worked as fertility poles.

After death, or upon falling naturally before rot and fungi set in, the plant can be worked into Saturnine talismans, especially those that aid in necromancy. Walking a pine forest the day after a storm may prove most fruitful for this. Such wood should be given more appropriate Saturnine offerings, such as tobacco smoke, brennivín, or another strong spirit, poured out while speaking your desire to take the wood and work it into necromantic talismans. Pine often shelters and nurtures berserkur (fly agaric), furthering its proximity to Saturnine work. The two, when worked in partnership, give great success.

A staff of storm-fallen pine, inscribed with staves of aiding flight and anointed with an oil of fly agaric, makes an excellent tool for spirit flight. For a more protective Martial tool, a staff of living wood, harvested and dried over time, inscribed with protective staves and anointed with some protective oils, would be most appropriate. The fresh pine needles growing in spring can be gathered and worked into a tea. When used along with spruce tips and honey, it makes an excellent aid for opening one up to the spirits of place. This tea may also be given back to the land as an offering. Drink this tea when offering herbs and other materia to the land before foraging so that the spirits may lead you to the most potent herbs for harvesting.

Plantain
(Grædisúra, *Plantago major*)
Moon • Venus

Pollen records show us that this was one of the commonly grown plants within the monastic garden of Skriðuklaustur in East Iceland. This location was used mostly as an early hospital and medical centre, established in 1493. The garden there was used to grow many healing herbs, including some non-native. The name *grædisúra* literally translates to "healing sorrel." It can be worked into all sorts of staves for healing and soothing skin complaints, cuts, and scrapes. Magically, it is worked for protection. The fresh leaf placed within a shoe will help one travel for longer without tiring. The whole plant, bound in red string and hung in the home, grants protection. The plant works well with Mary and Saint Christopher, who should be called on to bless it before hanging it in a vehicle or placing it within a shoe. It is also a plant of Freyja and Frigg, being one of the many healing plants that fall under her domain.

Rowan
(Reynir, *Sorbus sp.*)
Sun

One of the kings of Icelandic plant magic, reynir is worked for all sorts of protection. The best for this is the "flying rowan," found growing upon the branches of other trees. Rowan is said, like obsidian, to contain nine good and nine bad virtues. What virtues these are, exactly, isn't fully expanded upon. However, from the folklore, we are told that should one light a fire of reynir between two friends, their friendship shall suffer. The berries may be gathered and strung into necklaces to be worn as protection. Folklore also tells us of rowans springing up following the abandoning of babies in nature around Iceland. These trees were said to occasionally be heard crying as the spirits of the children likely assimilated into the land as tree spirits.

Southernwood

(*Artemisia abrotanum*)
Moon • Mercury

The third Artemisia species mentioned in this herbarium, southernwood is worked into love magic and gathered during a Venusian time. The plant has a wonderful camphor-like odour that reminds many people of cola. Like wormwood, it can be placed into bedspreads and cupboards to keep pests away from clothing. Sometimes called European sage, this plant also aids in dream work and can be placed within dream pillows and charm bags to aid in draumagaldur. An oil of these three Artemisia sisters (alongside wormwood and mugwort) makes for an excellent anointer of the temples, forehead, and dream candles. Dream staves should be reddened and then oiled with this blend for extra potency. Burning the plant works to clear spaces of unclean spirits, and a mix of the three Artemisias is potent for this cleansing. Like wormwood, watch out for overconsumption, as this plant contains some chemicals considered toxic to humans. A yellow dye can be made from the leaves of southernwood. Add it to a charm bag for love with Venusian plants.

Tansy

(Regnfang, *Tanacetum vulgare*)
Saturn • Sun

Tansy is a renowned herb for necromantic work, as well as cleansing and clearing. The dual action of clearing makes for a versatile plant with many magical uses. Tansies can be worked into oils for necromancy candles, and an oil of tansy would be an excellent choice to anoint a mullein Hag's Taper for calling in spirits. In Icelandic, it has many names, including *rænfang, reinfáni, daggarsmali, leiðabuski,* and *ormagras,* the latter of which is a name it shares with wormwood due to some of their shared properties. Medicinally, it works to soothe muscle and joint pain, and it is used for cleansing and purification of the body as a laxative and diaphoretic.

VIPERS BUGLOSS
(NAÐURKOLLUR, *ECHIUM VULGARE*)
Mars

Growing in much of Europe and temperate Asia, this pretty blue and pink flower, a member of the borage family, hides a spiky surprise. Just like its cousin, borage, the plant has small soft spines that make picking it without gloves something I don't recommend. The common name comes from its use as a remedy for adder bites; the root specifically was used for this. In magic, we can mirror this practice by working a decoction of the root into work aimed at repairing and healing land after it has been disturbed. This protective plant also happens to be one of the first to pop up on disturbed ground, adding to the potency of this work.

The spiny stem and leaves can be worked into malefica, and the blue flowers can be added to blends of fast healing. This plant, though used for healing, gives us the fast action of Mars, and its use as a medicine needed urgently to combat snake bites in the past shows us its swiftness. Work it for swift vindication or vengeance. The plant can be included in charm bags of harming and healing, and I have had great success working it with both staves and binding runes focused on malefica and protection. The names of the plant in Danish, Norwegian, and Swedish all reflect the snake connection, generally being called "snake's head."

WORMWOOD
(MALURT, *ARTEMISIA ABSINTHIUM*)
Mercury • Moon

An equally magical and dangerous plant, *malurt* is the name for both wormwood and mugwort in Icelandic, and due to this, among our group, we refer to it as *ormagras,* or "wyrm herb." Humans have been working with this plant since at least 1550 BCE. Best known for its ability to banish the unclean, both mundane and magical, we burn ormagras to rid spaces of unclean energies. The plant doesn't grow in Iceland, though in today's global world, the herb can be inexpensively grown indoors, as well as imported dried and ready for use in incense and more.

Known as the "green fairy," the spirit of this plant teeters on the edge of madness. It is worked with often to protect people and places from the unclean, not as careful and caring protector, but more of the energy of a somewhat unstable doorman keeping undesirables out of the club (though it is also prone to being undesirable). She walks the line between healer and harmer, where too much of a good thing can be quite bad. We utilise her in tincture form—ideally created and blessed within a Martial or Solar hour—to be sprinkled about the home when you feel a cleanse is needed.

We burn her in incense along with holtasóley to call in spirits, though not lightly, as, together and if not properly instructed, this pair may call in the wandering shades of madness and spirits with dark airs about them (those not unclean but wholly unsavoury). We reserve using this pair together for when we are called to do so by some spirit or entity that favours these conditions.

The etymological connection to the great wyrm, though somewhat strenuous, brings us to Jörmungandur, the world serpent. Though often thought of as a destructive force, we often see his perspective as that of a spirit who protects nature, playing his role, which, from the perspective of Þór and the Æsir, is that of the enemy. Ormagras has this energy: not caring for the trivial matters of sanity from a human perspective. She gives answers willingly when asked, often through visions. The frequent use of her willing help for some can end up being the temptation that eventually poisons the mind. In the case of ormagras, poisoning of the mind is very much a real danger if overindulging in the use of this plant. In its form of absinthe, the green fairy has led many brilliant minds to ruin. Work her in an incense outside or in a well-ventilated room.

Work her tincture, drop by drop, to enhance visionary work, and work her into an ointment with her cousin mugwort, which can be applied to the feet to aid in spirit flight. Burn alongside blueberry leaf for an aid to any divination.

Yᚲw

(Ýʀ, *Taxus baccata*)
Saturn

Ýr grows in gardens in Iceland but doesn't do so well out of urban areas. This plant of the dead works well with many staves of cursing, necromancy, and protection stemming from Icelandic tradition. Known to many as the tree of death, this plant was held sacred to many skálds in the past; sitting beneath the tree in fruit on a warm summer's day can be a lightly intoxicating event. The chemicals and oils evaporating from the tree on warm days were said to induce inspiration and may well help with spirit communication. Graveyard ýr is the most potent and should be taken with the permission of the guardian of the graveyard and the tree itself.

16

BESTIARY

Animals play just as much of a role in Icelandic folk magic as plants do. The Icelandic *Physiologus* exists in two fragments: *AM 673 a II 4to* and *AM 673 a I 4to*. These two fragments give us fantastical creatures and may well have played a role in the inspiration and appearance of later-mentioned creatures, such as Iceland's variety of deadly whales and monstrous seals, skates, and trout. Various animal remains are worked with in Icelandic folk magic, both older and contemporary, though some are less savoury than others.

We see plenty of examples in stave work: the brains of ravens, sheep knuckle bones, and cow skins. I've attempted to gather as many examples of these animal remains as possible and outlined their surrounding folklore, as well as examples of what found remains can be worked for. Some of this is based on planetary traits, some that come from folklore sources, and some from UPG. Animals are listed with their Latin binomials, as well as English and Icelandic names and associated lore.

I also want to stress that, while I'm including this chapter in the book, I don't encourage the poaching or purposeful killing of any creature to obtain its remains. Iceland can be a harsh place, and, as such, animal remains are more common to come across in nature, but we would be acting against the respect of these creatures and the natural world if we purposefully killed them for a feather, fur, or body part.

I have also included fantastical creatures in this section with a selection of Icelandic ghosts and spirits within a Phantasmarium. The Latin binominals for these creatures are, of course, just for fun but were chosen to reflect their main defining traits.

ARCTIC TERN
(KRÍA, *STERNA PARADISAEA*)

In Icelandic folklore, a kría's heart, when held on a person, will make others look on them with fondness and respect. Said to arrive at the first krossmessa in early summer and then leave Iceland by the krossmessa in autumn, this bird is fiercely protective of its nest. The remains of the kría can be worked with for defence and protection, and a kría servitor spirit would make a wonderful guardian over treasures or even oneself. We can work kría feathers into charms of protection for the home, as well as tie them onto our stangur or ritual clothing.

BLUE WHALE
(STEYPIREYÐUR, *BALAENOPTERA MUSCULUS*)

Blue whales have been said to rescue ships from so-called evil whales in the past and even have escorted some of these ships safely back to shore. However, one fisherman was said to have killed a whale by throwing a stone into its blowhole. The man was sentenced to twenty years on land. However, during his nineteenth year, he grew too impatient and went out on a boat. A whale attacked this ship, knocking the man into the sea. It was said to have wrapped its tongue around the man and swallowed him.

CHICKEN
(HANI, *GALLUS DOMESTICUS*)

According to folklore, roosters are said to lay eggs in their old age, from which hatch all sorts of nasty creatures. The back claw of a rooster's left foot is carried as a talisman for winning games. Mixing the blood from an all-white hen with the heart blood of an all-black cat, then applying it to your eyes, is said to give one powerful clairvoyant ability. Keeping a rooster's spur in a charm bag along with staves to win games makes for a useful bit of magic.

Common Snipe
(Hrossgaugur, *Gallinago gallinago*)

The following folklore shows us how the common snipe foretells the weather as well as one's fortune. If the first snipe you hear that year is singing to the south of you, then it bodes a happy life full of good food and a lack of austerity. It heralds marriage and a lack of sorrow. If the first snipe you hear sings at night, then sorrow and harsh times will befall you this year. If you hear it to the north, then your knowledge and wisdom will serve you well. If you hear it from within the clouds, then good fortune will be upon you. If you hear him from beneath you, then death may be close at hand. A common snipe's feathers can be worked into charms of good fortune, tied to charm bags, or hung within the home.

Cow
(Kýr, *Bos taurus*)

Calfskin has long been used as the ideal skin to draw staves on. White calfskin, in particular, has been used for dream and sleep staves. Within Icelandic folklore, cows gain the ability to speak on the nights of January 6 (Þrettándinn) and June 24 (Jónsmessunótt), or maybe we gain the ability to understand them. This is more fun than immediately useful, with the folklore telling us of farmhands terrified after overhearing the cows speaking.

Dealfish
(Vogmær, *Trachipterus arcticus*)

Fisherman's folklore says that catching this species is said to bring bad luck and shipwrecks, and it is to be thrown back to see whenever it is caught. The remains of the fish could be worked into a níðstöng for just this.

Dog
(Hundur, *Canis familiaris*)

Puppies born with vision are sometimes thought to become a skoffinn. Dog's blood is an ingredient in some stave workings, especially that of a black-haired dog. The hair of black dogs has been worked in many spells in European grimoire magic, and this black dog hair also shows up as an ingredient in some Icelandic spells. Dogs are also the poor creatures used to snap the root of holtasóley, and, as such, die from hearing the sound. This lore is an exact reflection of European mandrake lore.

EURASIAN WREN
(Músarendill, *Troglodytes troglodytes*)

This bird is regarded as a thief in Icelandic folklore. Crosses were put in the chimneys of homes to repel these birds. These hole-dwelling birds were thought to come out of the earth and, as such, were believed to be evil in nature. (This wren does nest in holes, dark crevices, and old nests, which is where this belief must have arisen.) It was believed that if the heart of a músarendill was worked into the handle of a knife, then wounds from this knife would be incurable. This heart was also worked into charms to know the thoughts of others, possibly alongside a stave worked for the same purpose.

The heart was to be dried in the sun and then wrapped in a knotted cloth and held when speaking to someone to know their true thoughts and intentions. The dried head of the wren was also worked alongside the svefnþorn to make one sleep until the head was removed from above them. The feathers, as well as remains of the wren, can be worked into charms of secrecy, unlocking, and thievery. One working I would suggest, inspired by folklore, would be to work a wren feather as a lock pick along with this galdur:

> *"Blæs eg svo bylur í lási*
> *og blístra af mannsístru;*
> *fjandinn með fúlan anda*
> *fast í lásinn blási;*
> *tröll upp togi mellur,*
> *taki á púkar allir;*
> *fetti [or: fitli] við fótarjárni*
> *fjandans ósjúkir púkar.*
> *Lyftið upp lásnum allir*
> *lifandi fjandans andar."*

This may be even better if the feather has been empowered and placed on a stave such as this:

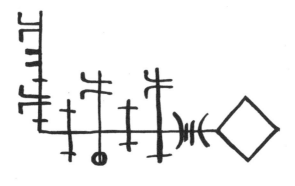

Fox
(Refur, *Vulpes lagopus*)

Other names for foxes in Icelandic include vargur, melrakki, and lágfóta. It is said that if foxes are seen near the town in autumn, then winter will likely be hard. Fox fygljur are not uncommon in Iceland, and some families are known to have fox fylgjur. The fox is father to the skoffinn and mother to the skuggabaldur. (These two fearsome beasts are mentioned later.) The arctic fox is well known as a tricky animal, elusive and quick. We can work with its remains for these virtues, mostly utilising bones in charms of stealth and cunning. Skulls of foxes can be worked as spirit houses for many Mercurial and Saturnine spirits and should be inscribed with various staves of the spirits one wishes to invoke into them.

Grey Heron
(Hegrinn, *Ardea cinerea*)

The grey heron is a rare winter visitor to Iceland, though when it is spotted, it indicates the following year will be excellent for fishing. Heron's claws have long been held as a potent magical item, attracting wealth from others, the Earth, and the sea. Folklore says you must shoot a claw from the right and left foot of the heron and catch them before they hit the ground, though scavenged remains are preferred in contemporary practice.

HARLEQUIN DUCK
(STRAUMÖND, *HISTRIONICUS HISTRIONICUS*)

In Icelandic folklore, the straumönd's head is removed and dried, then carried as a talisman of protection from "all evil and unnaturalness." This talisman would be best kept in a charm bag of protective materia along with staves and symbols for protection.

HORSE
(HESTUR, *EQUUS FERUS CABALLUS*)

In Icelandic and Scottish folklore, horse placentas were buried in the mýri. From this, a four-leaf clover would grow. This lore is often mixed with the lore of herb Paris in Iceland, another plant that is named "four-leaf." Horse skins have been used in older stave instructions, especially those for fast travel, resistance, and protection. These skins would also make perfect surfaces on which to work gandreið. As an animal of Freyr, their remains can be included in many workings and rituals that call on him. Horse teeth and bones can be used sympathetically for strength and fortitude. Their hair and tails can be woven or sewn into clothing or objects to impart these virtues. Finally, horseshoes can be used for protection and luck. They are placed above the door frame with the ends facing up, acting as a cup in which to catch good fortune.

POLAR BEAR
(ÍSBJÖRN, *URSUS MARITIMUS*)

The polar bear doesn't live in Iceland, but it does occasionally drift over, much to the terror of sheep farmers in the North. The bear was important in Scandinavia, and aspects of this animal still linger on as family fylgjur, as well as those who possess "bear-warmth" and don't often feel the cold, though some stories say this is only true of children wrapped in bearskin at birth. We find stories in Iceland of bears caring for lost people, as well as one story of a bear at Dýrhóll near Ólafsfjörður, who supposedly lived in a cave there.

Porbeagle Shark
(Hámeri, *Lamna nasus*)

Catching this fish brings one strength that will not fail all year. When the tide is low, one must not meet the eyes of the hámeri, or they will be stricken with cowardice. Due to this, fishermen cover the eyes of the shark as soon as it is fished.

Raven
(Hrafn, *Corvus corax*)

Ravens are most often associated with hrafnamál and prophecy. They have been known to hold meetings, which we call hrafnaþing, gathering like human parliaments and sometimes condemning one of their numbers to death, just as humans did while holding trials at the alþing in the Viking age. Their feathers have long been used as quills to draw staves and, after those of the water rail, are the most highly prised for this.

In Icelandic folklore, ravens are known as birds of greed, eating carcasses eyes first. They are believed to be always hungry. This is backed up by the fact that they have been known to eat their own eggs during harsh springs. Ravens are also believed to foretell the death of townsfolk by gathering on the rooves of their houses and cawing. They are said to be orderly creatures, sleeping on a similar cycle to humans; this is why if a raven is heard or seen in the night, it is believed to be an evil spirit, often called "night ravens" (nátthrafnar). This word is also used for people who appear at night asking for lodging.

Ravens often take up residency on farms over winter. These ravens are respected and sometimes even cared for; leaving food for them is recommended. Ravens have the power of speech, bringing news to and from Óðinn daily within Norse mythology, as well as mimicking human voices. Hrafnamál is the language of the ravens. Those gifted with the ability to speak hrafnamál can communicate with these birds of prophecy and learn all sorts of knowledge from watching and listening to them. The birds are believed to be able to foretell all sorts of disasters. In Vatnsdal, a girl befriended a raven and would feed it every day. One day, the raven didn't want to eat and convinced the girl to follow it out of town and into a field. When they reached the field, the girl heard a crash from behind as an avalanche fell on the town.

One method for obtaining knowledge of hrafnamál states to take the heart of a raven while it is still alive. If the bird flies two or more paces after this, the heart will become a talisman used to understand the secrets of ravens. To use this talisman, put the heart in your mouth whenever you desire to understand their language. After every time you use the heart, you should place it into a vessel that has not been used before. Because this method is difficult and cruel, there are other methods to interpret the language of ravens. We can "read" their flight, tones, and number of croaks. When setting out about your day, if a raven flies past you in the direction you're headed, close to the ground on your right side, this signals good luck. If the raven flies high in the opposite direction, you should reconsider your journey that day. If a raven sits on the roof of a church or house and shakes his wings, this foretells death in the village.

In folklore, ravens have also been said to "ward off evil spirits from the earth." Due to this ability, we can make all sorts of protective talismans from their remains. In particular, their feet can be dried and worked into necklace charms carried for protection. Working a few dried rowan berries into these charms brings extra protection.

Red-necked Phalarope
(Óðinshani, *Phalaropus lobatus*)

Óðinshani is said to show humans which water will not freeze from spring to long after midsummer and is said to peck at the water, which will not freeze again after spring has begun. This should be watched out for, as during deep snows, water sources can be easily obscured.

Rock Ptarmigan
(Rjúpa, *Lagopus muta*)

One day, Mary called together all the birds of the world and commanded that they build a fire. She then told them to show their love for her by walking through the fire. All the birds walked through the fire in their love for her, burning the feathers from their feet and leaving them bare, all except for the rjúpa. Mary was angered by this and decreed that from then on, it would be the most harmless and helpless of birds. She cursed the bird that its brother, the falcon, should never recognise it, not until, while eating the rjúpa, he sees its heart (at which he cries from grief). Other tales tell us that a blanket with rjúpa feathers inside should not be used by a pregnant woman, or she will be unable to give birth, and if she eats the egg of the bird, her children will be born with freckles. Due to this folklore, we could work the feathers of the rjúpa into charms of contraception as well as anaphrodisiac talismans.

ᛋᛖᚨᛚ SEAL

(SELIR, *HALICHOERUS GRYPUS* AND *PHOCA VITULINA*)

While close to Greenland geographically, there is not much crossover between the seal lore of Greenland and Icelandic folklore, as much of it follows more Northern European currents. It is noted in some books of Icelandic folklore that the men of the Pharoah chasing Moses, who perished in the Red Sea, became seals and that many of the races of seals come from them. Selkie lore is abundant within Icelandic folklore, however. Selkónan or Selkynjaða konan, the seal woman, is a commonly known story, and some people are said to be descended from seal women who married mortal farmers. Seals are said to become human on a few nights: the night of the thirteenth night of Christmas (Þrettándinn) and midsummer (Jónsmessunótt). This particular night is a common night for much magical mischief in Iceland.

The following excerpt sums up the sorrow that the selkie legend often focuses on. In this poem recorded in *Þjóðsögur og Ævintýri*, the mother selkie is forlorn and yearns to be with both her seven children that live in the sea and the seven she has on land.

> *"Mér er um og ó,*
> *ég á sjö börn í sjó*
> *og sjö börn á landi."*

Seal teeth could be worked sympathetically and carried on necklaces at sea to increase a catch. The selhamur or selskinna (seal skin) can be worked with for hamfari in the shape of this animal. I've had some experience with this during spirit flight, and if you can get your hands on an ethically sourced or secondhand seal skin, then I recommend trying this.

WATER RAIL
(KELDUSVÍN, *RALLUS AQUATICUS*)

Of all the birds of Iceland, the feathers of the keldusvín are supposedly the best for writing staves with. This bird is now rarely found in Iceland. The bird's feathers are prized and make better magical stave writing tools than a raven's feathers. One stave is recommended to be inked into the dried skin of this bird, a method that is impractical and uneasy to achieve, so it won't be included here. Hearing its call is supposed to bring ill luck upon those who hear it.

WISHING BEAR
(ÓSKABJÖRN, *ISOPODA*)

While no one knows exactly which isopod the wishing bear was, it is believed to have once been the size of a whale and the most evil fish in the sea. Saint Peter was said to have once come up against it, throwing a stone into its mouth and laying a curse on it. Upon swallowing the stone, it shrunk down to its current size. The same stone is still said to exist within it, and if you find it, the stone will grant wishes. Some folklore also says that the stone is to be held on or under the tongue while one speaks three wishes.

WHITE-TAILED EAGLE
(ÖRN/HAVÖRN, *HALIAEETUS ALBICILLA*)

The eagle is known as the king of birds. Previously male, the name of the eagle became *Assa*, a feminine noun. She waits patiently by rivers to catch salmon. Due to this patience, the eagle has been known in folklore as a lazy bird. The bird's sworn enemy is the músarindill, the Eurasian wren (*Troglodytes troglodytes*), which likely comes from examples of the two animals being found dead together. To make an enemy vulnerable, you must take an eagle feather from the animal's left wing.

Place this under the mattress this person sleeps on or the pillow they lay their head on, and the next day, the person will be gullible and agree to deals that leave them at a disadvantage. For improved memory, folklore tells that us that one must drink milk that has an eagle feather placed in it. An eagle's claw is supposed to hinder a forge; if placed in the forge crank, the forge won't work until it is removed. Eagle eggs may birth dragons if gold is placed under them. This follows the same magic as the method by which one turns a slug into a lindwyrm. Rescuing an eagle from having its claws caught in a salmon that was too large for it to carry is said to bring a life of good fortune.

Keep in mind that owning feathers, talons, eggs, or any other material from eagles is illegal in many areas. Always check the laws in your location and err on the side of caution.

White Wagtail
(Maríerla, *Motacilla alba*)

The tongue of a maríuerla, dried in the sun and then ground with mass wine, is applied to dice so that you win any game. This talisman can also supposedly be worked for opening and unlocking. Find more information about the lore of this sacred bird of María on page 184.

PHANTASMARIUM

The next section contains a little catalogue of the more mystical and fantastic creatures found within Icelandic folklore. As a catalogue of spirits, this phantasmarium can delineate the differences between the many types of Icelandic ghosts, nature spirits, and more. Sometimes, even locals have trouble discerning when a ghost should be classed as a skuggi or a syjpur, or when the being causing trouble is a púki or a tilberi. Let this collection of spirits serve as your guide to understanding things that go bump in the night on this island.

Abandoned Spirits
(Útburður, *Umbra perditus*)

These tragic spirits are the ghosts of children left out in the land to die. During hard times in Iceland, this would have been the fate of many children whose parents couldn't afford to feed or care for them, as well as many illegitimate children who were the result of infidelity and affairs. These ghosts are terrifying creatures, sometimes appearing as if they have aged as the living do, though unable to speak, with backward facing arms and legs, crawling on all fours. The following verse is associated with them:

"Kalt er mér í klettagjá	"Cold, I am in the cliff-gorge,
Að kúra undir steinum.	Huddled under rocks.
Burt er holdið beinum frá,	The flesh long gone from the bones,
Borinn var ég í meinum."	Born was I in pain."

As with many spirits, improper or non-existent burial leads the spirits to wander, lost and confused, Earth-bound, and unable to move on. This sad fate often ends with the spirit finding its way back to the mother, often being a terrifying ordeal.

DWARVES
(DVERGAR, *SPIRITUS RUPICOLA*)

The dvergar, or dwarves, of Icelandic folklore live in remote places, often deep within the mountains. These dwarves don't appear as much in stories outside of those about Nordic mythology, though there are areas in Iceland where the dwarves have been seen and heard singing. Dverghamrar, or the dwarf hammer, is one such place. On the south coast of Iceland, a local girl once heard the dwarves singing their songs at this spot. Dvergar are dwellers in the deep, so they rarely come to the surface world and, as such, are often regarded as deeper, darker spirits. They are more closely related to Iceland's cave systems, volcanoes, and darkness. Some see them as the antithesis of the elves, ruling in winter when the elves have retreated to their realm until summer comes again.

ECHOES
(BERGMÁL, *UMBRA RESONANTIA*)

Some ghosts we see are not much more than echoes or scars left upon the spiritual landscape. We can call these echoes psychic trauma. We all know legends of ghosts that appear at certain times and places, and some may seem menacing, though these echoes hold no power of their own. Many such echoes have been recorded around Iceland. Some take the form of apparitions, some are sounds, and some are even simply smells. Those that take on the form of apparitions can cross over with a few other categories of spirit mentioned in this section.

One such example is a man from Laxamýri, who kept fine horses and loved to race. He was once riding along a path to a river, and on his journey, he encountered another rider on a fine brown horse. He called out to the rider, only to find the rider sped up and rode fast away from him. Being fond of races, the man took this as a challenge and gave chase. He rode after the man, who didn't seem to notice what was happening around him.

As they approached a river, the chaser slowed, knowing this river was impassable on horseback. But to his shock and surprise, the rider on the brown horse sped up, and the horse jumped into the river, vanishing. The man later discovered that a rider on a brown horse had died in the river around the same time the previous year. Interestingly, this is one of many stories of ghostly horsemen repeating the events leading to their death along with their horses. These echoes are sometimes also called *skuggi,* though this can also refer to other types of spirits.

Elves
(Álfar or Huldufólk, *Spiritus summus*)

Elves, or huldufólk, are the inhabitants of the land in Iceland. Thousands of stories, both local and regional, are remembered and still told about the hidden people. To many of us, these spirits are the descendants of those who lived on the land before Kristintaka, as well as the spirits of nature and the land itself. As landvættur in their own right, they are inhabitants of fields, mounds, hills, and lakes. There are many ways to classify these spirits and the many roles they play. Some bring us warnings, some protect spaces, and some are simply overheard singing or speaking by lone travellers in nature.

Looking at these spirits from the human view of classification may not benefit us as much as it would to view them as individuals, the way we do other humans, seeing each as unique, with their own reasons, actions, and reactions. It is widely acknowledged that you don't disturb their dwellings. Some hidden people even adopted Christianity, building churches and spaces of worship to the Christian

God post-Kristintaka. The hidden folk are the bergbúar, the haugbúar, and other spirits that inhabit the stones, rocks, and mountains. Their capital city is widely agreed upon as being located at Ásbýrgi in the North of Iceland, a place I highly recommend visiting in a respectful and calm manner.

Following Ghosts
(Afturgöngur, *Umbra sequax*)

This is a category of all spirits, not just human dead. Many spirits have the potential to become afturgöngur. As mentioned earlier, many are divided into *skotta* and *móri*, though these seemingly human spirits may never have been so but have taken on a human likeness over time. One strange story from the North tells us of a sailor named Bjarni, who, while out sailing and fishing with his crew out in the deep ocean, came across a boat with no oars piloted by two strange, pale, robed men. The men of the ship called out to them, but they didn't say a word. The fishing ship was followed by this oarless boat for a few days before they finally came ashore. By this time, the oarless boat had disappeared. Soon after this ordeal, three of the ship's crew died.

These sorts of stories are fairly common in Icelandic folklore, with spirits showing up in strange guises and following those fated to die for some time before their passing. Those who are followed by harmless (if not creepy) entities are the lucky ones, as some afturgöngur are much more fearsome and track their victims until they die horrible deaths or are driven mad. Some afturgöngur are simply vengeful dead who perform tasks such as killing livestock or blighting land based on the way they may have been treated in life and the cause of their death.

One such ghost of a badly treated farmhand is still known to kill newborn cattle at Laxamýri. Some afturgöngur can be animals, including the ghosts of faithful dogs and even cattle. The ghosts of dogs have been said to be seen around towns, happily living in the areas they did in life and even sometimes interacting with humans as if still alive. One such ghost dog is said to haunt Vestmanneyjar, jumping onto the packs of travellers and slowly weighing them down until they collapse from exhaustion. Móri and skotta are the two most agreed-upon expressions of afturgöngur.

Fox-Cat

(Skoffinn, Skuggabaldur, and
Finngálkn, *Vulpes letalis*)

Skoffinn buries itself three days after birth, then reemerges three years later. It is the child of a male fox and a female cat. It has basilisk traits, so it kills with sight; it can be killed by using mirrors or with silver bullets, just like with dragons birthed from eagle eggs placed on gold. Clothing made from the hides of skoffinn and skuggabaldur is supposed to transfer its power of invulnerability to bullets to the wearer.

Like the skoffinn, the skuggabaldur buries itself in the ground three days after birth and emerges three years later. It is said to be able to kill with only a look (and can be killed by being shown its own reflection) and to be immune to gunshot. It also shares some traits with the basilisk and is the child of a female fox and a male cat. These animals have been known to speak, with one telling the crowd who killed it that, once it dies, they should tell the cat who lived at Bollastaðir of their deed. The killing was later spoken of in a house in Bollastaðir, when the cat, sitting calmly, launched at the one who told the story and wouldn't let go until its head was removed. The folklore sometimes conflates these three creatures but, at other times, tells of the skoffinn being hatched from a rooster's egg, much like the basilisk lore. The finngálkn folklore is the same, so this name may be three different versions of the same creature.

Great Serpents

(Lyndormar, *Draco serpens*)

Gold seems to have a particular effect on certain creatures in Iceland, including great serpents. A slug was once said to have been placed in a box of gold by a girl who wished to see if the folktales about lyndorm held true. When she returned to the box, she was shocked to see it bursting at its hinges with the now swollen lyndorm. In fear, she threw the box and wyrm into Skorradalsvatn, where the wyrm is said to have continued to grow, becoming the appropriate size for the large, deep lake. Many still claim that they have seen the wyrm, also known as the serpent of Skorradalsvatn (Ormurinn í Skorraldalsvatni), with many sightings occurring in 1858 and 1861, according to Árnason in *Þjóðsögur og Ævintýri*.

Noted lyndormar around Iceland include:

- Hvalvatns ormur
- Skorradalsvatn ormur
- Kleifarvatn ormur
- Hvítá ormar
- Skálfandafljóts ormur
- Hvammsfirði ormur

Heathback Whale
(Lyngbakur, *Balaenoptera eremus*)

This creature of folklore looks like an island. It lays still in the water for so long that heaths begin to sprout from its back until sailors pass by and land on the whale. Sometimes, the sailors set up camp and manage to stay a while before the whale senses them and begins to dive. The men must then hurry back to the ships before they are lost at sea.

House Spirits
(Húsandi, *Spiritus domesticus*)

House spirits play a role in Icelandic folk magic as the main protector spirit of a home unless otherwise warded. This is a title that many spirits can hold. A húsandi may have once been a púki, a human spirit, or a landvættur. These spirits should be reserved and have a special place in the home dedicated to them. Feed them with offerings of milk or food and regularly converse with them while going about your domestic business. Maintaining a good relationship with these spirits can help maintain a safe and cosy household. Other words for ghosts and spirits in Icelandic include *sveimur, slæðingur, lalli, fornyja, skufsa, vomur, daugsi, vofa,* and *vofra*.

Imps

(Púkar, *Spiritus familiaris*)

Many practitioners have a few púkar that help them complete tasks, such as stealing milk, tormenting their enemies, or completing domestic chores for them. Púkar appear in many different forms. These are often lesser spirits unless otherwise fed and cultivated by practitioners. They may appear in the form of physical animals, often small creatures such as insects or even mice. Naming and taming púkar is beneficial for those of us who work with spirits, giving us mutually beneficial relationships to aid in the development of our craft.

Land Spirits

(Landvættir, *Spiritus tellus*)

From the four great landvættir of Iceland to smaller regional landvættir, this term is a title given to spirits who hold a high rank in their local spirit ecology. We know the four rulers of the land in Iceland are masters of all other spirits beneath them. Any kind of spirit may serve as the landvættur to a field, a forest, a river, or any other natural place. To catalogue them all would be impossible, but we should concern ourselves with respecting them and approaching them before working with them.

Likeness or Apparition

(Svipur, *Umbra similitudo*)

These apparitions, appearing clearly in the likeness of the deceased, are always human spirits. Within folklore, we see these spirits appearing both in dreams and the waking world to relatives or just anyone who happens to be in the right place at the right time. Sometimes, they will inform the living of the location of their corpses; other times, they will express their dying feelings, which are not always negative or sad. Once, a svipur appeared to a farmer on nearby land and expressed his relief and happiness about finally being "out of his misery" in death. This type of apparition may well be the shades of souls passing on some last piece of information before they join the other shades of our ancestors, wherever they may be. They are also sometimes called *skuggi*.

Milk Suckers

(Tilberi or Snakkur, *Spiritus egenus*)

These spirits are born of human bone, blood, and sheep's wool. These creatures, briefly mentioned earlier, are entities of pure need. They suck the milk from cows and regurgitate it to keep their creators in good health in exchange for blood. The tilberi will feed from a "nipple," which it creates by biting the one who birthed it. It can complete any number of tasks for payment of blood via this wound. This is unsavoury magic that has lifelong consequences. Tilberi are hard to kill and may only be trapped, not fully disposed of.

Mound Dwellers

(Haugbúar, *Umbra tumulus habitantis*)

Many fornmenn of old are buried within mounds, known since the times before Kristnitakan. These spirits are revered by us. Many mounds have had the names of those buried within them associated with them for a very long time. These spaces must be respected and not disturbed. We can sometimes work with these spirits as the landvættir of places, though we would do best not to disturb the dead very often. Útiseta may be worked on these mounds if one has the experience and knowledge to do so. Some Haugbúar are not as asleep as others. One such mound on Grímsey is known as Stórhóll. This mound was said to be the burial place of two rich foreigners, and some shepherds have said that, on clear sunny days, the two spirits can be seen playing chess on a golden chess board atop the mound, one wearing a red dress and the other, green.

Noctural Ghosts
(Mara, *Umbra nocturnus*)

The mara are nocturnal ghosts who sit atop their victims, often violently attacking them and causing all sorts of problems. These spirits attack in the same style as spirits who "hag-ride" their victims by night on the mainland. They are often the vengeful dead (those who feel wronged in death), maybe due to the disturbance of grave sites or other such misdeeds. Within Icelandic folklore, these dangerous spirits have been known to kill, attacking whole groups of victims, sometimes in cycles of specific times. One such spirit became a problem in the town of Stokkseyri in South Iceland. The spirit was bound beneath a rock in town and is said to need re-binding every seven years. Once in recent history, this task was not accomplished, and the mara began to attack the town's residents again before it was finally re-bound.

Poisonous Pike
(Gedda or Vatnagedda, *Salmo venenata*)

The poisonous pike, a magical being supposedly found in Gedduvatn in the Westfjords, was said to be a powerful creature with an aura that dispels ghosts and spirits. It is also known as *vatngedda* and *eiturgedda*. The fat of this animal is said to cure pain caused by ghosts and spirits. To catch this fish, you must wear many layers of gloves of both human and skate skin and cast the line baited with a gold ring.

Resurrected Spirits
(Uppvakningar, *Umbra corporeus*)

These are terrifying draugar that are raised from the dead and sent after others, usually with preternatural strength. These are the terrifying Nordic "zombies" of old stories, raised by sorcerers to kill their enemies and only rarely thwarted by cunning or strong would-be victims. Jón Árnason lays out his method for resurrecting draugar in his work, which I have discussed earlier on page 38.

Stone Dwellers
(Bergbúar, *Spiritus petra-habitaculum*)

There are many creatures that inhabit the rocks and stones of Iceland, from the hidden folk to the dwarves, dark elves, all manner of land spirits, and even human and once-human ghosts. The term *bergbúar* refers to all those who dwell within rocks. These spirits need to be respected; their homes had best not be moved and offerings may be left for them outside their dwellings in hard times. Other names for these spirits include *steinbúi, angi, kettlingur, kyrpingur, putalingur, puti, smámenni,* and *vöggur.*

Treasure Spirits
(Fépúkar, *Umbra opes-custos*)

Some spirits are known to be guarding buried treasure. In Iceland, these have been noted as all sorts of spirits, from humans to ghosts to dragons. One such example is a spirit said to be the shade of Jón Lærði (more about him can be found on page 189. This ghost guards a hill under which he was said to have buried treasure. Such sites would be best left alone. It doesn't take a genius to work out what might happen to one who steals such guarded treasure.

Trolls
(Tröll, *Trollus sp.*)

There are many types of trolls in Icelandic folklore, from those who can only move about by night to those who were once human and have changed over time. We know of nátttröll, who turn to stone come daylight, causing trouble in the depths of the dark winter. We know of Grýla and other such named and even somewhat regarded trolls such as Bárður, the half-troll guardian of Snæfellsnes, Jóra, the angry troll of Hengill, and more. These fearsome creatures may well reflect more of the dark side of human nature than we wish to acknowledge. You can read more on trolls in Chapter Five.

Water Horse
(Nykur, *Equus palustris*)

The Icelandic nykur displays many of the same traits as its Scottish cousin, the kelpie. The horse can be distinguished from other Icelandic horses by simply looking at its hooves. If they face backwards, this horse is a water horse, and one should not trust it. Attempt to ride the horse, and you'll find yourself stuck to it, unable to escape before it lunges into a deep pool and feasts on your entrails. The only way to escape this beast is to utter its own name or the name of God. Praying a *Pater Noster* will cause this beast to flee. Speaking anything close to the word *nykur* will work also; the word *nenni*, a commonly used word in Icelandic, is close enough to be effective.

Waterfall Spirits
(Fossvættir, *Spiritus cataracta*)

Somewhat like the spirits of waterfalls in other Nordic countries, waterfall spirits in Iceland are not as dangerous as the Norwegian fossegrim. These spirits should be paid respect, and their flow should not be hindered; otherwise, they are prone to cause trouble in the surrounding area. Some tales warn us of travelling by waterfalls late at night. Seljalandsfoss, now a major tourist attraction, is said to be home to a waterfall spirit. As such, I recommend treating this space with a heightened level of respect. Those who die by drowning in rivers and waterfalls sometimes wind up the spiritual guardians of such places.

17

Náttúrusteinar: Magical Stones

Magical stones play a unique role in Icelandic folklore and folk magic. Often said to appear on the edges—or float to the surface—of deep lakes on Jónsmessunótt, these stones have a handful of uses. Some are known as óskarsteinar (wishing stones), and some are called hulinhjálmssteinar (invisibility stones). There are many types with many uses, and I recommend working with found stones like these as magical tools. We hold them in as high regard as many hold crystals and gems within other witchcraft practices. These stones can be many shapes, colours, and sizes; all are different and unique. Where they may not fit the exact visual aesthetic that semi-precious gems like amethyst and quartz do, they are just as potent, if not more, imbued with powers that often reveal themselves only to the one who finds them.

Magical stones have long been held in high regard within magical traditions, and we can see their importance, especially as magical objects. When looking at medieval lapidaries, Bishop Marbode of Rennes's *Liber de lapidibus* stands out in particular. Fragments of this could well influence a lot of the lore surrounding náttúrusteinar and their powers. Translated to Icelandic around 1200, fragments of this work are also present in the early fourteenth-century *Hauksbók*. It is likely that the connection between stone-like quartz and the spirits was observed in medieval Iceland. One medieval burial at Hofstaðir contained a skull with two quartz crystals in its mouth. Later magical traditions connect quartz with being a prime crystal for the housing and occasional trapping of spirits, as well as an aid in necromancy.

We know from archaeological records that green stones were hoarded or gathered at Reykholt, likely due to the idea that the church at Jerusalem was built upon a holy green stone, and as such, other green stones would hold similar virtues of purity or power. We know that these green stones were gathered for four hundred years or so, a behaviour which argues a belief in their power.

HEALING STONES

Nátturusteinar have been used to ease childbirth and aid in healing. One such stone to aid in childbirth was noted in the inventory of Hólar, the Northern centre of Christianity. I work one such stone alongside vallhumall (*Achillea millefolium*) oil to bring swift healing. This stone was found out in nature, on Jónsmessunótt, following tradition. I also use a white stone, gifted to me by a friend, for this sort of healing work. I enhance the stone's natural gifts with specific staves designed to aid in healing. Green stones in Iceland, specifically jasper, have also been used for healing in the past. This idea connects us back to the holy green stone of Jerusalem, as well as to the green stones of the biblical Aaron's breastplate. Generally, green nátturusteinar were also said to ward off devils and evil, likely due to their holy virtues. Green jasper was also said to help ease childbirth, a common theme for stone magic in Iceland.

It is said that stones that aid childbirth must sit in warm white wine, which is then consumed by the one giving birth, or the stone is to simply be placed on the belly during labour. Spherulites, known as *baggalútur* in Icelandic, are the stones still used this way in living memory, accompanied by galdur and Christian prayers. Also known as blóðstemmusteinn, these stones are also used for blood-stopping as well as being used to aid in labour. Further folklore and stories add more confusion about these stones. One source says they are supposed to be kept wrapped up in a white linen cloth and placed within a jar full of flour, or they will lose their power. Jars of flour are also said to help preserve the magical qualities of other stones, such as agates.

In contemporary practice, we can keep our blood-stopping stones in pouches of dried yarrow, lady's bedstraw, and white deadnettle. To use them, hold them over or on a bleeding wound and chant the following chant, gathered by Jón Árnason:

"Stemmist blóð þeim blæðir,
Blóð féll af gúðs róðu;
Almáttugum bauð ótta,
Af undum sárlega píndist;
Stattu í dýrð svo dreyri,
En það guðsson heyri;
Önd og blóðugar æðar
Er sá (sú) sæll (sæl)sem leysist.
Stemmist blóð, blæði hverki út né inn."

This is to be ended with the Latin *"Filium spiritum domino pater."*

Finding Náttúrusteinar

Árnason gives us a list of places where many náttúrusteinar may be found; however, remember that these stones can be found all over the country and, indeed, elsewhere in the world. The ponds atop Drápuhlíðarfjall in Snæfellsnes are said to contain many of these magical stones, but we do not recommend taking rocks and materia from that area of Snæfellsnes as the area on the peninsula where the hill is found is a protected site and removing the stones is illegal.

Further into the past, we see references to magical stones gifted by dwarves, such as the magical stones mentioned in Þorstein's *þáttr bæjarmagns*. Þorsteinn is gifted two stones, one of which turns the user invisible (clearly a hulinhjálmursteinn). In the saga, the other stone is triangular and tri-coloured, which influences the weather. Within oral tradition and contemporary craft, we do know of some stones worked with in weather magic. The hulinhjálmur staves, also found later, can be engraved or inscribed onto náttúrusteinar or onto pouches or parchment that one carries the stone in to enhance their effect.

One misconception of these workings for invisibility is that they are intended to make one truly invisible. Of course, in reality, these workings are illusionary, intending to make one go unnoticed as they go about their business. While there are plenty of workings for this, both contemporary and older, I believe that due to the wording of some of the folklore source material on náttúrusteinar, sometimes invisibility really means a lack of visibility through the weather or darkness.

Sometimes, the words chosen, to me, move more towards weather working of darkening the sky to hide someone or something, as well as calling in fog or cloud to cover an area. This would be another interesting dual aspect virtue: an object typically falling under the rulership of the element of Earth having the power to affect the sky and atmosphere, which fall under the rule of the opposite element. This is another example of dual aspects in many materia from Icelandic tradition.

Sometimes, the folklore surrounding these stones is incredibly vague. Some sources say that the best way to find them is to wait for Jónsmessunótt and watch them rise from the bottom of their lakes and ponds and dance on the water. Some are said to be found in crow and raven nests, eggs, or even inside the birds. This echoes other folk magic beliefs around Northern Europe of stones being found within toads, swallows, and other animals.

Another vague location from folklore sources is a magical well in Skagafjörður, said to have golden water, surrounded by tall crags on all sides. This well may well be a real location, with "golden water" referring to the water reflecting the midnight sun during Jónsmessunótt. The stones in it are said to jump up out of the water on Jónsmessunótt, making it a much easier location for collecting these stones, provided you can find the well.

Some nátturusteinar are said to grow in the sea and wash ashore. Plenty of ingredients and magical tools can be found along the seashore, so keep this in mind while you beach comb. Some believe that stones gathered at the seashore weren't stones at all but the giant seed of the tropical sea-bean (*Entada gigas* or *Mimosa scandens*). The lore around all of these varies, but the seeds are very different from the stones used in folk magic, both in living and older memory. The seed could well drift to Iceland with driftwood from anywhere along the gulf stream, as stranger things have washed ashore on this island.

Náttúrusteinar in Folklore

Icelandic folklore contains a resurrection stone (fans of the *Harry Potter* series may be familiar with such a mythical object). However, the method to obtain one is cruel and breaks a few environmental laws. It is said that one must find an eagle's nest with a living chick unattended. You must then smother the chick, and upon returning, the eagle will try all it can to revive the baby. It will bring all kinds of nátturusteinar to the nest until it finds lausnarsteinninn. The stone will revive the chick, and if no one is around to take the stone, the eagle will dispose of it where no man will find it. Similar uses for stones show up in Swedish trolldom with similar gruesome methods. Many other similarities can be drawn between Icelandic nátturusteinar and the magical stones found within Swedish trolldom. Methods of acquiring stones of invisibility and those that allow one to speak to or understand birds or other people are nearly identical. Perhaps this is due to the countries' shared cultural roots, or maybe because the magic of these stones is more than just folklore.

The óskasteinn (wishing stone) is another náttúrusteinar still worked in Icelandic folk magic. These stones were named so because one gets whatever they wish for when they carry the stone. Yet again, we have conflicting folklore around these stones, as well as within our living traditions and practices. Árnason says that one method of finding this stone, another said to be from the sea, is to look for it on Easter morning along the seashore.

The stone is a yellow-white colour and very similar to a bean. The other method involves stealing a raven's egg from the nest, boiling it, then replacing it and waiting for the other chicks to hatch. When they have all hatched, the boiled egg is to have a hole poked in it, and within it, one is said to find the small wishing stone. This should then be worn on one's elbow or kept in fresh new linen, or else it will lose its power. His other methods all involve aquatic isopods, and the folklore gets a little too murky to make much sense of.

Another story tells us that a woman out walking found a wishing stone on Tindastól near Sauðárkrókur in North Iceland. She picked up the stone and wished to find herself at the most extravagant party. Suddenly, she found herself at one, and she was gifted a golden cup by a strange man. In her shock, she wished to be back on the mountain, and suddenly, she was transported. She threw the stone back at the mountain and returned home with her golden cup. Was this a party of the Álfar living in the mountain? She later sold the golden cup to the king (presumably of Denmark) and was gifted three plots of land in Skagafjörður. So, maybe these wishing stones bring good fortune in all shapes and forms. We at least believe them to bring about wealth and grant material wishes.

Another stone is known in Icelandic as *sagnasteinn*. This translates to "history stone," although based on what it does, I would call this a "knowing stone" or a "sage stone." This stone is said to be found in the nests of ladybugs in the month of May, whereas another story tells us it is found in the nests of owls. Once found, it should be placed in a handkerchief that is stained with blood. Hold it up to your right ear, and it will tell you that which you wish to know. This sort of work undoubtedly needs the stone to possess a spirit of its own—or at least be connected to some spirit that does the work of retrieving or sharing information. Personally, I would be sceptical of this—a spirit wouldn't usually give something for nothing—so keep an eye out for trickery and deceit.

Another story about the origins of this stone is that, during Easter week, when summer comes, you can find it in a raven's nest on Good Friday. Around Good Friday mass, one must go to the nest, and upon writing some small text (or galdur), the raven will fall asleep as if dead. It would then drop this stone from its mouth. The stone should be taken, dried, and then placed under your own tongue to bring you the gift of understanding and speaking to the ravens. This working could come from the same belief of stones residing within animals, as well as the belief that, upon consuming part of an animal, one gains that animal's powers and abilities.

These more fantastical aspects of Icelandic folk magic make for great stories, but I don't recommend trying them out. Náttúrusteinar are plenty and often found by happenstance about nature, so no animals need to be harmed for this folklore to be put to the test. I would instead recommend experimenting with the crowberry. Dry them out and place them beneath your tongue to see if they will give you the ability to understand the animals they are named after.

A final knowing stone can supposedly be found within grey seafoam. This stone should be dropped into a lake, turning that body of water into a scrying pool for you to ask the spirits there to answer whatever questions you might have. This last method is obviously the easiest and most favoured. Any stones you find on the beach that make themselves known as sage stones should be thrown into a large body of water after being thrice asked a question. Sit and scry for the answer. A perfect location for this in Southwest Iceland is the remote and appropriately named Spákonuvatn (Fortune Teller's Lake) in Reykjanes.

Yet another stone spoken of to hold magical powers is the Skruggsteinn. This stone is said to come from the sky, hence the name, meaning "thunder stone." It is said that anyone who is lucky enough to find the stone can use it to "see" all over the world. This thunderstone is unlikely to be another thunderstone from the mainland (flint) as Iceland lacks chalk. Some stones are said to prevent births, and sulphur, known in Icelandic as *brennistienn*, is used for malefic work. The tradition of using a bezóar, a stone that was believed to work as an antidote for all things, made its way to Iceland as well. These stones are masses most often found trapped with the gastrointestinal systems of animals, though they can occur in other parts of the body.

This tradition of using stones that originated within animals is commonplace in much of Europe's witchcraft lore. In Swedish trolldom, these stones are found within the heads and bodies of birds and land mammals, most traditionally swallows and other small birds, though toads are also said to possess stones. In Iceland, this tradition was absorbed into much of the lore and folk knowledge as other magical stones. Both eagles and ravens were thought to possess healing stones both within their bodies and the earlier discussed notion of them bringing resurrection stones to revive their dead young.

It is worth closing this section by mentioning that in Iceland, especially within the Þjóðveldið, between the years 930 and 1262, the use of magical stones was prohibited by law and was taken as seriously as other witchcraft-related practices. After 1262, the church and state still looked upon the use of magical stones as witchcraft, and their use continued to be discouraged.

TYPES OF STONES

According to the Icelandic translations of *Liber de lapidibus,* as well as other sources of stone folklore and magic, the following stones (some of which can be found naturally occurring in Iceland) have powers and virtues associated with them:

Onyx: Said to cause supernatural disturbances in sleep, as well as social unrest if worn at night. Though, like many things in Icelandic folk magic, if worn in the day, it is said to bring good social status and make one more agreeable. It most often occurs in Iceland with white bands. In contemporary witchcraft, it is worked for banishing grief and instilling self-confidence.

Topaz: Previously worked as a blood-stopper stone. Supposedly, if placed in water, it was said to stop it from boiling. It is most worked nowadays for joy, good fortune, good health, and honesty.

Sapphire: Previously used for curing eye wounds and ailments, as well as reducing excessive perspiration. It was also said to prevent faint heartedness and envy within the wearer. It is one of the stones said to have a power to unlock doors. Still to this day, it is worn to ease depression and lows.

Amethyst: Granted protection from poisoning and relief from the effects of alcohol. Within contemporary practice, it is most often worked for sleep, dreams, protection, and psychic powers.

Emerald: Said to extend one's lifespan, as well as enhance sexual appetites and abilities. Its dual nature was to calm and soothe lust, as well as having the power to calm the sea. In contemporary practice, it's said to calm and bring peace to oneself.

Lapis Lazuli: Said to make people gentler with one another. Its full powers were supposed to manifest when set in silver, which is still a common pairing today. It is said in contemporary witchcraft to inspire strength, courage, and the truth.

Peridot: Previously worked to drive away trolls and unclean spirits. It was also said to bring good health and inspire restful sleep.

Bloodstone: Historically worked for invisibility and weather magic, and may well be one of the stones mentioned in saga literature. Bloodstone is worked in contemporary witchcraft to heighten intuition and increase creativity, as well as for protection and grounding.

Quartz: Worked throughout the Middle Ages in Europe as a stone that aided in communication with spirits and, as such, necromancy. It was also worked as a spirit trap, which is a stone to house angelic beings inside, then used as a medium to ask them for knowledge. Within many modern practices, clear quartz seems to have become a catch-all and general substitute, which is something I am not so keen on. While quartz works as a medium for spirits, it doesn't possess the virtues of any other stone one would wish to substitute it for.

Iceland Spar: A form of calcite, known in Icelandic as *Silfurbergskristall,* may well be the sólsteinar, or sunstones, of the Viking and Middle Ages. It was used as a navigator's tool; when held up to clouds that covered the sun, the stone was supposed to clearly show where the sun was through the clouds, allowing for navigation in cloudy weather. This physical power of "showing" where the sun was translates for us as a spiritual power to reveal the truth—or at least help us to see the reality of things. Silfurberg crystals that had been fractured or lost their clarity were called *rosti* and said to be less useful, both magically and physically.

Obsidian: Known as *hrafntinna* in Icelandic, it is said to have nine virtues, all of which may be beneficial to the one who comes across this volcanic glass. Associated with the raven, the stone has been said to aid in the understanding of hrafnamál (the language of the ravens). Areas like Landmannalaugar in the highlands contain fields of naturally occurring obsidian, though taking from these places is forbidden by law and the draconic spirits who make this space their home.

Agate: Agate stones also hold magical power within Icelandic tradition. These stones possess many virtues. One cannot be bested by magic if one holds one. For this purpose, it is best set in a ring of gold. The stone allows one to drink and drink but never get drunk. Poisoned food and drink are said to not "stay down" when consumed while wearing an agate stone. Agates are fairly easy to find in Iceland, but remember that removing anything from the landscape in most cases is illegal, and one can be fined high sums at the airport and have these objects removed before leaving the country.

Caring for Your Magical Stones

If we wish to follow folklore as an example, once you've found a few magical stones, you will need to house and care for them correctly. Some must be kept within a jar of flour, some wrapped in linen, and others, both. As with many plants and roots, the magic within them may be easily lost without proper care. I recommend finding or making yourself a ceramic jar and adorning it with symbols either during construction or afterward. This jar should then be filled with flour and should be used only to contain these stones.

If you wish to bring them along with you, I recommend a sturdy jar that is small enough to put into a bag or pouch. This jar should be easily sealable to keep all your stones safe and cosy. The jar can be adorned with all sorts of staves and symbols. If you believe you've found yourself a hulinhjálmssteinn, you could carve or adorn the jar with a hulinhjálmsstafur. If you're working with stones for healing, then any number of staves to promote healing would be appropriate. Decorate it with any of the staves mentioned later that most accurately fit the virtues of the stone or stones inside.

If you're creating your own ceramic jar, add colour to the jar using an appropriate glaze to enhance these virtues. This might be green for healing, and if making your own jar, going as far as using a wood ash glaze of healing tree woods would hopefully give a nice grey-green finish to the jar. Inscribe the linen used to wrap the stones with staves appropriate for their virtues, as well as adding dried herbs to the flour in these jars: birch leaves, angelica, and mint for healing stones; yarrow for blood-stoppers; or valerian root and other sour-smelling plant materia for jars used to house malefic or ill-natured stones like sulphur.

18

María, Freyja, Dýrlingar, og Syndarar: Mary, Freyja, Saints, and Sinners

Icelandic folk magic has a unique take on the Virgin Mary. To many of us who practice in Iceland, as well as to some Christians and those with only a passing interest, she is known as the queen of the elves. The notion that some elves, like some people, are Christian might sound incompatible with Neo-Pagan ideas of Nordic folk magic to some, but to us, this is accepted as fact in Iceland. María, or Mary, is heavily assimilated with Freyja, so we can see why the Lady of Álfheimar was aligned with the queen of heaven.

María's name is given to many places, plants, and things within Iceland. We know her caves, her hills, and all her sacred spots. We know which plants she cares for and which birds she watches over. As I mentioned before, although Catholicism was abandoned after the reformation, the people's reverence for Mary persisted. We even see evidence of runes used to carve Mary's name. One spindle weight thought to have been made in Greenland was found in Iceland engraved with a runic inscription naming Mary.

We have many stories of her being directly involved with the lives of people and animals around Iceland. Of the birds named after her, Maríuerla or Maríuatla (the white wagtail, *Motacilla alba*) is one we work divination and magic with. This bird has also been called *friggjaelda* or *friggjaertla* in the past. When first you see her in the springtime, you must greet her with the following rhyme.

"Heil og sæl, María litla mín.
Hvar er hún svala systir þín?
Er hún í útlöndum að spinna lín?
Það mun hún vera, hún svala systir þín.
Ég skal gefa þér berin blá
ef þú vísar mér á
hver ég vera á
í vor og sumar,
'vetur og haust."

"Greetings, my little Mary.
Where is your sister swallow?
Is she abroad spinning linen?
I know her to be, your sparrow sister.
I'll give you berries blue
If you tell me
How I shall be,
In spring, summer,
Winter, or autumn."

The rhyme should be chanted to the bird. This rhyme and the way she reacts to it will tell us how our coming year will be. If, during this time, she should take flight, she does not wish to help you. But, should she stay, you then need to ask her to fly in the direction your fortune for the year lies. She will then do so, and you should bear this information in mind for the coming year. The white wagtail comes to Iceland between April and September, and her appearance used to coincide with the arrival of merchant ships in the spring. This may well be where this association with fortune comes from. Within less savoury folk magic, the tongue of the bird is to be dried in the sun, then crushed and blended with mass wine. This mixture should then be scraped into the indents of a die, which is then said to never lose.

As for plant life, we work both Maríustakkur (*Alchemilla mollis*) and Maríuvöndur (*Gentianella campestris*) as offerings to Mary. These both have a connection to Freyja, and Maríustakkur is said to grow in areas inhabited by elves along with many other plants we work to honour and venerate the mother figure. Hofsóley (*Caltha palustris*) and Vallhumall (*Achillea millefolium*) are two other plants we utilise for any work involving the Virgin Mary. Although these two don't hold her namesake, they work wonderful healing and love magic, two virtues ruled by María.

Certain places are held as sacred to Mary and may well have been thought of as sacred to Freyja before the island adopted Christianity. Maríahellar, a small cave just on the outskirts of the capital area, is one such place. This lava tunnel cave is a gorgeous space, and candles may be left here along with petitions to Mary if one returns to clean them up afterward. Maríulind is another sacred spot. Redefined in more recent times as a sacred space to Mary within Iceland's magical landscape, this spring was blessed as a site sacred to María, and a statue of her was placed there. This spot holds a special place in our hearts, and a visit to the spring in Hellnar, on the Snæfellsnes peninsula, is recommended. Mary even has her own magical staves. Within contemporary folk magic, we use these to form occasionally extravagant displays of devotion, working colourful powdered herbs and other materia into these shapes in sacred places.

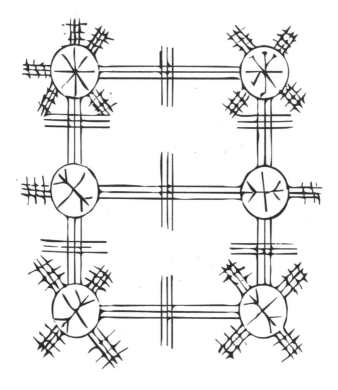

This first stave is from the collection *Lbs 5472 II* and is one that can be worked into more elaborate offerings. I have had great success in working this stave on a Sunday in the hours of Venus for aid in love and healing magic, as well as in the hour of the Moon for dream magic. A talisman of healing that works by venerating María is crafted by drawing this stave on either fresh linen or sheep skin within the hour of Venus. You then use the material to create a pouch, which should be filled with herbs sacred to Mary. All of those mentioned earlier in this section are appropriate, but you could also add maðjurt (*Filipendula ulmaria*) to aid in healing sleep. Other staves to María are drawn onto her altars, lined out in powdered herbs and berries, and sometimes drawn in nature, on beaches, or in areas where our work won't remain once the rain or snow has washed it away.

Another stave, known as Maríukross (Mary's cross), was recorded in *Lbs 5472 III.* We have used this stave to work with Mary, along with staves worked with spirits or entities associated with Mary. The simplest way to utilise Maríukross is to draw the stave out with powdered herbs, ideally dried and crushed birki laufar (birch leaves), bláber (blueberries), maríustakkur (ladies' mantle), and maríuvöndur (field gentian). I recommend gathering all these herbs together on a Monday or Friday, and, while powdering them, repeat the *Ave Maria* in whichever language you prefer over the herbs. Work the power into the shape of the stave to aid in all spells relating to the things that Mary and Freyja preside over.

As we now know, María is known as *álfadrottning*, a name shared with Freyja and sometimes Frigg. As the mother figure, Mary is kind, caring, and healing; she nurtures and protects her children. Folklore tells us that many elves also converted to Christianity in Iceland, and with this strong connection and importance of Mary remaining after the reformation, she holds a firm and earned a place within our magical practices. Some who may think she is too much of a Christian figure to work with should remember that her role at even the most archetypal level has always been that of a caring mother.

Mary, in Iceland, is not holier than thou; she doesn't care for one's creed nor which other gods one might pray to. She is open to all. Those who are weary of Christianity yet who practice witchcraft, especially using aspects of folklore that would simply not exist if Christianity hadn't solidified them in the public's consciousness, need to remember that without the questionable beliefs of Christian priests, Iceland would likely not have the rich history and tradition of Solomonic seal-inspired stave work. Almost all staves, especially more complicated ones, exist because of the heretical work of Icelandic priests and those common folk whose traditions assimilated Jesus and Mary with the Norse gods.

There is, at least within our practices, a dual aspect of Mary that aligns further with Freyja's personality. We occasionally call upon Mary and Freyja for vengeance. This is not normal curse work; we specifically call upon Mary the Mother to protect us and her children with force if necessary. This is usually done through prayer alone, as we aren't working curses, just asking that Mary take on the role of fierce protector. What she will do for us is up to her, but we pray to her for aid and ask that she intercede however she sees fit to bring offending parties to justice. Specific prayers are made for this based on our situation, usually describing what is going on and asking for her intercession. We usually surround these prayers with praying the rosary in Icelandic. An example I have found helpful in the past follows. (The Icelandic *Ave Maria, Pater Noster,* and other prayers can be found in the appendices.)

One mountain above Grunnavík in the Westfjords is known as *Maríuhorn.* This mountain may well have been the site of sacrifices to María in the old days. We know that many people travelled there to make sacrifices and that the power of María was held in high enough regard for people to visit this isolated and difficult-to-reach part of the island. Many believed that María had the power to influence the weather, and she was prayed to for aid in this way. This is why working her staves as a focal point for prayer can have so many different uses.

MARÍA MÓÐIR MÍN: MOTHER MARY PRAYER

"María, móðir mín,
Kirkja, systir mín,
Engill, bróðir minn,
Lát mig hvorki á vegum villast
Né á sjó látast
Né á vatni týnast
Né á eldi brenna,
Og einskis manns öfund
Á mér hrína.
Allt hið góða sé yfir mér
og með mér
Að eilífu."

"Mary, my mother,
Church, my sister,
Angel, my brother,
Do not let me go astray
Not at sea
Nor on water get lost
Nor in fire burn,
And nobody's envy
To myself bring.
All the good be upon me
and with me
Forever."

DÝRLINGAR OG HEILAGIR MENN: SAINTS AND HOLY MEN

Iceland's only official saint has been recognised unofficially since 1198, when he was canonized by the Icelandic parliament. Saint Þorlákur has since had a following among Christians in Iceland and, until recently, hasn't been worked with in folk Christian traditions as far as we know. However, we do call upon him on occasion, mainly for his patronage over Iceland and fishermen. He is the patron saint of the Catholic Christ's Church in Reykjavík, as well as more recently being recognised as a patron saint of autism. Along with the use of some staves, we call upon him to aid and protect fishermen while out at sea. We ask him to bless protective talismans to be worn within Iceland, as well as to bless other charms for fishermen. White lilies were and are the symbol for the diocese of Skálholt, so this flower may be given as an offering on small altars featuring the saint.

Another tale of a Saint from Iceland tells of Heilagur Ólafur or Saint Olaf. Once, he and all his men were sleeping and resting on their journey. The enemy surrounded them while they slept, but a small flea bit the Saint so hard that he woke up. It was because of this that the Saint saw the attackers and alerted his men. For the flea's help, the Saint blessed them with the ability to jump. It is said that while fishing in Iceland, a boy prayed to Heilagur Pétur (Saint Peter) for a good catch. Soon after, the boy caught a fish with a coin purse in its stomach that made him well off in life then after. Another Icelandic tale recounts how woodlice were once the worst fish in the ocean until Saint Peter cursed them, that they become small and docile. Since then, these isopods have been nothing but harmless.

Jón Lærði, or John the Learned, was a self-educated scholar, writer, poet, and craftsman. He was born in Ófeigsfjörður in Strandir in 1574. He was also called Jón Tannsmíður because he carved whale teeth. Later in life, he gained the name *Lærði* due to his intelligence and skill. He was also what we would consider a wizard or cunning man. In 1611, he was said to have quelled two dangerous ghosts in Snæfellsnes using his own galdur in the form of poems; two of these poems are still preserved. He was much loved by holy and common men alike, and when on trial for witchcraft and shipped to Copenhagen, he was able to appeal against it. He was finally sentenced in Iceland and, with the help of Bishop Brynjólf Sveinsson of Skálholt, was able to live the rest of his life in peace in the East of Iceland. His work, especially the two exorcism poems and his work as an herbalist and early unofficial doctor, makes him an essential piece of Iceland's magical history.

Sæmundur Fróði is one of Iceland's most famous sorcerers. In Árnason's telling from *Þjóðsögur og Ævintýri*, Sæmundur is said to have studied at a secret black school, where students were taught by occult writings on the wall, and the school's warden was kölski, the devil himself. The rules of the school dictated that the class who graduated were to leave one by one, with the last one being snatched up by the devil and damned to hell. Sæmundur was far too clever to be caught by such a rule, so he waited until he was at the door, about to leave, the sunlight streaming in and casting his shadow on the wall behind him. The devil came to him and was about to grab him when he turned and said, "I'm not the last; look, there is one still behind me."

The devil turned towards the shadow, and, in that moment, Sæmundur leapt through the door to safety. From then on, he was without a shadow, as the devil had claimed it from him. Sometime after this, Sæmundur was to return to Iceland, and, without a ship and in need of a swift return, he called upon the devil to make a deal: "Return me across the sea without getting my cloak wet, and you shall have my soul." The devil turned into a seal and swam Sæmundur across the sea. When they had nearly reached land, Sæmundur struck the seal on its head and swam the rest of the way, getting his cloak soaking wet. Again, he had tricked the devil and safely got out of a bad deal. Sæmundur became a well-known, feared, and respected priest in Iceland and was arguably the most well-known wizard priest in the country's history. Sæmundur died in 1133 and is buried at Oddakirkja in Rangárvellir, South Iceland. His grave was, for a time, used as a site for the sick to come and ask for healing.

Another notable wizard priest was Eiríkur í Vogsósum. His stories are many, including how he owned and wrote many books of magic, as well as when he summoned all the dead in one cemetery just to find one page of the grimoire *Gráskinna* that was buried there. He was also said to have duelled with Stokkeyri-Dísa, who was a worthy equal to his own power. As a dead magician, we can call upon Eiríkur to help teach us necromancy, as well as many other things, though be warned—he has as little patience for nonsense in death as he did in life.

Believed by some to be an elven changeling, Þorleifur Þórðarson was intelligent from a young age. He was a great poet and was soon considered a true skáld. He soon gained the name *Galdra-Leifi* because he was believed to be magical. He once banished a troll woman from nearby a farm, a great feat. He had many friends and was treated as royalty wherever he went.

Another wizard priest of note is Einar, *prestur og galdrmeistari*. He was a priest and master wizard. It is also said that he once saved the head of a drowned man to work divination, feeding and watering it with holy bread and wine and speaking to it when he needed answers. We can see this sort of work being done with skulls in many magical traditions, such as the skull acting as the vessel through which we can communicate with the spirit inhabiting it. Likewise, feeding such a fetish with blessed communion wine and bread would make for a powerful tool.

SYNDARAR: SINNERS

Galdra-Loftur, as mentioned earlier, was foolish enough to call upon the ghost of Grimmi, the bishop of Hólar and author of the infernal galdrabók *Rauðskinna*. But before this and his mysterious demise, he was known as one of the biggest pranksters in his school, often convincing other priests in training to play tricks on each other. He was said to have used gandreið on one of his parent's serving girls. One of his magical tricks trapped a kitchen girl in the wall, where her skeleton was later found. He is said to have read *Gráskinna* front to back, even when finding the whole text was no mean feat. The longer he spent studying at Hólar, the more his plans grew until the time came when he decided to call up the ghost of Grimmi and learn the location of *Rauðskinna*. He enlisted the help of an unfortunate classmate whom Loftur threatened to kill if he refused to help. The two of them set about raising Grimmi's spirit, and as we know, this ended in Loftur losing his mind and rowing himself into the ocean.

Grimmi, the bishop of Hólar Gottskálk Nikulasson, while being an ordained bishop, is counted within the category of sinners for two main reasons. Firstly, his name, *Grimmi*, which means "the cruel," gives us a hint about his character. Secondly, as we just learned, this supposedly holy bishop is credited with creating the darkest book of "black magic" that Iceland has ever known. Said to have been a pious man, Grimmi was often unnecessarily hard on members of the church and public alike. As he was a Catholic priest, we can see how his infamy post-Reformation would likely have been demonised and his infernal proclivities overexaggerated. Though, I personally think whether this is true or not doesn't matter. He has been interacted with in spirit with the utmost fear and respect. His sorcery is as powerful in death as it was in life, and we can't be sure whether this has been emphasised by hundreds of years of infamy or new knowledge beyond death. He is not a spirit to invoke. Remember the tale of Galdra-Loftur as a clear warning. Many have sought the location of *Rauðskinna* since his death, and none have succeeded in finding it.

Páll Galdramaður, a magician, lived in a small cottage in Húnavatnsýslu. It was said that he killed his wife with witchcraft by carving helrúnir into some cheese and covering it with butter. His wife ate the cheese and soon after was found dead. The townsfolk nearby discovered what had happened, and Páll was condemned to be burned. The day came, and once Páll had been burned, it was seen that his body was burned to ash, but his heart was still in perfect condition. The heart was pierced, and black insects flew from it.

GALDRABÓK
GRIMOIRE

19

GRIMOIRE

Many manuscripts contain staves and workings that have been touched upon by previous works on Icelandic magic. Sadly, some haven't been particularly accurate in their translation, losing the nuance that being able to understand them in their original language brings. The historical context around many of these translations has also been lost. Some are literal translations, which can give us some clues, of course, but without some understanding of the mindset of the recorders or, indeed, the creators of these staves, we lose a little of the understanding. Some symbols did, of course, exist in pre-Christian Iceland and in Nordic and Scandinavian traditions (rune alphabets and cruciform symbols of protection, for example).

However, many Icelandic magical staves, originating likely post-1500s, are heavily influenced by the Christian priests who penned them. You could argue that we see echoes of Agrippa's occult philosophy and the Christian understanding of natural magic in the minds of these post-medieval Icelandic priests and scholars. Many staves take clear inspiration from Solomonic and other grimoire traditions of high magic. Their forms and inclusion of planetary symbols show us a clear awareness of the importance of astrology and the heavenly hierarchy within Christian mysticism. Cipher alphabets, as well as those based on runes or otherwise coded symbols, are also present throughout many manuscript sources. We could take this to further argue that the priests recording or creating these staves and alphabets may well have been more than simply interested in this magic. The legends of Galdra-Loftur and other such infamous priests show us that Christian priests in Iceland clearly weren't as strict in their devotion to God as they should have been. The mindset of medieval Iceland was a dark and dangerous place. Restless dead, trolls, elves, and more haunted the countryside. Disappearances and otherwise mysterious happenings were still regarded as supernatural. Although the educated few paid less mind to this, the general population, to this day, holds some belief in elves and the huldufólk.

Staves are influenced by the time and place they were created or recorded. If we don't look at the world with at least a somewhat similar understanding of magic, including animism and natural magic, we lose part of their magic to lifeless instructions. Living animistic Icelandic tradition may well serve as the bridge to the full potential of many of these staves and workings. Of course, personal understanding and gnosis can lead to great discoveries in any tradition or path, and, as such, within our group and the wider magical community of Iceland, I have sought consensus and experimentation regarding the contemporary workings included within. The staves I list as my own come from personal gnosis, of course, but I have only included those that have been tried and tested by others both within and outside the island. Likewise, in cases where the inspiration or first steps of experimentation of a working wouldn't have made its way to my and our collective practices, I have mentioned the one, or thing, at its source.

CREATING MAGICAL STAVES

The methods of creating magical staves in our traditions are knowledge that many seek. Stave-craft is an art; as many who work with bindrunes and other such Nordic-inspired symbols will tell you, this can be hard work. Those with experience in sigil crafting and a level of self-knowledge that allows for complete honesty and deep intuition will have less of an issue creating unique and individual staves. Just as many are talented in one or two forms of art or divination, you will also find those who take to stave making naturally and those who do not. For those who do not, don't be discouraged.

Practice can indeed make perfect if you want something bad enough. Icelandic magical staves are much more than lines drawn on paper or etched into wood. For those who wish to explore the art of making staves, I will give two methods, both of which I have permission to share. The first is one that those who have any previous experience in sigil-making will recognise. Austin Osman Spare and his work on chaos magic and sigils in *The Zoetic Grimoire of Zos* serves as the inspiration. It is a contemporary method, practical, and easy enough to get the hang of. Instead of using the letters of the Roman alphabet, we utilise a mix of the elder futhark and various magical alphabets from Icelandic galdrabækur.

The first example follows Spare's method. We begin with a concept or goal we wish to move towards. Distil this concept or goal into a sentence as simple or complex as one wishes. I tend to make a note of how many times each letter pops up in the sentence and use the most common letter(s) as the main letter(s) while making the stave. For example, if "L" is the most common letter, I will use the character I choose from one of these alphabets representing "L" as the centre of the stave or the most prominent symbol found within it. If I have, for example, three "L"s, three "D"s, and three "E"s in my sentence, I will use a character for each of these letters in my stave, choosing to ignore the less common letters which only occur once or twice. The letters I mostly utilise have been wonderfully catalogued in *Lbs 3902 4to*. The manuscript *AM 247 8vo* also contains many alphabets one can use to create staves. Here is a selection of a few letters from the alphabets from *Lbs 3902 4to*.

A		N	
B		O	
C		P	
D		Q	
E		R	
F		S	
G		T	
H		U	
I		Y	
K		Z	
L		Þ	
M			

We can work with these letters to create staves in much the same way as Spare's method, even breaking the symbols down and rearranging them. If we feel the stave works—and soon after testing it out to make sure—we can use these characters as we see fit.

To render my enemy powerless

TRNDRMYNMYPWRLSS   OEEEEOEE

Vertical: Horizontal:

T R N D M Y P W L S   O E

T- R- W-   E-

N- D- P-   O-

M- Y-

S- L-

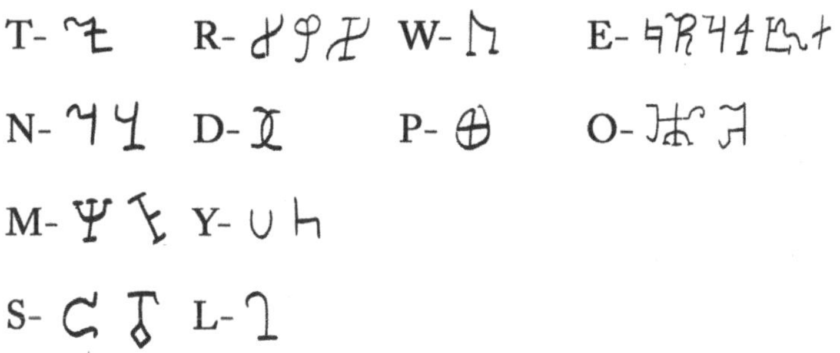

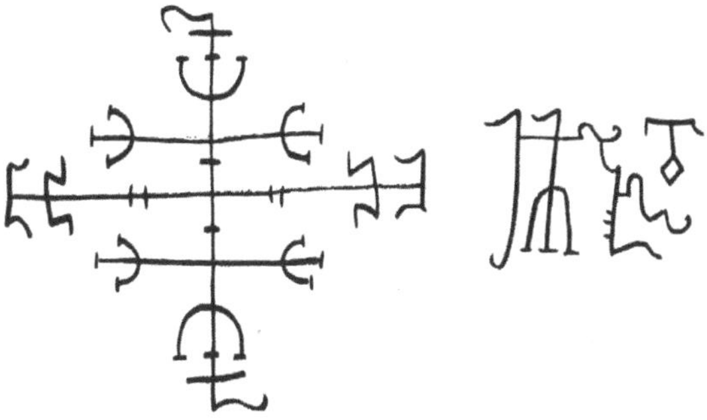

The second method is a lot more individual and works by asking spirits to give you a stave to help communicate with them or for some goal in relation to them. For example, this works well when asking plant spirits to give us symbols specific to communicating with them. The seals and staves I give in the herbarium (Chapter Sixteen) were gathered in this way. Sometimes, these staves appear to us as fully formed. The better we are at communicating with these spirits, the easier this will be. For example, if we want to deepen our relationship with the spirit of the field down the lane, we can go to this space, regularly communicate with the spirit, leave it offerings, and build a relationship with it. Then, ask it for a stave or symbol it wishes us to use to aid in communication with it. Knowledge and experience with the method of divination (ideally speculative divination) would help us well with this. Those forms ask us to interpret a much broader spectrum of things, such as mental images that appear to us.

Other methods of yes-no divination, such as flipping a coin or the Icelandic method of working with sheep knuckle bones, can help us get a quicker sense of whether or not we are on the right track. In a way, we could look at this as making galdur from seiður: grasping some mystery, revealed to us by spirit(s), and funnelled into a quantifiable symbol. Once that meaning is applied, it is, from then on, a static representation of that gnosis and work. This method takes time and practice, as well as a little prior experience with spirit communication. Remember that establishing relationships with places and spirits can be key for this method to work well for us.

VARIATIONS OF EXISTING STAVES

Opinions differ on the correct way to reproduce staves from the past. I believe that staves can be tweaked somewhat (not always in shape and design, and sometimes only in method). We know that magic doesn't end outside of Iceland, and working staves with alternative methods and non-Icelandic materia has yielded good results for many. We could also argue that the older the stave, the more it is "engraved into the universe," as in, the longer it has held the same purpose and function. Therefore, even with a slight variation in small lines here or there, it will not lose the power it possesses. Furthermore, we believe that the number of slight variants it has, all being worked for the same purpose, reinforces the stave itself. We can possibly reinforce this idea when thinking of the way that grimoire magicians can choose several varying names and, thus, varying aspects of demons and angels. The demon may well be the same, or it may be an aspect of that spirit that still gets the job done.

One solid example is working with ægishjálmur, a stave that already has many variants. Does our work have less of an impact depending on which stave we choose? Not at all. The impact will stay with us and what we have channelled into the work. For me, this is a good enough reason to experiment with our own variants. Though, as always, the warning of Egill remains the same: one shouldn't mess about too much with poorly made staves. For this reason, I would say that, unless you feel entirely compelled, you should create your own staves rather than trying to tweak others without a good amount of experience in the subject. Later, I'll share plenty of examples of staves and workings I've created myself, some based on other staves. We can tie our own traditions into our stave work, blending our local folk magic with Icelandic staves. You can find examples of this throughout the galdrabók later.

20
Stafir Fyrir Bændur og Sjómenn: Staves for Farmers and Fishermen

Fishing has always been a part of Icelandic culture. The seemingly barren nation supports itself on fish and sheep, so naturally, fishermen have been working charms and spells since the settling of the country. Fishermen's spells mostly concern themselves with either increasing the size of a catch or protecting the fishermen from bad weather (and, occasionally, sea monsters).

The following staves are worked to increase the likelihood of a good catch. They can be worked several ways, but I recommend carving them into birch or willow bark. Water-ruled plants like birch and willow don't offend the sea in the way that juniper and rowan do, but using fish leather or whalebone would be even better. If worked with whalebone or fish leather, the charm should be carved (for bone) or inked (for leather), then suitably blessed before it is worn about the neck or carried in the back pocket when at sea.

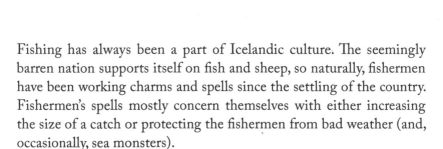

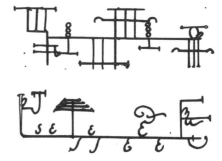

For whalebone or the bones of some other sea creature, carve the stave, then redden it with a drop of your blood before dipping it into the ocean three times. With each dip, speak over it, either asking the charm to do its job, signing the cross, or reciting the *Pater Noster* over it.

For fish leather, add a drop of your blood to some ink. Then, using this mixture, draw out one or more of these staves on the skin. Bless the charm with some words of your own, a sign of the cross, or three *Pater Nosters*.

VATNAHLÍFIR

This stave comes from the collection *Lbs 3902 4to,* found in older manuscripts. Originally, the instructions suggested the stave was to be "bare under one's right hand" and that this would protect from drowning. I suppose, more specifically, it would protect from drowning in a glacial flash flood, though opinions differ on this. Either way, to work this stave, draw it out on parchment and redden it. Work it into a charm bag with protective materia, or tattoo it under your right hand if you wish to be literal with the instructions.

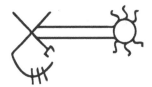

The *Huld* manuscript states that this stave is also finally empowered once the following words have been spoken:

"Guð gefi mér til lukku og blessunar í Jesus nafni, Amen."

These protective charms could also be accompanied by this galdur from *ATA Ämb 2 F16:26.* Work these words into your protective charms for those at sea or those sailing or flying over water:

"Helon Heloui Saa bonai lux tetram Cramatus."

FISH HEADS AND BONES

Fish heads and bones may be worked into protective charms to protect fishermen and return them safely to shore. In Iceland, this work is still important within contemporary magic, as fishermen still venture offshore for long periods of time to fish, just as they have done since Iceland's settling. Work protective staves alongside fish remains one finds along the seashore. Fish heads pointed in the direction of a victim are sometimes used as níðstöng, though one could create a stave for favourable wind and work it with a fish head, pointing it in the direction one wishes to send the favourable wind.

SO YOUR LAMBS HAVE TWINS

This stave is worked so that a farmer's sheep may birth two lambs. It is called *stafur til að fá tvílembt* (literally "stave to obtain twin lambs"). It comes from the collection *Lbs 3902 4to* and is to be created and hung in the barn. As this concerns livestock, I suggest a Jovial time and day for creating this stave. As we know, fé (cattle) were currency in the Viking age, and given that Jupiter is also the lord of increase, we would do well to work spells of increase in his times.

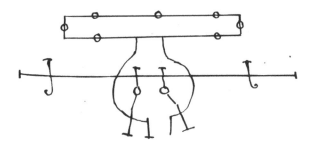

I suggest taking wool from the two sheep you wish to mate and binding it around a stick of wood with this stave carved into it. Redden the stave with your blood and hang it in the barn above the two sheep.

VINDHNÍFUR

This working is my own UPG, developed over a few years and based on a few specific staves, as well as some Dutch folk magic involving knives used to cut the wind. One must find a new, unused knife (ideally of iron, but steel will suffice). On the handle of this knife, one must inscribe the following stave. You must then wrap the knife in clean white linen. Take it to the highest point in your local area. If the very peak is impractical to reach, then somewhere high will do. Present the spirits of this place with an offering specific to them if local folklore dictates. If not, I recommend burning a large number of herbs and incense while singing their praises.

Ask that they bless the knife so that when it strikes the ground, the spirits from the sky down to the sea will listen and calm the wind in that area. Ask this in your own words and await a response. Once you are sure the request has been granted, take the knife to the sea or the lowest point in your area. Repeat the offering to the sea spirits and ask that they bless the knife so that when it strikes the ground, the spirits of the sea up to the sky will listen and calm the wind in that area. Once you have received the blessing from both of these spirits, test the knife out when the next storm or high wind rolls around. Remember to give offerings to the spirits every so often to help keep this knife working.

WIND STAVES

Fishermen don't just need protection. Having favourable winds was much more important in the past, but even with modern motors, many boats need the aid of the wind. Also, not just fishermen benefit from the wind; the wind may be necessary to blow certain weather away or call it in.

This stave from *Lbs 3902 4to* to call favourable winds could be worked into charms and talismans given to fishermen and sailors, engraved on blessed medals, or worked into woods and Mercurial materia for the best effect. Working them into the remains of sea birds may also prove useful.

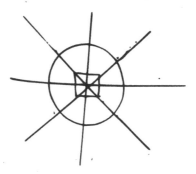

The next stave is worked to bring "norðan veður" (weather from the North, or cold winds and gales). Inscribe the stave on clear parchment, then take it out of the home and walk it north. I suggest working it into wood and animal remains to see how the effect may differ.

Staves also exist to protect fishermen from ill winds. The following stave is from the collection *Lbs 3902 4to* and works to protect from ill wind and bad wind spirits. This complicated stave could be carved or burned into a larger talisman and carried on ships to protect from bad weather and the tempers of sea spirits. Rowan would be a good wood to work with, though any protective wood should work well. Redden it as usual, although praying over it may also be appropriate before use.

Likewise, farmers can utilise wind magic to help save crops, livestock, and more. Other farm-related magic within Icelandic folklore includes *"Að spekja sauði eður bæla,"* the verbal spell to control unruly sheep. You should recite this three times as you drive the sheep out of their pen:

"Ber vængi kitta ditta,
Dynjandi nostra delicta.
Guð heilagi andi,
Gættu að hjörð minni.
Gefðu mér hana spaka,
Sendu mér hana heim.
Ég gef hana á þitt vald.
In nomine patris, et filii, et spiritus sancti, amen."

PROTECTION ON LAND AND SEA

This stave is for protection on land and sea—useful for fishermen and farmers alike. It may be inscribed on rowan wood or the wood of any protective local tree. I recommend working one of the prayers of protection over it, such as the *Pater Noster* or even one of your own design. It should then be always worn as a protective talisman. Should one feel the need to rejuvenate its power, simply redden it as you did upon creating it.

ÆGISHJÁLMUR: THE HELM OF AWE

Likely most recognisable as a "Viking" tattoo, this symbol is somewhat ambiguous. It wasn't likely to have ever been tattooed. It may be that the poems and galdur surrounding it came first. It might be that the symbol itself was invented to represent the helm of the same name mentioned in the sagas. The symbol itself is likely one of the older and more simple stave forms, probably favoured as a "base" stave by the priests who liked the symmetry of Solomonic seals. The cross formation appears again and again in staves of repulsion and protection, which makes it rather simple, much like the solar cross, and later, the biblical cross has been used as amulets of protection for an unknowable number of years.

We find many variants of the stave within manuscripts. I argue that they can all be used to work towards victory and inspire some aspect of fear within one's foes. These two focuses invoke for us two of Óðinn's names and forms: Sigtyr, god of victory, and Ygg the terrible. I have had success working the staves alongside these names and forms of Óðinn and have noticed that the symbols sometimes have the effect of banishing unclean spirits from spaces. However, as that isn't something "officially" attached to their lore—that remains my own UPG. This form is the most common and can be born on talismans and charms for either effect. I believe that its wide use and the fact that it is well-known give it a certain level of power.

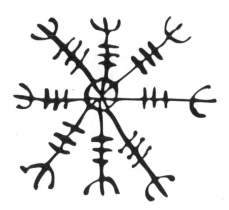

The second version is a larger symmetrical form. I suggest that this may be used as a talisman for success as well as obstacle removal, especially the removal of those who oppose one's path to success. It should be engraved into metal discs, burned or carved into wood, and reddened before use.

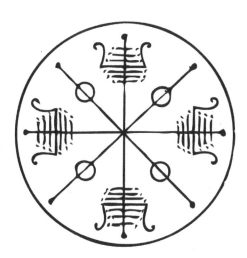

The last of the few ægishjálmur I will mention is this collection of nine variants of the symbol. Interestingly, we can work these nine variants with yarrow oil for protection. This is where we move a little more into the realm of banishment and repulsion. Create a yarrow oil infusion, then, using your læknisfingur (the ring finger of your right hand), draw out these symbols on oneself, the walls of a space, or objects to expel and repel unclean spirits. Tie this in with the *Pater Noster* on page 302 or one of the banishing chants found later on page 244.

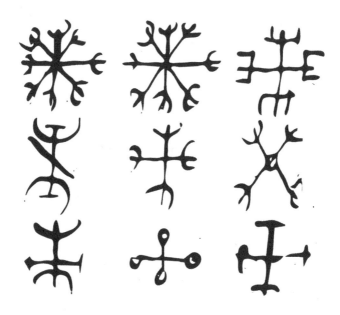

21

LUKKUSTAFIR,
HEILLASTAFIR:
LUCK STAVES

In Icelandic folk practice, good luck, or good hamingju, accumulates over time. Good actions and coming from a good family can affect this. We can look at staves for safe travel and good fortune as one goes about their business as luck magic. Some luck magic is intended for gambling and games, whereas other luck magic intends to give one general good fortune. Staves such as the luck ring found below fall into the former category, with other staves, such as Ólaf Tryggvason's róðukross, falling into the latter. These later staves keep us in good örlög (fate) and may subtly influence and maintain our hamingju over time. Living a life in a balance of good örlög shines clearly on those around us who skip past and brush over general misfortune: those who seemingly never fall into great ills, financial trouble, or woes. They are our friends and acquaintances who survive all forms of near misses. The later staves are said to maintain the flow of good örlög around us, saving us from scrapes with adversity.

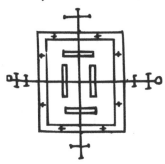

The above stave, known as the "luck ring," was intended to be carved or etched into a gold ring, most likely done in a Solar hour on the Sunnudagur (Sunday). The ring would then be worn to bring luck to any who wore it. This magic reflects much of the talismanic magic of grimoires like the *Black Pullet* and *Le Petit Albert,* with enchanted jewellery, relying on astrological timings and, occasionally, angelic influence. Once crafted, this gold ring can be further blessed with the use of an incense of Jovial and Solar herbs. In Iceland, the herbs we would use are túnfífill (*Taraxacum officinale*), einir (*Juniperus communis*), and lúpína (*Lupinus nootkatensis*), but any combo of Jovial and Solar herbs you wish to use would work. If you want to go all out with planetary virtues, I recommend working with Agrippa's planetary numbers and suffumigating the ring with a mixture of four Jovial herbs and six Solar herbs. You could also utilise a Solar planetary incense from one of the many old grimoires.

SOLAR STAVES

For extra Solar virtues, I recommend that this entire process take place on a board or table inscribed with one of these two Solar innsigli from *Lbs 5472 4to* mentioned back on page 18.

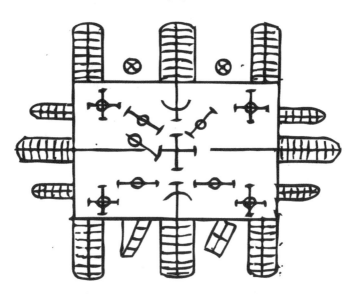

The board itself should be inscribed in the hour of the Sun on Sunnudagur. Anoint with a Solar oil, then suffumigate it with a Solar incense. If you can make this board from rowan wood, I recommend this. Otherwise, a simple pine board works well.

Another stave used to provide blessings of good luck and safety is the Varnarkross from *Lbs 5472*. This stave is drawn on fresh parchment and carried. I recommend folding the paper three times, then crossing it three times, and finally reading three *Pater Nosters* over it. If you have access to holy water (or really any blessed waters), I recommend sprinkling a little on this charm, then on yourself, before going on with your day.

The next stave, known as the *heillahringur,* is another recorded in *Lbs 5472.* This ring brings good fortune. It may be worked well as a tattoo or engraved into jewellery. It can also be used the same way as the previous stave. To bless it, I recommend using the same techniques as the previous stave.

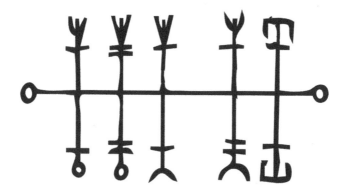

Róðukrossar pop up in many manuscripts. Personally, I maintain that these fall into the category of luck magic, subtly influencing one's fate and keeping one in good örlög.

This stave is said to:

> *"Varnar gegn illum öndum, forðar manni*
> *frá villu og er til heilla á sjó og landi."*

Translated, this means:

> "To protect against ill spirits, misfortunes,
> and bad luck, on land and while at sea."

It should be carried by your chest, within your clothes. This can either be sewn into clothes with a protective, ideally blessed, red thread, or can be inked onto some dried skin then carried at your breast. Redden the staves as with all staves and, just to be safe, pray the Lord's Prayer over this charm.

Another stave to keep one in good örlög and hamingju is Varnastafur Valdimars. This stave is found in the collection *Lbs 3902 4to* and is said to come from Germany and is supposedly ancient in origin. It is said to grant good favour and hamingju, and as such, is included in this category. There is some debate that as this stave is not the typical cruciform design of many others with similar virtues, it may well be of an older and more Pagan origin, though we cannot be sure.

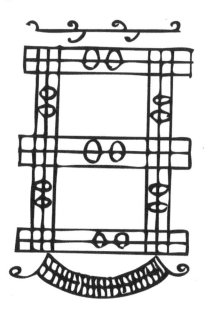

This piece of galdur is designed *"Að fá góðar heimtur,"* or to get good returns of luck and hamingju, for example. You should recite this every so often so that you don't walk into trouble or ill luck:

"Út rek ég fé mitt
Undir guðs garða,
Sting ég fyrir það stinnum
Verði og varðveizlu.
Des heitir,
En dýra móðir,
Sem svo
Sjáandi geymir,
Svo hvorki björn bíti
Eða bein slíti,
Lumsa sé úlfur
Og allar úlfsemjar
In nomine partris, et filii, et spiritus sancti, amen."

216

MERKURIUS OR MERKÚR INNSIGLI

This stave is my own UPG, working off the two Solar seals shown earlier. This stave can be worked to empower Mercurial workings, herbs, candles, and more. I recommend creating it on a piece of wood within a Mercurial day and hour and oiling the wood with a Mercurial oil. Create the stave and redden it with blood, then use this tool for all specific Mercury-related work. On the underside of the wood, you can even engrave these symbols of Mercury from Agrippa.

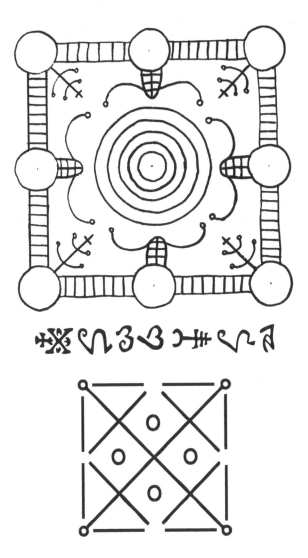

JÚPITER INNSIGLI

As we worked the Solar innsigli earlier, we can also work the Júpiter innsigli for enchanting and empowering work and materia with Jovial virtues of luck. Some combination of this with Solar materia makes for the best luck work. So, try further empowering your luck and increase your workings with this innsigli of Júpiter. Of course, use the day and hour of Jupiter for this.

SIGURMERKI

We find two examples of staves called *Sigurmerki* in different manuscripts. These staves are worked to bring victory in what you do. I suggest working them into talismans, crafted within a combination of Jovial or Solar timings and anointed with a suitable oil of plants that bring on these virtues of success and victory. Working these two staves into either side of an amulet for victory in all you do would be the best way to utilise them. The two staves follow on the next page.

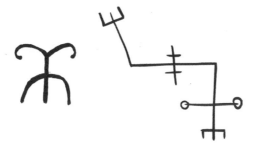

This stave below also works to these ends; found in the collection *Lbs 5472* and titled "for victory over problems," it can be worked into a suitable amulet to be carried. Empower it the same way as the previous amulet. Working Júpiters innsigli as the station on which they are empowered is also advised from my own personal experiences.

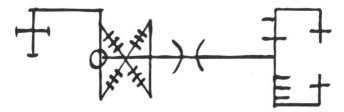

22

Varnagaldur: Apotropaic Magic

The overwhelming majority of galdrastafir are worked for protection of all kinds. Whether this is protection at sea, against enemies, ill-will, dangerous spirits and sendings, or even against simple misfortune, there is a protective stave for almost all situations. Add in contemporary stave work, and we can find one for just about anything one can think of. With its Christian influence, Icelandic magic contains many works that involve the invocation of Jesus, God, or both, as well as those that invoke Christian figures along with those of the pantheon. Invoking Jesus with the use of clearly Christian staves is just as potent as the work of invoking Óðinn or Freyja for protective magic. Here is an example of the simplicity of some protective staves. Clearly, this stave invokes Jesus, directly appealing for the aid of Christ to protect one from dark magic. The following stave is simple and can be carved into an amulet or talisman, thrice prayed over, and crossed before use. It can also be carved into rowan wood, prayed over, and crossed before being hung within the home to protect the space.

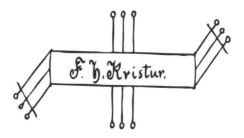

The next stave is worked to call upon Jesus for protection. As with the previous stave, it should be thrice prayed over and crossed and, ideally, sprinkled with some holy water or an infusion of Martial and Solar herbs. This stave can also be used to bless objects and materia. Draw it out on a large piece of paper in red ink. For a more permanent tool, inscribe it on a sheet of linen or burn or carve it into a wooden board.

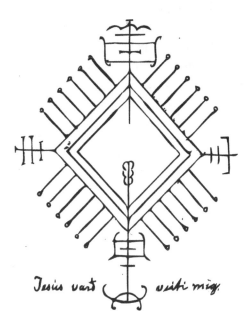

Jesús vard ( ) veiti mig.

To use this tool to enchant or bless objects and materia, I recommend creating it within a Martial hour on Sunnudagur (Sunday). Once the board has been carved or paper decorated with this stave, it should then be suffumigated with frankincense and copal while one prays the *Pater Noster* over it in whichever language you choose. Repeat the prayer six times, as six is a number of the Sun. Then, make six signs of the cross (the *Signum Crucis*) over it. Anoint this tool with some Solar oil, holy water, or otherwise blessed water (all the better if blessed by a priest). Methods for blessed water and chalk can be found later in this chapter.

Moses and Aaron are two biblical figures who pop up in Icelandic magic. There are three staves attributed to them (one to Moses and two to Aaron). All three are found in the collection in *Lbs 5472*, recorded from older sources, as are many within this collection. The Staff of Moses stave can be utilised to empower the stangur, staff, or any other rod or wand the practitioner works with. While this method doesn't pop up in any historical evidence we have found, the inclusion of this symbol on tools has been part of contemporary practice, at least. The use of both the Staff of Moses (Figure 1) and Aaron's vönder (Figure 2) on staffs and tools for direction magic makes perfect sense. Both empower and add protection by holy association alone. The inclusion of Aaron's Shield (Figure 3) on ritual clothing, as a tattoo, or even as a protective amulet of any material offers this same protection and safety from unclean entities by its biblical and, therefore, repellent power over unclean spirits. The "shield" is a clear reference to Aaron's breastplate of biblical fame.

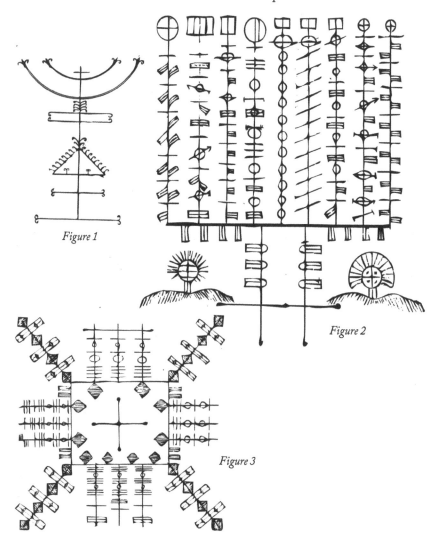

Figure 1

Figure 2

Figure 3

As with the previous staves, once the stave is carved or otherwise decorated on the tool or amulet of your choice, pray three or six times over the object, cross it thrice or six times, then anoint it with a Solar or holy water or oil.

As we've discussed, cursing and sending various entities and spirits to attack one's enemies is common in Icelandic folk magic. There are plenty of staves used to protect yourself from these attacks. This varnastafur, protective stave, is another contained within the *Lbs 5472* collection. The equal-armed form has a very shield-like design, though this doesn't always indicate a protective stave. This stave can be worked in a few ways. When tattooed on the body, it offers protection. However, it seems to do more when carved into reynir (*Sorbus aucuparia*) or einir (*Juniperus communis*), making it more of an active than a passive stave. I suggest working it in combination with protective plants from your local area and seeing how it feels.

The following stave comes from *Lbs 4627* and is another stave with a shield formation worked against ill magic. If you fear you are about to be—or have already become—the target of any negative magic sent your way, carve this stave into reynir. Redden it with a drop of your blood, and wear this talisman around your neck.

Many other staves are worked to protect from ill will and ill magic. The following staves can be worked the same as the stave above. Figure 4 and Figure 5 are both from the collection *Lbs 5472*.

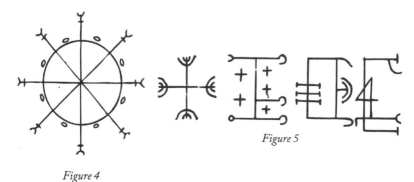

Figure 5

Figure 4

Sendingar, as discussed earlier, are spirits—sometimes those of long-dead humans—sent to terrify or harm others. These sendings can vary in strength, and folklore tells us they can even shapeshift, sometimes taking the form of insects. Most notably, one story tells of how a wizard was able to trap a sending that was sent to kill him. He managed to trick the sending into taking the form of a fly, which he then trapped in a glass. Another folk story tells of how a widow in Hvalfjörður was able to lure sendings sent against her neighbour and trap them in a pit she had dug on his property.

Two reasonably well-known staves are recorded to work against ill sendings. They were originally found in another manuscript but were recorded in the collection *Lbs 5472*. They can be worked independently or together, but I recommend working them in a few ways. They could be drawn on either side of the lid of a bottle—a working used to trap a sending. They could be inscribed or carved into a stone, which would then be used to cover a hole that sendings have been trapped within. They could be tattooed either separately or on each shoulder blade. In dire circumstances, they could be drawn out in saliva on the passive hand.

I recommend working them into the home, carved near the doorway or windowsill to add an extra line of defence. Those who wish to work them into jewellery-making should engrave them on either side of a flat silver or gold necklace and wear it about your neck at times when you feel you may be victim to malefic work. When carving them into wood or stone to carry as a charm, make the sign of the cross over them or hallow them with prayers to Óðinn, Jesus, Þór, or whomever you wish to ask for aid in protecting you from negative sendings.

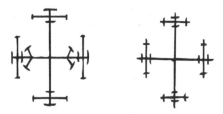

Another stave to protect against unclean spirits comes from Lbs 4375 4to, called *stafur á móti öllum anda*, a stave against ill spirits. We can work it in many of the same ways as the other staves in this section of the book. It can be put on fresh parchment and reddened, as well as placed into protective charm bags that we can carry on our person, created in a Solar or Martial timing.

NINE SEALS OF PROTECTION

The leechbook manuscript *AM 434a 12mo*, from around 1200, gives us nine useful seals of protection from various things. These are excellent practical talismans that are easy to make and use. Ben Waggoner gives excellent translations for these in his book *Norse Magic and Herbal Healing*, which are as follows:

La Va: Against the judgement of men

Io Ax: Against physical cruelty

A Gar: Against afflictions in this world

Io Hoth: Against the course of a fire

Ame Ne: Against madness and frenzy

Ag La: Against all evil terrors

Na On: Against the walking of ogres and trolls

In: Against kings' battles

Ia Him: Against a demon's blows

I recommend working the first talisman during a Solar hour. Considering it's above all else within the solar system, the Sun doesn't fear the judgement of men. The second would be best to work into Martial work, invoking this planetary energy against injustice. The third would also fall under Martial powers, this time within Mars' protective energies. The fourth could be worked in a Saturnine timing, as fire needs food for it to expand, and the limiting and binding powers of Saturn hinder this. The fifth can be worked in a combination of Lunar and Mercurial timings. Because the Moon inspires lunacy, so too may it calm the mind, and working in Mercurial powers of clearing channels make these two the ideal combination.

The sixth would fall under the powers of the Sun, dispelling creatures and entities considered unclean. The seventh may well work within the Venusian powers of persuasion and manipulation, the advisors in the king's ears being the ones making the real decisions. The eighth falls again under Solar or Martial work, either or both being ideal timings to work it under. And finally, the ninth, I suggest falls best under Solar timings and powers. Individually, these make powerful and practical amulets, and I highly recommend creating and carrying them.

PROTECTION OF THE CARDINAL DIRECTIONS

The next four staves were recorded by Jón Árnason in his magnum opus, *Þjóðsögur og Ævfintýri*. They are intended to work collectively and should be used all together on one charm or otherwise all tattooed. They protect one from each of the cardinal directions. They may also be used to work as the cardinal points of a magic circle, scratched into the earth where you set up your space, or even decorated on four rocks, each reddened and then set at the cardinal points.

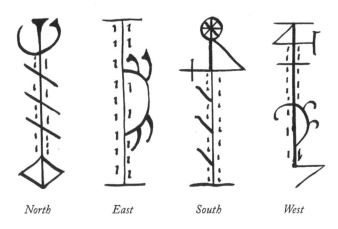

| North | East | South | West |

To the North, you should place the first stave, associated in Iceland with the element of Air and the landvættur Gammur, the great eagle who rules the skies.

To the South, you should place the second stave, associated in Iceland with the element of Earth and the landvættur Bergrisi, also called Járngrímur, the giant who watches over the land.

To the East, you should place the third stave, associated in Iceland with the element of Fire and the landvættur Dreki, the dragon who watches over the East.

To the West, you should place the last stave, associated in Iceland with the element of Water and the landvættur Griðungur, the giant bull who watches over the West.

TH< NIN< RING$ Of <HARL<MAGN<

The Nine Rings of Charlemagne, known as *Karla-Magnúsar hringur*, is another charm that crosses from general good örlög to being more apotropaic and active in its effect. This charm is quite extensive in its virtues, and I argue that the best effect is found with it after following a nine-day ritual for each of its nine rings. These nine rings are broken down into three sets of three.

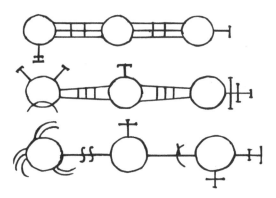

There are nine rings in total, and each is said to have a separate power and effect. Shown above are all nine rings, divided into groups of three as they are drawn. The first of these sections gives the following virtues:

- Protection from one's mind being troubled, the pranks of evil spirits, and attacks from one's enemies.
- Said to quell all fear within one's heart and protect one from sudden death.
- Said to cloud the minds of one's enemies with confusion to make them turn from you and second guess their plans to fight. The rings are filled with holy words and the name of God.

The rings of the second section give these virtues:

- Grants healing of wounds made by the sword.
- Aids in helping one to know their way forward and avoid being misled by weather, loss of direction, or falling prey to being misled by evil forces.
- Spares one from persecution by wrathful and evil men.

The third section grants these virtues:

- Grants one popularity among men and sees one win in all legal disputes.
- Combats and staves off all fear (similarly to the second ring from the first section).
- Spares one from falling into debauchery, ill habits, and vices of all kinds.

These qualities and virtues would make one very noble indeed. Whether the charm can grant all of them may need to be tested, though it works well to steer one in good örlög and hamingju, sparing one from many ills.

ÉG SIGNI MIG MEÐ FIMM SÁRUM JESÚ CHRISTI
I SIGN MYSELF WITH THE FIVE WOUNDS OF JESUS CHRIST

"Ég signi mig með fimm sárum Jesú Christí,
Míns endurlausnara,
Fyrir öllum minum óvinum,
Sýnilegum og ósynilegum,
Og öllu skaðlegu eðli
Heims og himins,
Lofts og lagar.
Í nafni f-ður og sonar og heilags anda.
Amen."

ÁGÆT BÆN MÓTI ILLUM ANDA OG GLETTINGUM
A PRAYER AGAINST EVIL AND MISFORTUNE

"Ég signi mig með sex sárum míns lausnara, Jesú Kristí,
móti öllum skaðlegum öndum og öllu voveiflegu eðli
Heims og himins,
Lofts og lagar,
Svo ill galdraskeyti
Ónýt verði."

BÆN MÓTI GALDRI:
A Prayer Against Witchcraft

"Gefi guð það ljúfur,
Galdur hrífi mig aldri,
Hús mín hæsti Jesús
Haldi og geymi frá galdri;
Sendi ég sannleiks anda
Sjöfaldan mót galdri.
Fjandinn og illsku undur
Aldrei hjá mér staldri."

Another brynjubæn (protective prayer) comes from Ólafur Davíðsson in volume two of *Íslenzkar Þjóðsögur*, calling on God to protect from evil and various troubles. However, as the wording says *drottinn minn* and is not capitalised, you could arguably tweak this to apply to Óðinn. It contains no Christian connotations, save the word *drottinn*, meaning "the lord."

"Ver þú mig, drottinn minn,
Fyrir voðavörgum,
Frá draugum og djöflum
Og frá öllum,
Illum hlutum,
Frá eitri og galdri,
Öfund og svikum,
Fyrir illum orðum
Og ógóðu tilliti auganna."

It asks for protection from many ills, including draugar, devils, bad magic, poison, ill words, and, lastly, the evil eye. It's very useful in a pinch.

Sewing things into clothes to offer protection is a common theme in folklore. The following two staves give protection if worn within clothing. They can be secretly sewn with red thread, in a Martial time, into the inside of the clothing of the one you wish to protect.

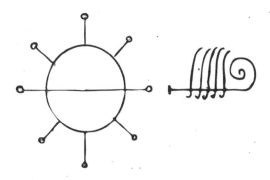

ROWAN FOR PROTECTION

Rowan is a highly protective wood, and the following staves can be carved in order to perform workings of protection.

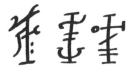

Rowan wood may be the base that the following stave can be carved into. It is called *Stafur móti óvin þínnum,* a stave against your enemies, and is worked into protective spells and charms when you are sure that there are actual enemies working against you. Carve it into rowan and redden it, then carry it on your person until you are sure the threat has been removed or dissipated.

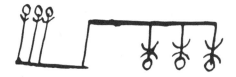

DIVINE PROTECTION

There are plenty of seals and staves associated with various biblical figures—some I discussed in greater detail earlier—but some are simply less complex and work for many of the same purposes. We have staves assigned to many biblical characters, all granting protection in their own right, though I suggest working with them as focal points for saint work if this is part of your practice. (We have had great success utilising staves of Mary this way.) The stave then becomes a tool to help us connect with that figure and ask for help with whatever their patronage may be.

SOLOMON'S SEAL

The power of the legendary King Solomon is known to many in occult circles. Whether this king ever existed is up for debate alongside many biblical figures, but his legacy is profound. Many readers may be familiar with the seals of Solomon and Goetic work pertaining to demons and spirits. We find mention of him even in the Far North, with staves being attributed to him, as well as many biblical figures. There are plenty of variants and other staves, also named sigils of Solomon. More specific work with this stave involving its associations with plants can be found in *Icelandic Plant Magic*.

This Solomon's seal stave comes from *JS 379 8vo*. It is to be carved into surturbrandur (lignite) and reddened with blood, then carried for protection. However, it may also be used in the same ways as many of Solomon's seals from other Icelandic grimoires and stave collections.

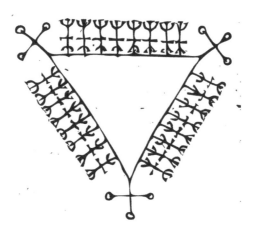

JOHN'S SEAL

Johannes innsigli, the seal of John, is included in *Lbs 3902 4to*. Like many of these biblical sigils, it can be worked against all sorts of óhreinn andi and other unclean spirits.

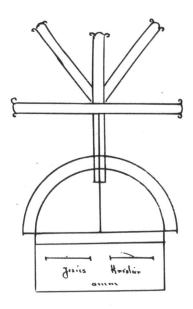

The following staves below can be worked in this manner as well. I recommend working them into protective talismans as well as charms pertaining to the patronage of the saint they are named for.

HOLY SPIRITS MARK   PAUL'S SEAL

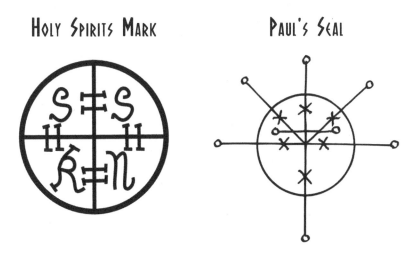

Mark's Seal

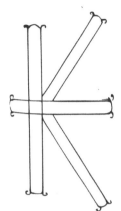

Daniel's Seal

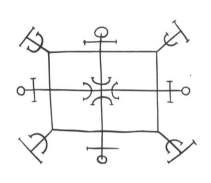

Saint Olaf's Seal

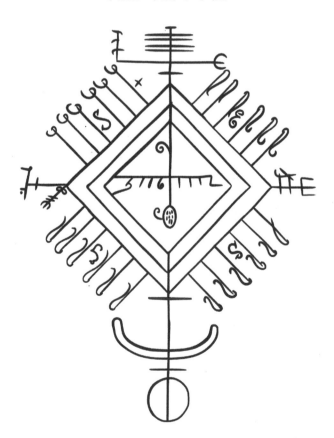

RAVEN PROTECTION CHARM

This charm, mentioned in Chapter Seventeen, is made from the remains of a raven's foot. Don't hunt ravens for these remains, as killing them can also serve as an omen of death for oneself. Work with acquired feet from roadkill or otherwise ethically acquired feet. Dry the foot in salt for at least two weeks. Once dry, remove it from the salt and dispose of the salt. Wrap the foot with red thread, including a few rowan berries in the charm if you want. Do this within a combination of Martial and Saturnine days and hours.

BLESSUÐ KRÍT OG VATN: BLESSED CHALK AND WATER

The use of blessed krít or kalksteinn chalks and water shows up in many paths around the world. With Catholic magic's influence on Iceland, we find the use of empowered chalks useful for our stave work. Drawing out staves with specially blessed and crafted chalks is a good way to make use of materia, as well as creating another practical tool to help us go about our work, especially in an urban and concrete landscape. Blessed water is also worked with in so many witchcraft traditions and world faiths. Working with blessed water for cleansing tools, space, and things can be a wonderful way to utilise lakes we hold sacred. In Iceland, at least, we can ask for the water we use to be gifted to us by the spirits of the lakes and ponds we work with, giving us an animistic method of working a tool that, in many faiths, has more to do with divine power than being grounded within our own land.

To bless chalk, I recommend working simple plaster of Paris with ground materia. When these materials are blessed with some power, whether that be from a church, well, sacred spot, or with the name of Óðinn, Týr, or another divine Pagan force, our chalk is turned into a potent tool of magic. Chalks worked to draw staves can utilise plenty of materia and are especially good when blessed by Óðinn. Potent herbs and plant materia, such as the ground leaves of hvönn (*Angelica archangelica*), ground bones from animal remains such as horses, the ground or pulverised feathers of birds, and the ashen remains of blót fires burned in the honour of the Norse gods are some—but definitely not all—of the excellent options to use with chalk. Chalk worked to draw protective staves does well when utilising the ash from fires of reynir and einir. This ash, blended with water and plaster of Paris, as well as protective ground rowan berries, makes for a powerful mix. When blessed in the names of Óðinn as protector, as well as Ása-Þór, we have a useful tool to add layers of protective virtues to our apotropaic magic.

When working with chalk to draw staves to get what we wish, as discussed in the next chapter, we could use herbs such as draumagras (*Equisetum arvense*). This herb is easily ground when dried and can be added to chalks for this, along with materia like blue lotus petals or other plants used for dream work outside of Iceland. Indeed, even the water used to blend with the plaster of Paris could be blessed or infused with plant materia. There are so many ways we can personalise this work and utilise those plants we feel called to work with.

Blessing water evokes a very Christian mental image, though we should do away with the idea that blessed water may only come from a church. Of course, we know this is not the case, as many faiths and paths utilise the world's most valuable resource in this way. Blessing water to use for cleaning and cleansing is one way we can work with it. We may ask spirits of the land, as well as deities and planetary forces, to bless water. Galdur and the vibrations of our magical words are, indeed, also enough to charge water for specific purposes. We may invoke spirits of the land, asking them to bless this water for us, wording our request as something like this, for example:

"Austri, Vestri, Suðri, Norðri, I call to the four corners of the world.
I ask the landvættur here in this space:
Vome forward and bless this water,
That I may work it to (protect/inspire),
That they may impart some of their power to it,
That it may become a vehicle for (protection/inspiration).
By the spirits of the land, the four corners of the world,
And my own spirits, guardians, and guides. May this be so."

This, of course, should be worded in the most appropriate way for where you are and which spirits you're invoking. This can be done alongside a suitable offering. Nothing is free, after all, and we shouldn't treat spirits and their help as charity. Asking specific ponds and lakes for their water also requires specific wording from us. Blessing some water for specific purposes by the names of Óðinn and Ása-Þór gives us a potent cleansing water or sprinkle for clearing unclean spirits. We may also work the names of Óðinn as Ygg (the terrible) to bless water used to create chalks with which we draw ægishjálmur. This sort of tool is highly specified but extra potent. We can also take inspiration from strands of traditional witchcraft as well as high magic and Christian esotericism, with blessings worked on chalk that utilise wording such as:

"I exorcise you, crafted chalk, bound of rock, infused waters, and (ground bone/herbs/materia). By the power of (Óðinn/God/María), may you be pure and direct in your virtue. (Protect/inspire) as you were intended and work to aid in the crafting of staves, sigils, seals, and symbols that work towards the ends I desire. Be now blessed in this/these names and undeviating in your virtue."

While blessing water and chalk, we can work this same example of various or singular names of deities and spirits, commanding that this tool be undeviating aid in singular or multiple virtue(s), solidifying its purpose and binding it to specific tasks. The combinations and ways we can work these two tools are not easily exhausted, so I encourage you to experiment with this and find out which offerings the spirits you call upon want in exchange.

23

ÓSK OG VILJI: WISH AND WILL

Plenty of manuscripts of Icelandic magical staves contain staves titled "stafur til að fá bón sína." This translates best to "stave to get what you wish or request." Óskagaldur (wish magic) sounds airy and fantastical, but within Icelandic magic, the use of staves to petition higher forces is common. Within our practices, we also utilise some of these staves to petition spirits directly. Just as in continental Europe, magical petitions may be written out, ideally on flakes of birch bark or on fish skin, and offered to the spirits or gods in the hope of a favourable return.

For this sort of work, we should always consider bio-degradable materials; it's even better if these materials are related to the spirits you are petitioning. For example, birch bark is excellently aligned with many dísir and landvættir. We have good results with our methods of petitioning the landvættir like this, and though this is based on continental Northern European folk magic, the spirits of Iceland seem to function in the same way. This sort of thing is not strictly documented in folkloric sources specific to Iceland, but like many examples from the continent, it works just fine.

The simplest of wishes can be worked with the myriad of "wishing" staves found throughout Icelandic grimoires. We find that writing out petitions on paper—whether virgin parchment or otherwise—along with one of these staves reddened with a drop of blood can be burned along with any herbs or incense you wish to help realise your goal.

Specific instructions are given with each stave listed in this section where appropriate based on any lore, as well as our own experiments and corroborated UPG.

We can combine wishing staves with wishing stones. We see wishing stones in a few stories, mentioned earlier in Chapter Eighteen. When we believe we may have found a wishing stone, we can engrave this stone with a wishing stave in the hopes that it may speed along any work or wishes we have been laying. Many of the wishing staves here could be appropriate for this sort of work.

Wish work often revolves around aspects of abundance and fulfilment: of course, we wish for what we don't have. Due to this, I recommend working Jovial materia into many methods of wish magic, from working Jovial powders into the shapes of these staves and using them on altars as magical foci to working with Jovial timings to make the best of this abundant energy. Of course, if our wish isn't related to Jupiter at all, we should utilise the most appropriate planetary force. If our wish is for new love, by all means, work a wish stave with Venusian materia and timings, though I recommend other staves for the best results in these areas.

Commonly, we find wish staves worked to acquire knowledge. For this, one would do well to work with Mercurial materia and timings. Many wish staves can also be worked alongside draumagaldur to acquire knowledge one wishes for through dreams. There is an overlap here that gives the reader the perfect opportunity to experiment, coming at this from both angles, as it were. Try both a wish stave and a dream stave and see which works best for you. Of course, if our wish is highly specific, we can work on creating our own stave to help us achieve this end.

$$Q t^c \text{75} P \delta \delta \delta \delta \, aa \, \int \int \int$$

I've had good results working these letters alongside wishes to acquire knowledge both in dreams and when walking the land. I recommend carrying a charm to get what one wishes, drawn on fresh parchment and bundled up with Jovial herbs in a charm bag. Create this in a Jovial day and hour, maybe working a little Mercurial time or materia with it if your wish requires a few hurdles to be jumped before it can materialise.

One wish stave I'd suggest working along with a wish stone is my own UPG. It was designed based on Jovial symbols, and the focus was "to aid in the manifestation of what I wish." This design is one I've worked with alongside what I believe to be a wishing stone for quite some time now. Feel free to try the same if you wish.

Otherwise, for faster results, I recommend working any of the following staves as focal points for spells for specific wishes. Draw any of these out on virgin parchment, place them at the centre of your working space, and work them into spells in whatever way you wish. You can add materia that falls under the most appropriate planetary virtue or use whichever methods you work with best.

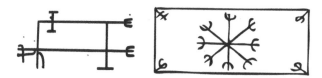

These wish staves could be accompanied by this galdur from *ATA Ämb 2 F16:26*. Read the following three times as normal, then three times in reverse, and you shall receive that which you want for yourself.

The correct verse: The reverse:
"Sprend manns hoc flide tum boll."   *"Boll tum flide hoc manns sprend."*

FJANDAFÆLA OG ANDAFÆLA: EXORCISM AND CLEARING

The use of staves and galdur for exorcism or the deterring of spirits is common within Icelandic magic. Many poems and stories of exorcisms have been recorded throughout time, tales of wise folk binding and banishing ghosts and spirits. These acts of exorcism and clearing need their own separate section to go into a little more detail than simple protections from these forces. The use of herbs and tools to rid places of spirits comes to us through folklore and tradition. As animists, we have a deep respect for the land, and we now acknowledge that sometimes it is necessary to banish spirits from places, even if these spirits are harmless.

The proper removal and treatment of unclean spirits is essential for a healthy "pest-free" practice, in my opinion.

Within our practices, we see unclean spirits take many forms. The dead can linger and cause trouble. Some human spirit may, in death, devolve into something more trollish. Part of one's spirit may live on as a púki, becoming the imp of another practitioner or having its own agency. Malignant entities may linger or come into being over time, accumulating power and agency like dust in the corners of a room. Tilberi can go from milk-sucking familiars to vengeful, ever-hungry monsters following families for generations.

ROSAHRINGUR MINNI

Rosahringur minni, sometimes called "the circle of lesser protection," is, in my opinion, an underappreciated and under-used stave. The traditional method of its use is, of course, complicated, requiring the skin of a brown female cow and the blood of a black male cat killed under a full moon. Luckily, the stave works well without either of these items. It can be inscribed on skin or even protective wood. It should be reddened in blood as with all other staves, but you may also wish to add some protective or exorcism oil as a final glaze. Create and consecrate this charm under a full moon and place it within the house to protect it from spirits and ghosts. These words, found in *Lbs 4375 8vo*, were typically spoken alongside the charm while it was waved around in a space while re-applying the oil used to consecrate it:

"Komi mér hjálp af jörðu,
sigur af sólu,
sæla af tungli,
stoð af stjörnum og styrkur af
englum drottins."

"Help comes to me from the Earth,
Victory from the Sun,
Bliss from the Moon,
Support from the stars and strength
from the angels of the Lord."

Fjandafælir and Andafælir Staves

Some of my own personal UPG around exorcism includes this stave I developed (also found in *Icelandic Plant Magic*), which we can use in two ways. The first involves four specific plants for aiding in banishing unclean spirits. Birch twigs, rowan leaves, northern cudweed, and juniper are bound together and burned in a space within which this stave is placed.

Be as creative with the placement as you like, and make sure to really smoke the space out with the herbs. Do this while chanting:

"Fjandafæla, fjælir fjanda,
Birki styrkir anda.
Reynir vernaðar mig frá föllnum,
Einir hreinsar mig frá djöflum."

"Cudweed, banish demons,
Birch, strengthen spirit.
Rowan, protect me from the fallen,
Juniper, cleanse me of devils."

The second way we can work this stave is alongside burning northern cudweed, bilberry leaves, and coltsfoot leaves. We place the stave within a space the same way as before, then smoke the space out with incense. Do this while reciting this galdur continually until the spirits have been cleared:

"Meinar þú morðinginn	"Do you murderer,
mér nokkuð granda,	Intend to kill me?
frá Guði ég sveia þér	From God, I damn you
ofan tilfjanda.	Down to the Devil.
Þar kvalirnar þér mest,	May the torture there,
þúsund neta smiður,	You, maker of a thousand nets,
í helvítið heitt of breitt,	In a hot, wide Hell,
halda þér niður."	Hold you down."

Andafælir (banishing spirits) is a word often used interchangeably with *fjandafæla*, though *Anda-* indicates spirits of all kinds, whereas *fjanda* more often refers to devils and unclean spirits. We can look at these staves as a parallel to the use of sweetgrass and lemongrass. Burning lemongrass is said to call in spirits of all kinds, after which we must burn sweetgrass to dispel the negative ones. Andafælir staves cover the banishing of many types of spirits, whereas fjandafælir staves won't have the same effect.

The one major andafælir stave we utilise in contemporary practice comes from the collection *Lbs 5472 IV 4to*. It may be used in the same way as the fjandafælir stave I created, along with protective or banishing herbs and materia.

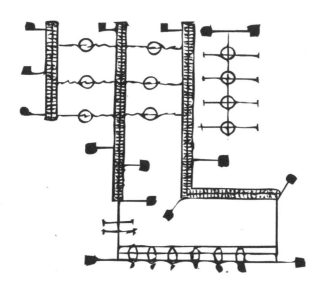

PRAYERS OF BANISHING

Ein góð bæn, or "one good prayer," collected by Árnason in *Þjóðsögur og Ævfintýri*, is shorter, easier to remember, and works as a good exorcism of spaces and places when paired with all manner of appropriate herbs, charms, and more. I recommend working it with herbs as incense. Burn the incense within the space to be cleared, along with banishing staves if you need more efficacy while chanting the following:

"Ég særi þig, óhreinn andi, frá mér og mínum og öllum þeim skepnum sem ég les þessa bæn yfir. Vertu mér og mínum svo fjarlægur sem austrið er vestrinu.

"I curse you, unclean spirit, from me and mine and all the creatures whom over I read this prayer. Be as far from me as East is from West.

Ég særi þig, óhreinn andi, fyrir guðs orða kraft svo sem hann útkastaði þér úr himnaríki"

I hurt you, unclean spirit, by the power of God's word as He (the devil) was cast from heaven."

These words are shorter and may work better if speed is required. I recommend this to clear away all sorts of lesser unclean spirits. The words alone may work just fine, but work it the same way as the above prayer if needed. It reads:

*"Hafðu nú hvergi frið
Héðan af, ég bið,
Gefi mér Jesús guðsson lið
Svo gæfunnar öðlist hæsta mið.
Amen."*

"Ye shall have no peace, from here on out.
Jesus, I beg you, son of God, grant me aid.
Rid us of these unclean spirits
and bring us victory over them.
Amen."

Another prayer, simply known as an "old prayer" or *Ein Gömul Bæn*, is from Ólafur Davíðsson's *Íslenzkar Þjóðsögur*. It invokes the lord of Sunday (God), Jesus, and calls on Saint John. It reads:

*"Velkominn vertu, sunnudags herra;
Þú ert mönnum mætastur,
Sjálfum Kristi mínum kærastur;
Þú munt bera vort bóð*

Fyrir voldugan guð
Undir eið og gullstíl.
Þar kom fram einn sannkristinn mann,
Sankti Jóhannes heitir hann.
Settu þig níður, sankti Jóhannes,
Og skoðaðu mínar undir.
Hver hefur þolað mein og hríð
Fyrir alln kristinn lýð,
Fyrir konu og fyrir mey,
Fyrir svein og fyrir mann?
Hver sem þetta versiðlesa kann
Níu nóttum áður maður deyr,
Þá er hann skilinn við alla vítis neyð,
Dýrt er drottins orðið, um aldir alda. Amen."

This chant, collected by Árnason, is used to aid in banishing unclean and vengeful spirits:

"Flýðu og farðu,	"Flee and fly
Fjóstu og brenndu,	Freeze and burn
Angri þig allar kindur,	All that have
Sem skírast kuma,	And ever will
Heðan í frá	Walk the Earth under God
Á himni og jörðu.	Despise you,
	In heaven and Earth.
Hreki þig allt og hrífi,	Shake you all
Haldinn versta kífi,	And hurry out,
Verði þér aldrei rótt	Night and day
Hvorki dag né nótt,	Shall contend your route,
Hátt lé lágt	Up and down,
Í hverri átt."	And all about,
	Evil spirits, I cast you out."

CLEANSING CHANT

This galdur is something I use for all sorts of quick cleansings. Whether it be for myself, tools, spaces, or other things, I work it with the askur, filling the bowl with water and adding a little consecrated salt. If you want, you can add a pinch of ground angelica root, ground juniper, and rowan berries. I then dip my læknisfingur into the water. Tracing out the following stave with my finger, I speak these words aloud:

"*Fjón þvæ ég af mér*
Fjanda minna,
Rán og reiði
Ríkra manna..."

The first part of the whole chant is usually enough and the most convenient to work with, but the full chant can be found below:

"*Svo að þeir glaðlega*
Mér gangi á móti
Og hlæjandi
Mig augum líti,
Ást drep ég hendi,
Lýk ég fésakir,
Lýkég fjörsakir,
Lýk ég enna mestu manna sakir.
Guð læiti mig
Og góðir menn,
Sjái hver á mig
Sældar augnum
Ægishjálm
Er ég ber
Í millum brúna,
Þá vo tignarmanna.
Öll sé mér veröld þjón
Að vinum.
Haf vatn millum gaupna þér."

This bannfæring (banishment) is read to accompany all kinds of workings of banishings and clearings. It calls on devils to sink back down to the dark depths of hell and invokes the name of the archangel Mikeal to crush their skulls and defeat them.

"Allir hlutir nú ami þér,
Af því að þú ery kominn hér.
Sökktu nú svartur niður.
Ó, þú helvítis hundspottið,
Hafðu nú hvorki ró né frið,
Brenni þitt brjóst og kviður.
Þú mátt ei hót við Mikeal.
Hann moli þína höfuðskel;
Hrepptu svo ætíð eilíft hel."

LAYING SPIRITS

Icelandic folklore is full of dangerous spirits, many of which require proper laying and binding. As mentioned before, such a spirit in Stokkseyri must be re-bound every seven years. This work is hard and often dangerous, requiring powerful staves, herbs, and many less savoury ingredients. Folklore tells us of many methods of laying spirits, such as using bones, skin, and even the internal organs of animals and people to bind these dangerous spirits. Rocks and other seals placed over holes are also useful methods. Much of this work sits behind initiatory barriers and is much less commonplace than the other magic contained in this galdrabók. For the keen-eyed, you may see how this sort of work may be performed in the folklore, ingredients, and magic mentioned throughout the book.

This is mentioned along with the staves against sendings earlier, and I recommend working various protective staves to trap spirits within holes and places of the earth if they cannot be banished otherwise. Some sources talk about making a hole within human bones, which are plugged and buried. Again, this work is impractical and possibly illegal. Working staves on rocks placed over holes is one way we see these spirits "laid down." Others include binding spirits to the supporting walls of houses, using the home itself as a trap, placing staves all around the building, and wording your galdur to bind the spirit to the home until the day it crumbles. As always, we should take a compassionate approach to human spirits and try to help them move on, dispersing their energies if needed. In particularly nasty cases, we may have no choice but to lock them away.

WORKINGS FOR WEALTH

The last workings in this section concern money. Where this might not seem to fit as clearly into workings of wish and will, under capitalism, at some point, I'm sure we've all wished to have more—or at least to keep what we have. A few staves are given in manuscripts as aids for merchants, buying and selling well and saving money. The first few are known as *kauploki*. These staves are used to ensure exchanges are favourable, and are often classed as merchants' staves. These few come from the collection *Lbs 3902 4to* and may be worked into all manner of charms for good business. They can be easily added to green heillapyngja, full of Jovial materia, and placed above the doors of businesses. These can also be inscribed on fresh parchment, reddened, and carried when making deals or haggling.

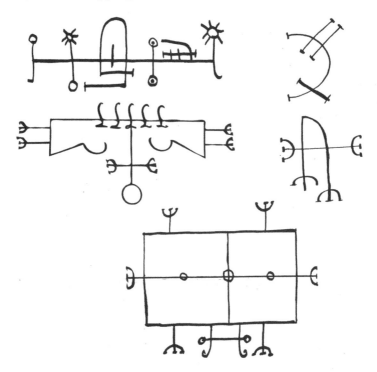

These next two staves are from *Lbs 5472 II 4to*. The first is worked to protect your money and can be carved into the lid of a box that you keep cash in. For a more modern approach, those who keep their cards both within their phone cases and use phone pay methods could place the stave, drawn on fresh parchment, within their phone case. This is best created within a Jovial time and day for associations with wealth, though for the purpose of protecting and reserving, we could call on Martial or Saturnine materia for this sort of working.

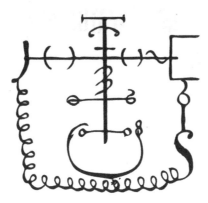

For the more frugal among us, this last stave may very well help you in a pinch. It is a stave to make money last and can be drawn on parchment and reddened during a mix of Jovial and Saturnine timings. It should then be placed within one's wallet or phone case. The stave is meant to make one's money last and go further, so it is well worth a try in this day and age.

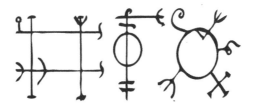

24

Ástagaldur og Ástfanginn: Love Magic and Infatuation

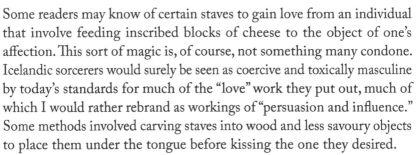

Some readers may know of certain staves to gain love from an individual that involve feeding inscribed blocks of cheese to the object of one's affection. This sort of magic is, of course, not something many condone. Icelandic sorcerers would surely be seen as coercive and toxically masculine by today's standards for much of the "love" work they put out, much of which I would rather rebrand as workings of "persuasion and influence." Some methods involved carving staves into wood and less savoury objects to place them under the tongue before kissing the one they desired.

Such a method shows up in this folktale. Around the year 1820, two young men were studying magic in Eyjafjörður. One night, one of the men went up to the girl he wished to court and kissed her. She thought this strange but began to feel love towards the man. Realising something was going on, she said aloud, "If there is anything here trying to beguile me, it shall end in a sad fate." This was enough to break the man's spell, and she returned to normal.

Remember the warning of Egill when working love magic: the poor farm boy who only wished for the love of the landowner's daughter nearly killed her with improperly performed love magic. The following workings are aimed more towards the art of seduction, persuasion, and inviting new love in while not specifically targeting any one person.

It isn't a wonder that some of the staves worked for love are the most visually appealing. The following stave comes from *Lbs 5472 II 4to*, and though it is called a stave "to get a girl," we can tweak the wording to "acquiring new love from anyone should we seek it."

Inscribe the stave on some Venusian materia within the hour and day of Venus for the best measure and, if possible, during one of the astrological seasons ruled by this planet. Like many of the staves mentioned so far, we can work the stave on materia as the focal point of our work or on a bag full of relevant materia. For this working to attract love, we can do either, though carrying a small pouch inscribed with the stave full of Venusian herbs is an easy way to get what we want from it. Fill a charm bag with any Venusian materia you wish and draw or embroider the stave onto the bag in a Venusian time.

The next stave can be worked slightly differently from its original method in contemporary practice. We can work the stave into a large wooden plate and work it to empower and ensoul Venusian workings. I recommend oiling the plate with a Venusian oil while you do this. We can then use the plate to empower charms of love, seduction, friendship, romance, and more.

We can work with stones such as rose quartz, carnelian, and others for our spells of attraction and persuasion. I recommend finding a flat pebble of each stone and engraving the following simple staves into them. Carry the carnelian when you wish others to find you irresistible and carry the rose quartz when you wish to find new romance. These staves also come from *Lbs 3902 4to*.

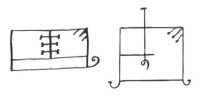

This next stave is from the same manuscript. I recommend working it into candle spells to attract new love. Carve it into a red or pink candle, redden it, anoint it with a Venusian oil, and light it every Friday in the hours of Venus.

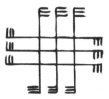

Aphrodisiac magic could well involve the commanding and compelling magic of switching someone's affections from another onto oneself. This is not magic I recommend, as many "stafur til að fá stulku" staves to *get* a girl are manipulations of free will. Certain galdur and words have been used for this, such as these from the galdrabók *ATA Ämb 2 F16:26*:

> *"Ég lít á þig, en þú legg á mig ást og elsku af öllum hug. Sit þú hvergi, þol þú hvergi, nema þú unnir mér. Þess bið ég Óðinn og alla þá sem kvennrúnir kunnu að ráð að þú í heimi hvergi þolir né þrífist nema þú elskir mig af öllum hug."*

I won't include a translation of this galdur as it is wicked and made to bend another's will, causing them suffering and torment until they direct their love towards the caster. Within the galdrabók, it comes with a couple of accompanying staves. As Sæmundsson states in "Galdrar á Íslandi," the wording of this spell is inspired by a section of Skírnismál, invoked in this instance like many Bible passages: using stories to bring about the same occurrences.

GEGN ÁST: ANAPHRODISIACS

We can look to various workings of sympathetic magic that promote love and reverse-engineer them to do the opposite. The use of "Adam and Eve" plant magic (that is, those plants with two roots that could be seen as man and woman) is one such example. Usually worked to promote and sometimes bind love between a man and woman, we can use these roots to do the exact opposite by splitting them apart. Plants like hjónagras (small white orchids) with their different roots can be used for this.

If we want to work this sort of magic on those closer to us, we could work the personal effects of this couple into our magic, taking some water the couple have both bathed in, gathering hairs from each of them, or otherwise acquiring something they both use or have used alongside this plant. The plant should be unearthed, and a hair from each person in the couple may be tied tightly to the different roots so that, as the roots wither, they become weak at the points the hairs tie. The roots will eventually fall away at these points, and as they do, the couple's love will wither and die. This can be done with many plants, not just this orchid. Check your local laws first to see if the orchid is endangered or protected in your area.

This sort of work can also be worked with the aid of a rose. Gather some sharp thorns from a rose, along with a black candle. Carve the names of the couple into the candle along with this anti-love stave. Redden it with blood and place over some personal effect of the couple, or work such an effect into the candle itself, if possible. Pierce the candle with the rose thorns. As you do this (ideally within a Saturnine hour in the day of Venus), speak the names of the couple and that you wish them to part ways over it. Anoint the candle with a Saturnine oil or some combination of Saturnine herbs and rose oil.

Busla's infamous curse mentioned on page 287 is a perfect example of anti-love magic. The wording of this curse can inspire plenty of our own workings.

25

Andasæring:
Necromancy

As mentioned briefly earlier, necromancy has played a role in Icelandic magic since the Viking age. From draugur being woken up to do all sorts of evil deeds to the monstrous offspring of cats and foxes buried only to re-emerge later, Iceland is full of necromancy. We have staves that compel the dead to serve as our spies, reveal to us the identity of thieves, and more.

The first working I'll talk about is far too complicated to try practically. I have found success in using the stave that it centres around to adorn tools, candles, and jars of incense intended to be worked as offerings to or used to call in the dead. In Icelandic folk magic, the stave is used to wake the dead, reanimate corpses, and raise draugur. To do this, it is supposed to be carved into the skin of a horse's head and reddened with a mixture of blood from a seal, a fox, and a man. This spell is then to be recited over the grave:

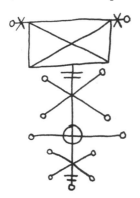

*"Þykkt blóð, þreytast rekkar.
Þjóð mörg vos öld bjóða,
grand heitt, gummar andast,
glatast auður, firrast snauðir.
Hætt grand hræðast dróttir
hríð mörg, vesöld kvíða,
angur vænt, ærnar skærur.
Illur sveimur nú er í heimi."*

I personally wouldn't recommend using it this way without experience with the dead, necromancy, and spirits of this nature. However, if one feels inclined, I recommend following good graveyard etiquette, learning a little about the name and life of the spirit you're waking, as well as gaining permission to wake anything from the presiding guardian spirit of the graveyard or cemetery you are working in. The stave is also said to have the power to drive away evil spirits, following the dual action theme that is ever-present in Icelandic folk magic, though I suggest using one of the many banishing spells or prayers should you need a spirit removed.

We also find one more complex stave, named draugarstafur from *Lbs 3902 4to*. This stave is a bit of a mystery; we don't know what it was intended for, though some have their thoughts. I've included it here without a working. It may very well pertain to necromancy, but it also might not be intended to be worked in the way we would expect. Either way, it is a good example of a more complex mixture of runic symbols and a pictogram, and we can only assume that it means a spirit summoned from beyond the grave.

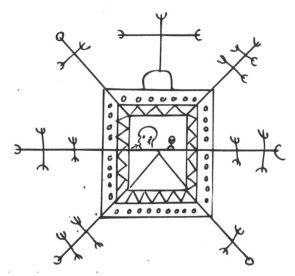

Necromancy aimed at coercing the dead into revealing the identity of thieves is also found within the galdrbók *ATA Ämb 2 F16:26*. This work ties into the idea that the dead have knowledge beyond the living and, as such, can be convinced to part with it. We see a few staves that concern asking the dead for information. More on these can be found alongside specific materia within *Icelandic Plant Magic*.

26

SJÓNHVERFING: ILLUSIONS

Of all the illusionary works recorded in Iceland, the hulinhjálmur is likely the best-known outside of the country. This magical "helm" is to be worn about your person when you wish to go unseen. There are several traditional ways we can work this stave, even more so when using it alongside continental techniques. The simplest is to draw it out on fresh parchment within the hour and day of Saturn, speak over it your wish to go unseen, and go about your business. There are many other methods, such as utilising it in candle spells and lighting the then-empowered candle when you wish to be out of sight and mind altogether (which is a useful technique to avoid any divination being done on you).

It could be made into a charm, reddened with blood, and worn. You could use it on a charm bag filled with Saturnine and concealing plants. If you want to add European influences, you could draw the stave on a pouch made from snake or lizard skin and fill it with bláhjálmur (*Aconitum napellus*) seeds. The stave can also be worked with the remains of foxes, rabbits, mice, and other animals that have a skill for avoiding detection. Other plants that align well with this stave are smjörgras (*Bartsia alpina*), völvuauga (*Atropa belladonna*), and stóriburkni (*Dryopteris filix-mas*), though other fern species (burknar) will also work. Outside of Iceland, there will be plenty of options for this sort of magic, so we encourage you to experiment.

The traditional method of working the Hulinhjálmur is a bit grotesque, and I don't recommend it as you can work the stave in less complex and costly ways. In traditional folk magic, the stave would be created with a special ink consisting of three drops of blood from the left index finger, three drops from the right ring finger (leech finger), two drops of blood from the right nipple, and one from the left. These need to be mixed with six drops of blood from the heart of a live raven, then melted with the brain of the raven and some pieces of a human's stomach. The seal must then be drawn out on lignite and pressed into the brow.

Needless to say, beyond the gathering of blood from your own body, this method of working the stave is highly impractical. If you want to use the blood method, I recommend taking great care when doing so, and bear in mind that a simple red ink and the use of a raven's quill have worked well enough in the more recent past. The stave can still be created on lignite, but this material is somewhat hard to get hold of nowadays, and finding a piece big enough for the details of this stave will prove difficult.

Another form of hulinhjálmur was recorded in the collection within *Lbs 5472*. This variant takes a longer form, made of near-mirrored characters. This version may be tattooed around the left arm for passive use to get somewhat less noticed in your day-to-day life. I recommend also working this into a charm, either carved into some Saturnine wood like yllr (*Taxus baccata*) or even reynir (*Sorbus aucuparia*). I have found reynir to be a suitable help in working this stave despite its differences in traditional virtues. The charm may also be worked into a Saturnine oil, adorning the lid of the bottle or jar you keep it in. Speak galdur over the stave once it has been drawn (perhaps with the same ink method as before) within a Saturnine day and hour and carry it with you. Suffumigate any finished charms involving this stave with Saturnine incense or ilmreyr (*Anthoxanthum odoratum*).

As we learned earlier, various magical folk across Iceland's history have used illusions and deception in their work. Halla of Straumfjörður, for instance, tricked merchants under their own noses and later disguised horses and carts as tufts of grass. There are two parts to the work: the use of objects or talismans, enchanted at certain times, often inscribed with staves, and specific galdur used in a pinch to hide or otherwise conceal things. This can be performed as short verbal spellwork, some sympathetic magic, and, occasionally, the use of enchanted clothing.

Enchanting clothing is commonplace in most magical traditions. The sewing of reynir fruits into pockets is something practiced in Iceland and is popular in Scotland—at least in living tradition. Clothes can also be dyed with certain plants to instill the plant's virtues and it's even better if some colour is involved. Staves can be sewn into clothing; this is something we employ a lot in living practice. Many of the protective and illusionary staves mentioned previously can be employed this way: reddened on the inside of the fabric or by dipping the needle in a drop of blood before sewing.

Though it is more of a stave used to exert your influence, the following stave from *Lbs 3902* fits well in this section. The manuscript tells us that "to control one's mind, make this stave in your palm, you can then change the minds of your neighbours." While I don't recommend the unethical attempt at controlling another's mind, I do see this stave having use in winning arguments or otherwise being convincing in small matters.

The stave should be made in the palm with spittle. As this is a more active type of magic, I recommend drawing it in the dominant hand using the leech finger of the other. You may wish to speak some galdur over the stave while doing so. I recommend pouring your desire for control, or sheer will to get the result you need, into the stave and telling it exactly what to help with. Once you have set this firmly, place your hand onto the target in a mundane manner—such as touching a shoulder or shaking hands—and establish firm eye contact when greeting them.

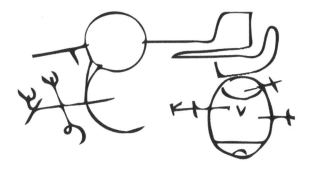

27

Draumagaldur: Dream Magic

Dream magic, as mentioned earlier, is another pillar of Icelandic magic. It sometimes crosses over with wish magic if what you wish is to receive knowledge via the medium of dreams. However, some magic is highly specific for dream work. Some herbs are worked in many ways as dream herbs, both following the folklore as well as contemporary workings (mentioned in Chapter Sixteen), such as maðjurt (*Filipendula ulmaria*) and vallhumall (*Achillea millefolium*). Plenty of staves can also be utilised for dream magic. Many of them can be carved or drawn onto candles and burned before bed, but some need more specific and less accessible materia.

These staves, recorded by Jón Árnason, are used for dream magic, although with this specific medium, I would call this "dream necromancy." These six staves are to be inscribed onto a human skull, which is then kept close to the bed and asked to bring you the information you need while you sleep. The skull used, if coming from an animistic perspective, should be the skull of someone in life who either was very intelligent or had some form of prophetic gift. Of course, acquiring a human skull is both incredibly difficult and unsavoury, even when doing so via legal alleys.

For making this working practical, I suggest using the skull of an animal whose physical traits work in favour of gathering information. For example, a winged animal (one able to fly far and receive information) gifted with speech, such as a raven or other corvid, would be a good idea. The skull of a cunning fox, a small mouse able to slip in and out of spaces unnoticed, or a rabbit able to disappear underground and come back with wisdom from the Earth would work. The skull of a black cat, an animal much associated with stealth as well as the occult, would also be a wise choice. Of course, the skull should be acquired legally and ethically. Then, it must be cleaned and ritually cleansed, blessed, and consecrated for its new purpose.

The second stage in this working is to decide whether you will work with the lingering spirit of the animal that once inhabited the skull or whether you will thoroughly cleanse it and use it as a vessel for some other spirit or entity who will retrieve you this information, aided by the virtues of the animal whose skull it will use.

Once the skull has been physically cleaned and otherwise consecrated, paint these six staves upon it. I recommend doing so within a combination of a Mercurial and Saturnine day and hour since we are working to enhance the virtues of communication and knowledge through the medium of necromancy. You can design an appropriate ritual around the inhabiting of the new tool based on the information on birthing spirits in Chapter Twenty-Eight.

The Stockholm manuscript *ATA Ämb 2 F16:26* also gives us this bit of galdur to aid in sleep disturbances and headaches. The following should be written on parchment and placed beneath one's head:

"Milant vá vitaloth jeobóa febaoth."

DREAM STAVES

There are also many staves specifically worked for dreaming and the acquisition of knowledge through dreams. The following staves can be found in the collection *Lbs 5472 I 4to* and may be worked in many ways. I find them best carved into candles and reddened as you would any stave. These should then be burned by your bed before sleep.

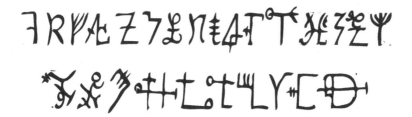

28

BIRTHING SPIRITS

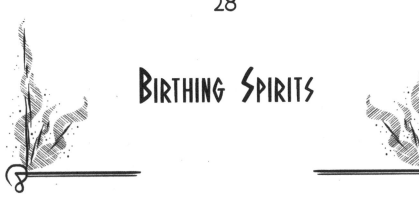

The creation of entities plays a role in the folk magic of many countries, and in Iceland, we have plenty of folklore to support the birthing of familiar spirits. As you now know, there are many types of birthed spirits within Icelandic folklore. From monstrous patchwork fylgjur created from animal remains to milk-sucking tilberi and tricky imps, we can look to Icelandic folklore for instructions on how to birth these spirits to aid in our witchcraft.

Púkar are imps, most often servitor spirits, that can be set to work in many ways. Most often, these spirits are sent about in folklore by wizards to spy on people for all manner of reasons. There are many folk stories of them sitting in the roofs of churches watching the townsfolk. We also see stories of púkar who torment common folk, sometimes being fed by bad habits such as swearing. Púkar are also passed on when a practitioner dies, which is a common theme in folk magic. In Icelandic folk magic, it is advised you pass your púkar on so that they don't run wild and cause mischief.

We can work with púkar in contemporary magic as we would with any other familiar spirit: engaging with them as we would with other spirits we make pacts with, creating sigils to work as foci to empower them, and sending them on specific tasks (ideally those that make our lives easier). We can name and birth our own púki working with plant roots, for example, or other materia. We can work roots in rótblæti, using them as houses for our púkar, or work the existing spirit of the plant into something new, making a pact with it to become a púki. This changing of roles is something commonly seen for many spirits in an animistic framework, and through making pacts with these spirits, we can give them a new role to fill.

As part of my own UPG, I've developed this stave I use to ensoul rótblæti and work materia into various vessels for spirits. It can be worked into a wooden plate or disk (ideally burned or carved into it). This stave should be reddened before the surface is oiled with some Saturnine oil. I make this tool in a combination of Saturnine and Mercurial times. Once you've acquired a root to work with, and have cleaned it, carved it, and prepared it for ensouling, redden the stave, then place suitable materia around the centre of it. The root should then be sat in the centre. We work this chant at the end of reading out a contractual agreement we have created to bind the spirit in certain ways:

"Rót sem eitt sinn var,
gef sjálfa þig upp og hýstu andann sem gengur inn í þig."

Contracts are an important part of working with spirits, just as they are when starting a new business or employing someone in any mundane task. As with humans, relationships with spirits can sour when there is misconduct, so we should be smart about how we offer payment and what that payment is. Rótblæti must be properly cared for and "fed and watered" semi-regularly (or as often as your contract entails). According to folklore, we should most often feed our servitor spirits with blood, honey, milk, and offerings of actual food.

Blood may be the best if working with a pacted spirit, but the spirits we work with may reveal to us their favourite offerings if we take the time to ask. Setting aside a bowl for these offerings in front of the space where your rótblæti live is ideal.

We should then consider creating a seal or sigil for the spirit, as having a "calling card" makes it easier to contact as well as to settle our familiar spirits. Naming our familiars can also be a method for us to limit these spirits, just as creating seals can be. Most importantly, we should include various clauses in the pacts we make with them, saving us from any trouble later. An example of this type of clause might be including that the spirit should dissipate after the vessel is destroyed when writing out a contract with a familiar spirit.

The materia we place around the rótblæti should follow the main virtues we wish to ensoul the spirit with. Of course, the root it is made from plays a role in this, too. Working a root of Angelica as an alrune or general home for a spirit works well due to the plant's many virtues. Working a root of some baneful plant, such as bláhjálmur (*Aconitum napellus*), into the home of a shady Saturnine spirit used for spying or bringing knowledge would also make sense.

We can work various roots of Icelandic species into rótblæti. Angelica, as a perfectly protective and potent plant ally, would make an ideal vessel for other spirits, as well as a useful plant familiar on its own. This sort of rótblæti should be given great care and respect. I've also had success working with roots of bláhjálmur (*Aconitum napellus*), hagabrúða (*Valeriana officinalis*), njóli (*Rumex longifolius*), and hjónagras (*Pseudorchis albida*).

Once we have considered all these points, prepared our ensoulment stave surface, cleaned, prepared, carved the root, brought together our *materia magica*, and finished off our written contracts, we can get to work. Open the space you will use as normal, sitting with your prepared materia, surface, and supplies. I recommend having a small amount of blessed water on hand. (A blessing over water can be found on page 236.) Work this to hold a "baptism" of your root fetish, giving it a new name and marking this next step within its spiritual life. Read out its contract. Sign your own name, the name of the spirit, and seal it with a drop of your own blood. Keep this contract safe afterwards, ideally in the same space you root fetish lives.

Once you have read the contract, as well as the above words in Icelandic (or your own version), we can finish the work. I recommend taking the rótblæti in your hands, raising it to your mouth, and blowing three times, each time envisioning life being breathed into the vessel as the spirit of your familiar fills it. We can then end our work, placing the vessel somewhere appropriate in the home or in our working space.

PÚKAR: IMPS

Now that you know a little about imps, it may be worth attempting to acquire and work with your own. This aspect of traditional witchcraft often involves asking the man in black to gift an imp or familiar. You can go this direction if you wish, but we can also work within contemporary (and somewhat Neo-Pagan) guidelines and ask Óðinn instead, or venture out into the land alone and ask the spirits there if one of them wishes to become your imp. *The Chilling Adventures of Sabrina* gave us, in my opinion, pop culture's most authentic animistic familiar invitation. This can be done with offerings and patience. The following ritual is one way I would approach the land when asking the spirits of my local place for a willing familiar.

TO CALL FOR PÚKAR

Venture out to the land, ideally in an area you know well and have established a connection with. Bring with you some food you have made yourself, as well as some incense to repel negative spirits. Call out to the land, letting it know you have made this offering for the spirits and wish to acquire a púki. Leave the place and return the following day to clear away any remains of the offering. If it seems as though it has been well accepted, then ask that the spirit return home with you. Prepare a small vessel for your púki to live within. Something simple, like a jar, works in a pinch, but you can be as intricate in the design of this vessel as you wish. Do keep in mind that simple is best for púkar. These are almost always low-level spirits that work for us and are not the same as various familiars with whom we have more contractual and formal relationships.

Púkar are more often called on for small mischiefs and tasks rather than larger goals. Place this jar in your home with the lid open and call out to the spirit that followed you home. Tell it that this jar is where it can live and work under your care. Once you feel it has inhabited the jar, close it and sit with the spirit. Try to ask for a name. If this is new to you, it may take some time, but simply ask it to reveal its name to you and let the name come to you. I like to make small sigils for my púkar once I have their names.

A púki can be set to various tasks. The folklore, as well as my own experience, has shown them to be useful spies, following and keeping tabs on people nearby. They are also good at small jobs, like keeping various plants and places safe during storms and protecting small trinkets. Púkar can be set to watch over gardens, helping plants grow. Remember to have a good divination practice that helps you communicate with your púkar. I use the Icelandic method or sheep knuckle bones for easy yes-or-no divination to verify whatever it is I'm asking them to do. This way, I'll know if they can do it and generally collect data on all the variables surrounding what I'm asking them to do, as well as using the bones to weed out potential tricky responses. I recommend, for those going into the land and inviting spirits back home, using this sort of yes-or-no divination to help work out whether the spirit coming back with you has good intentions or not.

I also recommend working plenty of protection on your home to prevent you from bringing any óhreinn andi back inside. Always remember that when connecting with any spirit that could potentially cause trouble, you should use caution and play it safe. When getting to know your púki, remember that spirits who change roles often change form or type over time. Some púki may well be the remaining shades of long-dead folk. Some may be detached fylgja. Some may well have been húsandi or landvættur themselves.

The "metaphysics" behind this role-changing is complex and unique, and sometimes the once-great vættur of a particular forest may have become a púki over time. Maybe its forest was lost or deforested, or its power decreased from a lack of offerings once Christianity came to the land. As we know, energy cannot be created or destroyed; it can only be transferred. This universal law governs all things found within the material realm, corporeal or otherwise.

29

Að Sjá Þjóf:
To See a Thief

Iceland has always been prone to resource scarcity. Even in today's world, this mentality often rears its ugly head. In the old days, resources meant survival. Many lived on the edge of poverty, owning little (if anything). During the vistarband, all who didn't own property equal to three cows were required by law to work for a farm, pledging themselves to the landowner for the year. Due to this lifestyle and other times of abject poverty, alongside the role of honour and loyalty in Icelandic society, it is clear to see why thief finding plays such an important role in Icelandic folk magic.

The askur is one of the main tools used in Icelandic folk magic to divulge the identity of thieves. Plants may be laid in the bowl to help discover the identity of thieves. Some plants may be worked with to help catch thieves. I suggest working a few plants alongside the staves of thievery. Elsewhere in the world, we can utilise local thief-catching plants or general thorned plants to help us in our work. Even using a rose bush would make sense, giving the added Venusian virtue of temptation and seduction to lure the thief in. More on those specific plants can be found in *Icelandic Plant Magic*.

As for methods that don't require plant materia, we can look to techniques of divination—specifically, stave work and magical candles. The following stave can be worked into a candle to discover thieves in dreams, sometimes calling on the spirits of the dead to tell us the identity of these thieves. Carve the following stave into a candle, redden it with blood or plant materia, then place it beside your bed and burn it before you sleep. One can also carve this stave onto wood and place it beneath your head. Traditionally, this is done for six consecutive nights. This stave is from the collection in *Lbs 2413 8vo*.

Working the stave this way may require a little added help. For this, I recommend burning a little oneiromancy incense before the work is done. My recommendation for plants suitable to this within Iceland is a mix of bláber (*Vaccinium sp.*), hófífill (*Tussilago farfara*), and Maðjurt (*Filipendula ulmaria*). Plants from elsewhere in the world that would also be suitable include mugwort, sage, bay laurel, blue lotus, lavender, chamomile, mullein, vervain, and wormwood, to name a few. Burn these in the room you will perform this dream divination before bed.

We find another stave to reveal a thief in the galdrabók *ATA Ämb 2 F16:26*. This stave employs the use of the askur and vallhumall to locate a thief. The words used to activate the stave and spell give us a perfect example of the blending of Christianity and Norse Pagan beliefs in a dual-faith spell. In Icelandic, it reads:

"*Óðinn, Loki, Bladur, Marður, Týr, Birgir, Hænir, Freyja Gefjun, Gusta og allir þær og þeir sem Valhöll byggja og byggt hafa frá heimsins upphafi, þá gefi mér það að mér veitist þessi hlutur.*"

Then, in English, I would translate it as:

"*Óðinn, Loki, Frey, Baldur, Marður, Týr, Birgir, Hænir, Freyja, Gefjun, Gusta and all those who inhabit Vallhöll, and have built the realm from its beginning, grant that which I ask.*"

Some plants grow by stealing nutrients from others. These parasitic and semi-parasitic plants can be utilised in workings of thievery to aid us with these Mercurial virtues. There are staves to persuade one to become a thief. Carving a thief summoning stave into the underside of a guest's dinner plate, then having them eat from it, is said to convince the victim to steal from their hosts. This sort of work would have been used in Iceland to damn those one didn't like, possibly to cheat neighbours and besmirch their name and reputation. I recommend the following contemporary approach to working with the traditional stave.

This thief summoning was recorded by Jón Árnason and works as a spell to torture the thief until they return the items they stole. We can work this by itself, or, if we have already divined the identity of the thief and are certain of who they are, alongside an image of the thief and a black candle. We can work the following staves into the candle or draw it over the photo of the person. Be aware that this can be quite heavy work and may not be for everyone. Alternatively, you can draw the staves out on parchment or carve them into wood and work the chant, holding the stave in your hand when the thief comes before you.

> "May you go mad and swell up in great agony,
> And may you never have peace until you come before me
> With the things that you have stolen from me.
> May Thor and Óðinn help."

But if the thief has eaten what he stole, then you must read this:

> "You shall spew up the things that you stole.
> So shall your body be fully bloated,
> and everything be torn up from the inside.
> Now your guts must howl, all clawing each other from the inside.
> May I fall on you with words so fitted,
> that your breast and torso may be burning,
> As if hounds' bit, tearing around your heart.
> May all your breast and mind become confused.

I forbid you to glance at a holy book.
A branch shall come out of your neck, worst one,
And these true prophecies shall do you harm.
Vomit now or else burst completely.
May Thor and Óðinn help in this,
So that the thief may have nowhere to hide."

In the original Icelandic, this reads:

"Svo skal búkur þinn
Blásast fullur
Og innan rifinn
Allur vera.
Nú skulu gaula
Garnir þínar
Og þær allar
Innan klórast.

Felli ég á þig
Svofelldum orðum
Að brjóst þitt og búkur
Brannandi veri
Sem þig um hjartað
Úr hálsi koma, vestur strákur
Og skulu þau áhrínsorð
Þér til meins standa.

Spú þú nú
Eða springdu allur.
Þar til hjálpi
Þór og Óðinn
Að þjófur afsaki sig eigi."

Árnason recorded another stave, used to discover the identity of a thief and invoke the Norse gods for help, along with the following working. This stave can be carved into a candle and reddened with blood. You then need to invoke the names of María, Jesús, Óðinn, Þór, and Satan, then sit with this in a quiet room alone. Meditate on the identity of the thief, and it will come to your mind's eye.

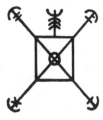

The following stave comes from *Lbs 4627 8vo* and works to help us discover the identity of a thief via oneiromancy. Work this carved into a candle or a piece of wood or drawn on parchment and reddened with blood. Place this charm under your pillow, and you will dream of the thief.

This stave from *Lbs 5472 IV 4to* and works in the same way as the above.

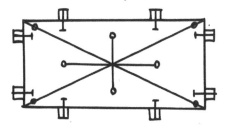

The next stave, from *Lbs 5472 III 4to*, is worked for general protection against thieves. It can be carved into boxes used to hide or conceal certain objects or wealth. If you own a safe, this would be the most appropriate stave to carve into it. We can also work it on parchment paper, redden it with blood, and then put it into a safe or place it under the things we don't wish to be stolen. Placing it over a doorway or entrance to a room containing precious objects may also be enough to prevent theft.

Mentioned in many books that discuss Icelandic magical staves, another lock-breaking stave gives us this useful galdur, which we can work with many, if not every other, lock-breaking stave. I shared the stave in my previous work, *Icelandic Plant Magic*, but we can utilise the galdur itself with any lock-breaking charm. This sort of work can be used to "un-pick" magical wards, galdraskjöldur. When encountering such wards, we simply hold up our lock-breaking charm towards it and recite the following:

> *"Tröll öll taki í mellu,*
> *taki í djöfull, so braki."*

This translates to:

> *"All trolls reach into the lock,*
> *The Devil reach into it, so that it will break."*

If this proves unsuccessful, take it a step further and recite this galdur, based on my translation of a passage known as the "Locks Verse of Thieves," while you visualise blowing into a lock that represents the ward:

> *"So I blow a storm into the hole,*
> *And then has come my luck,*
> *I breathe over human fat,*
> *That it shall be unstuck.*

I take hold with this hand,
The Devil with putrid gasp
And by the storm and by my will
Now shall rot its grasp."

If this doesn't work for you, we can work the following stave. This stave is called Þjófalikill, recorded in the collection *Lbs 3902 4to*. The traditional instructions tell us to draw the stave onto wet goat skin in blood by using the little finger of your right hand. Hold this charm in your preferred hand while attempting to open locks. If this is not enough, combine it with the lock verse or use it in place of the lock breaker stave on parchment.

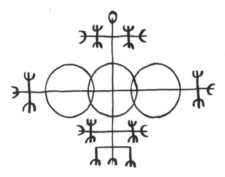

The last bit of lock-breaking magic involves the use of human fat gleaned from a recently dead corpse. This magic was used to break shackles as well as the locks on people's property. Some of the fat was placed on the keyhole, and this verse was then recited:

"Blæs ég svo bylur í lási,
og blístra af mannsístru;
fjandinn með fúlan anda
fast í lásinn blási;
tröll upp togi mellur,
taki á púkar.
Lyftið upp lásnum allir
lifandi fjandans andar."

Human fat was also used to create torches that burned until they were extinguished with blood, and it was worked into sharpening magic used to make knives never go dull. This is not something I recommend replicating.

ÞÓRSHAMAR

Having this charm on one's person is said to be enough to allow one to know who has stolen from them. The following stave should be engraved on copper, ideally from a church bell or clock, though regular copper should do.

The talisman should be reddened with your own blood during mass on Whitsunday between the reading of the epistle and the gospel. Make a small spike from copper, poke the spike between the eyes of the face on the stave, and say:

"Rek ég í augu Vígföður, "I poke you in the eyes Víföður (Óðinn),
rek ég í augu Valföður, I poke you in the eyes Valföður (Óðinn),
rek ég í augu Ása-Þórs." I poke you in the eyes Ása-Þórs (Þór)."

The thief will then feel intense pain between his eyes, such as that of a migraine. If the thief does not return what was stolen, then the process is repeated, and the thief is said to lose one eye. If the goods are still not returned, the process is repeated a third time, with the thief ending up blind.

Such a talisman was found in the possession of a merchant in Húsavík in 1858, given to him by a woman suspected of witchcraft. This charm was made of brass and had a small hole in the eye that a spike could be inserted into.

THIEF PROTECTION BOX

One pair of staves is recorded to be able to protect items from thieves. The two are called *blóðuxi* and *molduxi,* simply translated as "blood-oxen" and "earth-oxen." The two are to be carved into the lids of boxes, which are then filled with valuables and placed somewhere, maybe hidden in plain sight. This protective working is held in high regard.

30

Healing
and Helping

Healing works in Iceland had long been a mix of magic and medicine. With herbalism being illegal in Iceland until recent times, the use of herbs has long been held as mystical. Healing in Icelandic and Scandinavian folk practice has inspired a few practices, tools, and staves of my own design, such as the lækningastöng mentioned on page 128.

The left ring finger is called the *græðifingur* (finger of healing). For works of magic, I recommend using the *græðifingur* for anointing or copper knives and surfaces for carving and working. Some specific examples of herbal healing with staves can be found in *Icelandic Plant Magic*.

HEALING AMULET

Looking to older spells from across Scandinavia, an amulet was found in Sigtuna in 1931 and has been dated to the eleventh century. Inscribed on the amulet was the following rune poem:

"Þór/Þurs sárriðu, þursa dróttinn!
Fljú þú nú! Fundinn er[tu].
Haf þér þrjár þrár, Ulfr!
Haf þér níu nauðir, Ulfr!
Ulfr. Njót lyfja!"

"Boil/Spectre of the wound-fever,
lord of the giants!
Flee now! You are found.
Have for yourself three pangs, Wolf!
Have for yourself nine needs, Wolf!
Wolf. Make good use of the healing!"

This sort of healing charm is worked to remove the spirit of disease or infection from its host. We can look at the cultural context of the old-world belief of the porous body to make sense of this. The belief that "disease spirits" entered the body and caused problems is not one we hold strongly now with the advancement of modern medicine, but by looking at it from an animistic perspective, we can see there may well be spirits that rule certain diseases and conditions. Of course, should one need medical attention, these spells should not be seen as the only remedy. Work them alongside medical treatment if necessary.

Create the charm on parchment during a Venusian day and hour. You can also include some Solar virtues to help cast out any malignant energy if you wish.

VENUS INNSIGLI

This stave is a contemporary stave worked to empower and focus Venusian virtues. Work it as a tablet or plate used to empower and ensoul Venusian things. Place healing charms on this plate, as well as Venusian herbs, charm bags, and stones used to heal, and speak over them at Venusian days and hours to emphasise these virtues. Likewise, you should create this board in a Venusian day and hour, carve the stave, and redden it with blood, then oil the plate with a Venusian oil blend.

H<ALING <HANT$

The following chant comes from *Runic Amulets and Magical Objects* by Bernhard Mees and Mindy Macleod, a book I very much recommend giving a read. This chant was found engraved into a "healing stick" and is very much the historical evidence and inspiration for the lækningastöng as a specific tool:

> *"I pray Earth to guard and high heaven, the sun and holy Mary and the lord God himself, that he grant me leech-hands and a healing tongue to heal the trembler when a cure is needed. From back and from breast, from body and from limb, from eyes and from ears; from wherever evil can enter. A stone is called Svart ("black"), it stands out in the sea, there lie upon it nine needs, who...then...should, shall neither sleep sweet nor wake warm, until you pray this cure which I have proclaimed in runic words. Amen, and so be it."*

This galdur is my own UPG. It is easy to memorise and can be utilised while drumming and preforming rituals of healing. Ideally, it would be used after the source of the illness has been identified and various exorcisms of the body have been performed. Though this is not working under the porous body mentality of the old world, we can sympathetically draw out illness with song and exorcising it away. This chant invokes one of Óðinn's many names and should be used alongside healing that involves staves and herbs:

> *"Ég ákalla Njótur, nafni Óðins,*
> *Soothe (me/name/area of pain).*
> *Alleviate the ills of (my/their/its) body and being.*
> *Work your healing,*
> *By stave, blood, and herb."*

Another personal chant I've found helpful to aid in healing is this simple invocation of the rune Wunjo. As the rune of comfort, Wunjo may be worked while healing, especially to bring about magical healing rest and sleep:

> *"Ég ákalla Wunjo,*
> *Ég kalla á mátt þinn.*
> *Ég ákalla Wunjo.*
> *Ég ákalla Wunjo."*

Do this while tracing the rune on the thing or person that needs the aid of this calming force. Maintain a steady drum beat and really feel the words and power of the rune flow through you.

We can also look to the verses of Sigdrífumál for some healing words, working with verses from written sources in our healing work. In Sigdrífumál, we have a reference for healing runes and what they should be carved on:

"Limrúnar skaltu kunna,	"Limb runes should you know
af þú vilt læknir vera,	If you will be a healer
ok kunna sár at sjá;	And know about wounds;
á berki skal þær rista	Carve them on the bark
ok á baðmi viðar,	And carve them on twigs
þeim er lúta austr limar."	Where the twigs are pointing to East."

The most useful verbal charm we can take from Sigdrífumál is the ending, which is used to close ceremonies but also can be worked to finalise our workings—especially those of healing—by announcing our thanks to the spirits and deities we may have invoked to work the healing.

"Heill dagur,	"Hail Dag,
heilir dags synir,	Hail Dag's sons,
heil nótt og nipt;	Hail Nat and Nipt!
óreiðum augum	Look down upon us
lítið okkur þinig	With benevolent eyes
og gefið sitjöndum sigur.	And give victory to
	the sitting.
Heilir æsir,	Hail Æsir,
heilar ásynjur,	Hail Asynjus,
heil sjá in fjölnýta fold,	Hail bounteous Earth!
mál og mannvit	Words and wisdom
gefið okkur mærum tveim	Give to us noble twain,
ok læknishendur,	And healing hands in life!"
meðan lifum."	

TWELVE APOSTLES HEALING CHARM

This working is my own UPG based around folk Catholic practices and a stave called the *Twelve Apostles* stave. The stave comes from the manuscript *Lbs 3902 4to,* and to the best of our knowledge, is designed to represent the Twelve Apostles. One method of working it that I have used is to call upon the Twelve Apostles using this stave as a healing charm. The stave itself can be written out on fresh parchment and may then be folded and placed within a hiellapyngja containing healing materia. The bag could be green or light blue cotton or even purple to bring in more Catholic associations of godliness and divine might. The prayers of the Twelve Apostles are then prayed over this charm; though there are twelve, this takes a surprisingly short time to complete. After this, the verbal part of the spell ends with "í Jesus nafni," as the Twelve Apostles only work miracles and healing via Jesus Christ within the Catholic faith. The charm is then given to the one who needs healing or placed inside their pillow or under their bed.

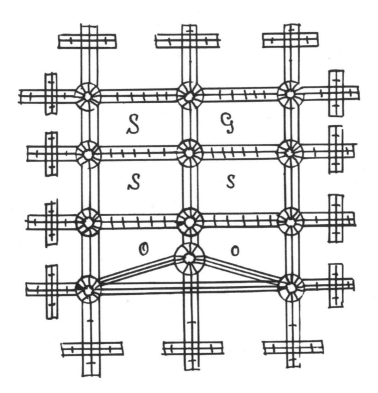

LÆKNINGA STAFUR

The following stave, from *Lbs 3902 4to*, is worked for healing. It can be carved into various woods and materia, but I recommend working it into the healing stick mentioned on page 128 or charm bags. Birch wood and bark would be the ideal wood to work this onto within Iceland, though there are many hundreds of other appropriate species elsewhere. In my experience, this stave has worked well with birki (*Betula nana*), vallhumall (*Achillea millefolium*), and maðjurt (*Filipendula ulmaria*). Outside of Iceland, oak (*Quercus robur*) and European white elm (*Ulmus laevis*) are two woods I recommend for this purpose.

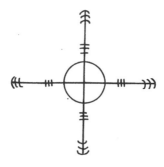

A CLEANSING PRAYER

This cleansing prayer comes from *ATA Ämb 2 F16:26*. As the prayer includes the phrase "cleansing oneself in the dew" in its opening line, I recommend working this while cleansing oneself in the morning dew of Jónsmessa. The prayer is long and hard to memorise, but invoking these words and powers alongside the regular ritual of rolling naked in the morning dew is potent.

"Þvæ ég mér í döggu og dælum, í brunabirtu þinni. Drottinn minn, set ég þitt blessuð bílæti millum augna mér, þvæ ég frá mér alla fjandmenn mína og þeirra formæli, þvæ ég frá mér rán og reiði ríkra manna. Holl sé mér veröld til vina og velgjörninga, hollt sé mér frón að fé og fengisemi, allt sé mér hollt sem ég þarf að gjöra, tala og hugsa. Þess bið ég þig, Drottinn dýrðarkóngur, að hver sá maður sem mig lítur á þessum degi renni til mín ástaraugum og verði mér svo feginn sem blessuð mey María varð sínum blessuðum elskulega syni þá hún fann hann við ána Jordan og þá hún fann hann í musterinu og hafði harmandi að honum leitað. Einnig bið ég þig, Drottinn drottanna og kóngur kónganna, að frá mér hverfi og frá mér

snúist öll ógæfa og ólukka, vondska og vélar allra þeirra er mig svíkja vilja
í orðum eða með orðum, í gjörðum, í göldrum eður með göldrum eða með
hverju móti þeir vilja mér fyrir koma. Heyrðu bæn mína, dýrlegi Drottinn
minn. Þér trúi ég og treysti ég til allra góðra hluta. Amen."

SÆRING GEGN IKTSÝKI: CHANT AGAINST ARTHRITIS

The following chant, collected by Ólafur Davíðsson in *Íslenzkar Þjóðsögur*, is used against rheumatoid arthritis (though, of course, a historical charm is no substitute for proper medical care). Chant this while moving your hands over the appropriate area of the body:

> *"Susannamm af logum lesti,*
> *Danielem af grauf olmra dyra*
> *Og þá sveina af ofni brennanda,*
> *David af synda sauri,*
> *Moyses af valldi heidinna þioda.*
> *Paulum af bondum,*
> *Enn Petrum af sio."*

BALANCING CHARM

This is my own UPG, created to bring about balance. I include it here as it may be used to empower medicine and herbs intended for balance, as well as used within a space to emanate calming and balanced energy. Use it as you see fit, as it can be worked in almost any way, even carved on wood, reddened, and left within a space.

31

BÖLVANIR: CURSES

Malefica makes up a great deal of many magical practices worldwide. (Imagine telling the wise woman of the village that cursing the corrupt landowner hoarding resources was evil and that she should accept her fate of starving over winter.) If we look at magic as "black and white," ignoring one side of the coin, we miss a wealth of knowledge and inspiration. After all, to make anti-venom, we first need the venom itself. What can harm may also heal, and vice versa.

The following staves can be used to binding or for smaller acts of hexing.

BÖLSKJÓÐA: CURSE BAG

Cursing bags are just as practical as healing heillapynjga. Though we call them a different name, the method is the same. Fill a small pouch with specifically selected and charged materia, then place it in an appropriate place. For curse work, this is usually the doorsteps, porches, or commonly walked paths of our enemies. Minor inconveniences and petty pains are easily cast when using bölskjóður.

Gather your malefic materia, and ideally, within the hour and day of Saturn, enchant this materia. I recommend doing this on the Satúrnus innsigli mentioned earlier. The following stave is from *Lbs 764 8vo*. Called *ónæðisstafur*, it is used to cause misfortune and nuisance. Work it into these bags. It can be either embroidered or drawn on the bag itself, or drawn on fresh parchment, reddened with blood, and then placed within.

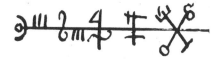

INSPIRING FEAR

One stave used specifically for inspiring fear is found in *ÍB 383 4to*, called *óttustafur*. I include a method for using this alongside plant materia in *Icelandic Plant Magic*, though we may also work this stave without the use of plants, drawing it onto the doorways or pathways of our enemies' property with chalk designed for malefica. Get creative with your methods with this one.

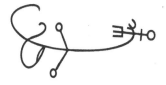

The sixteenth-century stave below is also worked to inspire fear. Carve it into wood and wear it at your breast when you stand before your enemy. I would suggest hiding it within a layer of clothing so as not to give away the reason for the aura of fear you are emanating towards your enemy.

HARMING WORDS

Spoken words and chants are one of the main ways we can utilise galdur or spoken magic to harm. Doing so out of protection is better than outright cursing any who cause you the slightest problem. Sometimes, it pays to think ahead when wording a curse or other form of malefic magic. Our feelings may change later, but some curses work like floodgates, unable to be shut until they have run their course. Personally, I would try to lean cursing more towards justice than vengeance. Wording it towards a fair and just outcome, unless otherwise required, is one way we can avoid falling victim to our own hubris, cutting off one's own nose to spite their face.

The following stave is my own creation, worked to bring one to justice. Create this stave within a Martial day and Mercurial hour, utilising the might of Martial virtues along with the swiftness of Mercury. It's best worked into a white or red candle. Once all is in place and the stave has been carved on the candle, redden it while speaking these words:

"Forseti, seat of justice,
I ask that you intercede,
Balance the scales,
Right what was wronged.
Tyr, vindicator,
Swift arm of justice,
Fall upon those whose names I speak.
(Insert name/names)
Óðinn, all father,
Hear my plea,
Right this wrong,
As your child, I ask this."

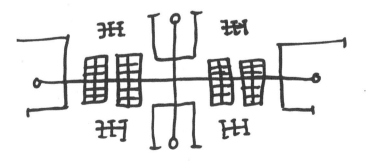

This prayer calls on Forseti, goddess of law and justice, as well as Tyr, the contemporary Norse warrior god of justice and retribution. From a purely animistic perspective, avoiding the use of deities, we could invoke Martial spirits, or simply spirits of óhreinn andi around us, asking them to be the ones to dispense justice. Personally, that method is a little too open-ended for me. Inviting random spirits to harm others is likely not going to lead to an ending either party desires, so the more specific you can be, the better. For other theistic options, we could call upon Óðinn as Bölverkur (curse worker) or Haptaguð (fettered one) for the binding and cursing of others like so:

"Bölverkur, ég ákalla þig,
Bind and curse (insert name),
That they may feel your
wrath and fury."

"Haptaguð, ég áklla þig,
Fetter them, constrict them,
That they may cease to move
against (me/us/name)."

BUSLA'S CURSE

Drawing inspiration from saga material, we could take the infamous curse of Busla and work it into our own curse work. The curse itself was cast upon King Hring, who was about to execute Busla's foster son Bósi the following morning. (The full curse, including the part binding the king so he is unable to rise from bed and wake his attendants for help, can be found within the poem.) She then finishes the curse with the following:

"Tröll og álfar,
Og töfranornir,
Búar og bergrisar
Brenni þínar hallir;
Hati þig hrímþursar,
Hestar steði þig,
Stráin stangi þig,
En stormar æri þig,
Og vei verði þér,
Nema þú vilja minn gerir."

"Trolls and elves
And sorceresses,
Goblins and giants
Shall burn your halls;
Frost-giants shall fright you,
And stallions ride you,
Straws shall sting you,
Storms drive you mad;
May you ever be damned,
Unless you do what I want."

The translation I've included is from Stephen A. Mitchell's *Witchcraft and Magic in the Nordic Middle Ages*. Note that this translation is more polite than the original text.

SATÚRNUS INNSIGLI

This contemporary seal of Saturn is my own UPG, tried and tested mainly with cursing and hexing materia. I recommend inscribing this onto a surface of wood, metal, or rock. Do so with either the binding chalk in the recipe section or by inking it into the surface and washing it once dry with Saturnine herbs within a Saturnine day and hour. This surface can then be utilised to empower all works of Saturnine virtue, as well as serve as an altar space from which to cast them.

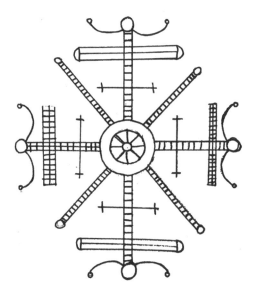

CURSING FOOD

This next piece of malefica comes from *ATA Ämb 2 F16:26*. This nasty curse uses rune staves carved into food (specifically fish and cheese) to curse one's enemy so they are unable to do anything more than vomit and spend the day uncomfortably going to and from the bathroom.

This particular working came with a remedy. It states that should the spell work longer than intended and one wishes to reverse it, then the victim must be fed warm milk mixed with albúmín. Albúmín was a word used from the 1600s to 1800s to mean many white substances (and now refers to a type of protein made by the liver). In *Galdra á Íslandi*, Sæmundsson states that, in this context, it likely means either dried whey powder or the dried membrane of egg white, two things that would have been much more likely found in rural Iceland.

MAKING A BÖLSKJÓÐA

As the malefic counterpart to a charm bag we discussed earlier, this sort of malefic work can be crafted and hidden on a person's property or home. Some curse work in Icelandic folk magic is hidden under the bed of enemies, some buried on their land, and some tied to their livestock. These are all methods we can use to employ our malefic work, whether it be to seriously curse or gently hex.

I suggest empowering all of the cursing materia one would use within the day and hour of Saturn and even using the Satúrnus innsigli as a station on which to charge it should one wish. The materia itself should also be gathered within a Saturnine time. Examples of the contents of these bags could include:

- Vensusvagn (*Aconitum napellus*) seeds and flowers.
- Holtasóley (*Dryas octopetula*) roots, leaves, and flowers.
- Graveyard dirt or the dirt from cursed or otherwise negatively influenced ground, or certain spots we would consider álagablettur (touched by some magic, often bad). Even areas of blighted ground work well for many curses.
- Ground bone.
- Ashes from previous malefic spellwork.
- Brennistein (sulphur).
- Lúpina (*Lupinus nootkatensis*) seeds and dried petals.
- Other Saturnine plants and materia worked to harm, hex, bind, and banish.

An example of a useful powder to place within a bölskjóða is the binding powder, found in *Icelandic Plant Magic*.

FOR CREATING BAD WEATHER AT SEA

This stave comes from the collection *Lbs 3902 4to*, and it is worked to create bad weather at sea. This sort of work is not done lightly, as, like the níðstöng, it is designed to stir up and aggravate the spirits of the sea.

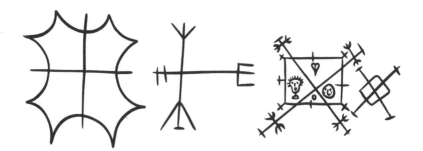

32

MAGICAL ALPHABETS

These magical alphabets can be worked with the stave creation method on page 199. They are all from various manuscripts, and some have further connotations such as names and maybe even specific uses. At the time of this writing, manuscripts containing all of these alphabets are available to read on the website *handrit.is*. Runic alphabets from Denmark, and Norway, as well as the Elder Futhark, are also included below.

DANISH AND NORWEGIAN

DANISH FUTHARK	NORWEGIAN FUTHARK

ᚠ	ᚢ	ᚦ	ᚨ	ᚱ	ᚴ		ᚠ	ᚢ	ᚦ	ᚨ	ᚱ	ᚴ
f	u	þ	a	r	k		f	u	þ	a	r	k

ᚼ	ᚾ	ᛁ	ᛆ	ᛌ		ᚼ	ᚻ	ᛁ	ᛆ	ᛕ
h	n	i	A	s		h	n	i	A	s

ᛏ	ᛒ	ᛘ	ᛚ	ᛦ		ᛐ	ᛒ	ᛘ	ᛚ	ᛦ
t	b	m	l	R/y		t	b	m	l	R/y

€LD€R FUTHARK

ᚠ	ᚢ	ᚦ	ᚨ	ᚱ	ᚲ	ᚷ	ᚹ
f	u	þ	a	r	k	g	w

ᚺ	ᚾ	ᛁ	ᛃ	ᛈ	ᛇ	ᛉ	ᛊ
h	n	i	j	p	E	R	s

ᛏ	ᛒ	ᛖ	ᛗ	ᛚ	ᛜ	ᛞ	ᛟ
t	b	e	m	l	ng	d	o

These next few alphabets are found within *Lbs 3902 4to*. The first two are known as Völvurúnir (Völva's or witches' runes), the second as Haugbúarúnir (the runes of the mound dwellers), and the last are known as svörturúnir (black runes). These are the alphabets I work with most out of the long list found in *Lbs 3902 4to*.

VÖLVURÚNIR

A	B	C	D	E	F	G	H	I/J	K	L	M

N	O	P	Q	R	S	T	U/V	W	Þ	Æ	Ö

A	B	C	D	E	F	G	H	I/J	K	L	M

N	O	P	R	S	T	U/V	Þ	Æ	Ö

HAUGBÚARÚNIR

A	B	C	D	E	F	G	H	I/J	K	L	M	N	O

P	Q	R	S	T	U	V	X	Y	Z	Þ	Æ	Ö

SVÖRTURÚNIR

A	B	C	D	E	F	G	H	I/J	K

L	M	N	O	P	R	S	T	Þ	Æ

A	B	C	D	E	F	G	H	I/J	K

L	M	N	O	P	R	S	T	U/V	Þ

33

INCENSE, OILS, BREWS, AND BLENDS

Within this chapter, I include a few blends found in *Icelandic Plant Magic*. Readers should know that many more recipes can be found in that book, as it deals more with herbal materia than this text. For some blends I chose to include in this text, I have given suggestions for plants that aren't native to Iceland that would be appropriate to include.

PLANETARY OIL AND INCENSE BLENDS

The following recipes can be worked as both oil and incense blends. Oil blends are usually worked to anoint candles or yourself before spells and rituals that require certain planetary virtues. Please be cautious when anointing yourself with oils. Some herbs are toxic or cause skin irritations, and allergic reactions may occur. Research what plants are safe to use on the body, avoid broken or sensitive skin areas, test reactions on small patches of skin, and do not consume any of these mixes. Keep oil mixes away from your eyes and nose and out of reach of children and pets.

When anointing candles, I use candles that match planetary colours. These blends can also be used to anoint any planetary innsigli. When working them as incense, burn the most appropriate blend for the work you're doing.

SOLAR BLEND

- 4 parts dandelion or hawkbit petals
- 1 part juniper berries, crushed
- 1 part rowan berries, crushed
- 1 part eyebright flower heads, dried
- 1 part Scot's lovage leaves or flowers (*do not use this in oil blends intended to anoint skin*)
- 1 part yellow rattle flowers, dried

Other herbs and plants that are not native to Iceland that I have had success working into Solar blends include sunflower, goldenseal, chamomile, frankincense, rosemary, and rue (*not for use on skin*).

LUNAR BLEND

- 2 parts bogbean flowers, dried
- 2 parts moonwort leaves and stalk, dried
- 2 parts sweet cicely flower heads
- 1 part marsh cinquefoil leaves and flowers, dried
- 1 part chickweed leaves
- 1 part forget-me-not flowers, dried
- 1 part fairy flax flowers, dried
- 1 part poppy seeds
- 1 part Iceland purslane leaves
- 1 part willow leaves, dried

Other Lunar herbs I have worked with for Icelandic staves and folk magic include mugwort, lemon balm, wormwood, and marshmallow.

MERCURIAL BLEND

- 2 parts bartsia flower heads, dried
- 2 parts clover leaves, dried
- 2 parts cinquefoil, any part of the whole plant, dried
- 2 parts caraway seeds or flowers
- 1 part cornel berries, dried

- 1 part valerian root, dried
- 1 part harebell flowers, dried
- 1 part grass of Parnassus flowers, dried

Non-Icelandic Mercurial herbs I've had good success in working with in this way include bittersweet, dill, southernwood, lavender, fennel, lemon verbena, lemon grass, aspen, and mint.

VENUSIAN BLEND

- 2 parts angelica root
- 2 parts bilberry leaves or berries
- 2 parts Arctic thyme leaves and flowers
- 1 part birch leaves
- 1 part chickweed leaves
- 1 part crane's bill flowers
- 1 part fleabane flowers
- 1 part heather flowers and leaves
- 1 part lady's mantle leaves
- 1 part yarrow flowers
- 1 part water avens flowers and leaves

Non-Icelandic plants I have had good success working into Venusian oils include nightshades, hollyhock, thyme, feverfew, geranium, pansy, primrose, raspberries, and daffodils (*do not use nightshades or hollyhock on the skin*).

MARTIAL BLEND

- 2 parts bearberry berries or leaves
- 2 parts gentian flowerheads and leaves
- 2 parts pine needles
- 1 part thistle spines
- 1 part couch grass
- 1 part sundew

Martial plants from outside of Iceland I've had good results from include other thistle species, teasels, rose thorns, hops, dragon's blood, cinnamon, snapdragons, and peppers.

JOVIAL BLEND

- 2 parts lupin flowers
- 2 parts meadowsweet flowers
- 2 parts cinquefoil flowers
- 1 part Arctic thyme
- 1 part couch grass
- 1 part dock leaf
- 1 part fireweed flowers (*do not apply to skin*)
- 1 part Sitka spruce needles

Jovial herbs I work with that aren't native to Iceland include linden, hyssop, agrimony (*avoid skin contact*), and borage.

SATURNINE BLEND

- 2 parts black cottonwood leaves or buds
- 2 parts bartsia
- 1 part Scottish asphodel
- 1 part bearberry leaves
- 1 part bistort leaves
- 1 part crowberry leaves or berries
- 1 part cornel leaves or berries
- 1 part harebell flowers
- 1 part knotgrass

Toxic saturnine plants that aren't native to Iceland that I grow and work into these oil blends include Daturas, other nightshades, ivy, yew, Solomon's seal, cypress, and elm. Wear gloves and never apply topically if you include any of these toxic materials.

GREEN OINTMENT

As mentioned earlier on page 34, this green ointment is based on the folk story of the midwife who helped an elf woman give birth. It is a potent salve that aids in útiseta, spirit flight, and general communication. I recommend working this blend in olive or almond oil as a base. It is traditionally worked by anointing the eyelids, palms, wrists, and temples, though, in practice, please avoid getting any in or around your eyes.

The blend includes the following:

- Engjarós (*Comarum palustre*)
- Bláklukka (*Campanula rotundiflora*)
- Hóffífill (*Tussilago farfara*)
- Gullmura (*Potentilla crantzii*)
- Blóðberg (*Thymus praecox*)
- Hvönn (*Angelica archangelica*)
- Sortulyng (*Arctostaphylos uva-ursi*)
- Alaskaösp (*Populus trichocarpa*)

Take a good handful of each of the herbs on this list and infuse them in your chosen carrier oil for a few hours. Strain the oil, then combine it with beeswax, melt the two together, and then allow it to cool in small tins. These tins could even be inscribed with my personal stave for spirit flight, mentioned in Chapter Ten.

Within my other work, *Icelandic Plant Magic,* readers will find a chapter about the plants we associate with specific deities, as well as blends of incense, oils, and more relating to these beings. The blessed chalk recipe found on page 235 is a perfect way to blend plant and animal materia into a potent magical tool.

◊ APPENDICES ◊
AND GLOSSARIES

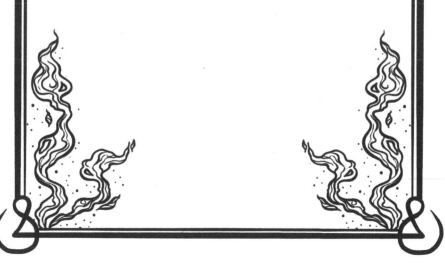

Prayers and Words

Prayers

Bæn til Heilags Þorláks
(Prayer to Saint Þorlákur)

"Almáttugi, eilífi Guð, þú gerðir heilagan Þorlák að biskupi og leiðtoga fólks þíns.

Megi fyrirbænir hans stuðla að fyrirgefningu þinni og kærleika okkar til handa.

Lát heilagur Þorlák vera fordæmi okkar og að við mættum boða það sem hann trúði á og sýna það í verki.

Við biðjum þess í nafni Drottins okkar Jesú Krists."

"All-powerful, ever-living God, you made Saint Thorlak bishop and leader of your people.

May his prayers help us to bring forgiveness and love.

May we be inspired by the example of St. Thorlak and proclaim what he believed and put his teaching into action.

We ask this in the name of Jesus our Lord."

SANKTI PÉTUR (SAINT PETER) PRAYER

"Sankti Pétur 'for á fjalli,
Flutti með sér grautardall,
Settist niður og át úr allt,
Þá var Pétri orðið kalt,
Sté hann kalt
Og sté kalt.
Sankti Pétur reri fast,
Þá daginn tók að dvína;
Hann gekk upp á hauðrið fljótt
Og þaðan upp á háan klett
Og barði upp vettlingana sína."

FAÐIR VOR

"Faðir vor, þú sem ert á himnum.
Helgist þitt nafn, til komi þitt ríki,
verði þinn vilji, svo á jörðu sem á himni.
Gef oss í dag vort daglegt brauð.
og Fyrirgef oss vorar skuldir,
svo sem vér og fyrirgefum
vorum skuldunautum.
eigi leið þú oss í freistni,
heldur frelsa oss frá illu.
(Því að þitt er ríkið, mátturinn og dýrðin að eilífu.)
Amen."

SALVE REGINA (ICELANDIC)

"Heil sért þú, drottning,
móðir miskunnarinnar,
lífs yndi og von vor, heil sért þú.
Til þín hrópum vér, útlæg börn Evu.
Til þín andvörpum vér,
stynjandi og grátandi í þessum táradal.

Talsmaður vor,
lít þú miskunnarríkum augum þínum til vor
og sýn þú oss,
eftir þennan útlegðartíma, Jesú,
hinn blessaða ávöxt lífs þíns,
milda, ástríka og ljúfa María mey.
Bið þú fyrir oss, heilaga Guðsmóðir.
Svo að vér verðum makleg fyrirheita Krists.
Amen."

PATER NOSTER

"Pater noster,
Qui es in caelis,
Sanctificetur nomen tuum.
Adveniat rgenum tuum.
Fiat voluntas tua,
Sicut in caelo et in terra.
Panem nostrum quotidianum
Da nobis hodie,
Et dimitte nobis debita nostra
sicut et nos dimittimus
Debitoribus nostris.
Et ne nos inducas in tentationem,
Sed libera nos a malo.
Amen."

AVE MARIA

"Ave Maria, gratia plena, Dominus tecum.
Benedicta tu in mulieribus,
et benedictus fructus ventris tui, Iesus.
Sancta Maria, Mater Dei,
ora pro nobis peccatoribus, nunc,
et in hora mortis nostrae.
Amen."

SÁLMARNIR: PSALMS

PSALM 4 AGAINST BAD LUCK

6   *Færið réttar fórnir og treystið Drottni.*

7   *Margir segja: "Hver lætur oss hamingju líta?" Lyft yfir oss ljósi auglitis þíns, Drottinn.*

8   *Þú hefir veitt hjarta mínu meiri gleði en menn hafa af gnægð korns og vínlagar.*

PSALM 91 FOR EXORCISM AND PROTECTION FROM EVIL SPIRITS

3   *Hann frelsar þig úr snöru fuglarans, frá drepsótt glötunarinnar,*

4   *hann skýlir þér með fjöðrum sínum, undir vængjum hans mátt þú hælis leita, trúfesti hans er skjöldur og verja.*

5   *Eigi þarft þú að óttast ógnir næturinnar, eða örina, sem flýgur um daga,*

6   *drepsóttina, er reikar um í dimmunni, eða sýkina, er geisar um hádegið.*

7   *Þótt þúsund falli þér við hlið og tíu þúsund þér til hægri handar, þá nær það ekki til þín.*

8   *Þú horfir aðeins á með augunum, sér hversu óguðlegum er endurgoldið.*

9   *Þitt hæli er Drottinn, þú hefir gjört Hinn hæsta að athvarfi þínu.*

10   *Engin ógæfa hendir þig, og engin plága nálgast tjald þitt.*

PSALM 3 FOR HEADACHES AND BACKACHES

5   *Þá er ég hrópa til Drottins, svarar hann mér frá fjallinu sínu helga. [Sela]*

6   *Ég leggst til hvíldar og sofna, ég vakna aftur, því að Drottinn hjálpar mér.*

7   *Ég óttast eigi hinn óteljandi manngrúa, er fylkir sér gegn mér á allar hliðar.*

PSALM 67 FOR SEVERE FEVER OR IMPRISONMENT

2 *Guð sé oss náðugur og blessi oss, hann láti ásjónu sína lýsa meðal vor, [Sela]*

3 *svo að þekkja megi veg þinn á jörðunni og hjálpræði þitt meðal allra þjóða.*

4 *Lýðirnir skulu lofa þig, ó Guð, þig skulu gjörvallir lýðir lofa.*

5 *Gleðjast og fagna skulu þjóðirnar, því að þú dæmir lýðina réttvíslega og leiðir þjóðirnar á jörðunni.*

6 *Lýðirnir skulu lofa þig, ó Guð, þig skulu gjörvallir lýðir lofa.*

7 *Jörðin hefir gefið ávöxt sinn, Guð, vor Guð, blessar oss.*

8 *Guð blessi oss, svo að öll endimörk jarðar megi óttast hann.*

HALLOWING THE VÉ

In Ásatrú and heathen practices, the sacred space one creates is called the vé. While this is a heathen practice, we utilise either this sort of sacred space or the more traditional magic circle for many workings. The vé should be set up with three sticks or posts, forming a triangle. Each post must then be hallowed with an offering, such as burning tobacco or pouring a little brennivín as you walk around the space. While you do this, you may also call upon the gods to hallow it. For example, you could ask Þór for protection, Freyr for abundance, Freyja for protection, Óðinn for knowledge, or Frigg for peace.

A simple example of this would be to approach each post. Pour or blow your offering of smoke or liquid, then say:

"I call on Óðinn, hallow this vé, protect this space from unclean spirits,
Fill it with your knowledge and wisdom.
I call on Þór, hallow this vé, protect this space from the forces of chaos,
Fill it with your strength and might.
I call on Freyja, hallow this vé, protect it from ill will,
Fill it with your might and magic.
I call on you Freyr, protect this space from rot and decay,
Fill it with your life and abundance.
I call on you Frigg, protect this space from discord,
Fill it with your peace and care."

ADDRESSING THE DWARVES

As mentioned, the spirits of the land must first be addressed before we perform any work in their space. We call upon the four cardinal directions, the four dwarves that hold up the sky—Austri, Vestri, Suðri, and Norðri—asking them to allow our work and offer us protection. We chant the following once we have set up our simple working space, keeping in mind that we may need to disassemble it should the spirits wish us to. We chant this and repeat algir two or three times before repeating, feeling out what the spirits say. If all is well, we can continue with our work.

> *"Kom Austri,*
> *Kom Vestri,*
> *Kom Suðri,*
> *Kom Norðri,*
> *Algir, algir."*

BLOOD-STEMMING CHANT

This blood-stopping chant was collected in Jón Árnason's *Þjóðsögur og Ævfintýri* and is to be used in conjunction with a blood-stemming stone, or, in contemporary practice, a white healing stone and some yarrow oil.

> *"Stemmist blóð þeim blæðir,*
> *Blóð féll af guðs róðu;*
> *Almáttugum bauð ótta,*
> *Af undum sárlega píndist;*
> *Stattu í dýrð svo dreyri,*
> *En það guðsson heyri;*
> *Önd og blóðugar æðar*
> *Er sá (sú) sæll (sæl)sem leysist.*
> *Stemmist blóð, blæði hverki út né inn."*

End this with the Latin *"Filium spiritum domino pater."*
This Latin blood-stemming chant comes from *ATA Ämb 2 F16:26,* preserved in the State Historical Museum of Stockholm. This galdrabók is

the best example of a sixteenth-century Icelandic grimoire. The following verse should be read three times, with one *Pater Noster* between each verse:

> *"Sangvis maneat in te,*
> *Sic ut fecit Christus in se,*
> *Sangvis maneat in tua vena,*
> *Sicut fecit Christus in Sua pena,*
> *Sangvis maneat fixus,*
> *Sicut quando Christus fuit Crussifixius.*
> *Pater Noster."*

A further bit of magic from the same manuscript tells us that to stop a nosebleed, one should write *"Consummatum est"* in noseblood on one's own forehead. However, this seems far less practical than the tried and tested blood-stemming chants.

Appendix II

Names of Power

Names of the Gods

Many of the Norse gods, as well as other figures in contemporary folklore, are referred to by more than one name or title. For example, Óðinn has many names, and we can look to Norse mythology for many of them. The way we refer to Óðinn depends on the kind of magic you are trying to work.

Óðinn, when called on for workings of necromancy, should be addressed as Hangagúð, Hangatýr, Valtýr, and Valföður. For workings of acquiring knowledge, call him Síðhattur, Þekkur, and Svíðar. And for workings of victory, refer to him as Sigtýr, Sigþór, and Sigtryggur.

Freyja is also known as the Great Lady, Gefn, Hörn, Mardöll, Sýr, and Valfrejya. She can also be called Álfadrotting, as, alongside Mary and the assimilated Maríu-Freyja, she is the queen of the elves. Drotting is also suitable as she is a queen.

Freyr, Freyja's brother, is known by name as Yngvi. This is unique in that we know his personal name beyond simply *Freyr* (meaning "lord"). He could be called *Drottinn*, as he is a lord and king. This is often the title given to the Christian God also. He is also called *Árguð* (god of harvest), *Ballriði* (bold rider), *Folkvaldi goða* in Skírnismál (meaning "foremost of the gods"), *Svía Goð* (god of the Svía, ancestors of modern

Swedes), and *Veraldargoð* ("god of the world," and maybe "protector of the world," a role I argue is equal to Þór's role as protector of the people).

Þór has many names, including Ása-Þór, as Þór of the Æsir, to distinguish him from others who share this name. He is also called *Einriði* (lone rider) and *Harðhugaður,* meaning "brave soul" and "strong spirit"; literally *harð* (strong) of *hugur* (will). Véurr is a name we could associate with his sacredness at human shrines and a name that is perhaps used to call upon him within a more sacred context than his general aspect as the defender of humanity.

The devil has many names in Iceland. Andskoti, Kölski, Freistari (the tempter), Myrkahöfðingi (the dark lord), Djöfull (devil), Fjandi, Djöfsi, Skratti, and many more. All of these names can be worked into bölvanir, hexes, and work involving the man in black figure.

GLOSSARY

A

Andar: Plural spirits, a general term.

Andasæring: Necromancy. Divination involving the dead. Literally meaning spirit conjuring and banishing.

Andi: Singular spirit. The word for the concept of spirit, as well as any spiritual being or entity.

Andskoti: One name for the devil, a curse word.

Athöfn: Rituals, magical workings, and more formal spell-work.

Á

Ákalla: To invoke, to call on.

Álög: A general term for magic, enchantment, and hexing. See *Galdur*.

Ársgangur: The year walk. A tradition hailing from Sweden but utilised in Iceland in slightly different ways.

Árshringur: The Wheel of the Year. The yearly cycle of seasonal festivals.

Ásatrú: The Pagan faith in Iceland, following the Norse pantheon and its reconstructed religion.

Ásatrúarfélagið: The Norse Pagan religious organisation of Iceland.

ᛒ

Bannfæring: Banishing, all works of removal, curses, and malefica.

Bikar: A chalice or goblet.

Blæti: A fetish, created from many things. However, if specifically a root, the *Rótblæti* is most appropriate.

Blót: A ceremony within many heathen and Ásatrú practices honoring the Norse gods, *landvættir,* and other spirits.

Brúða: Poppet, idol, doll.

Bænir: Prayers, singular *bæn.*

Bölvun: A curse. Plural *bölvanir.*

Bölskjóða: A cursing bag.

ᛞ

Dísir: Singular *Dís.* In pre-Christian times, *dísir* appear as female-presenting spirits of nature. They sometimes appear as omens of death, and it is said that to lose one's *dísir* means death will surely follow. Within a modern context, they are seen more as ancestral spirits, though they are mostly considered protective spirits of families. *Dís* may also be higher spirits, such as *Vanadís* (nature goddesses, for lack of a better word). *Dísir* are often tied to fate and have a connection to the *Valkyrjur.*

Draugur: Within a modern context, an apparition, sending, or ghost seen or sent by practitioners. However, within sagas and older stories, this word specifically referred to the very physical raised dead sent by angered magicians, capable of killing and very much feared.

Draum: Dream.

Draumagaldur: Dream magic.

Draumstoli: To have one's dreams, or ability to dream, stolen.

Draumvitjanir: Dream visits. Visitation by spirits and beings in dreams.

Dúkka: See *Brúða.*

Dvergar: Dwarves. Less Tolkien, more somewhat creepy underground spirits.

ᛖ

Efling: To empower or strengthen.

f

Fjölkynngi: While the term is less often used with all the typical taboos of a Christian society, the word means "knower of many things" or someone wise in many arts.

Foss: Waterfall.

Fossvættir: Waterfall spirits. Singular *fossvættur.*

Freyja: The Norse goddess of magic, war, fertility, and love, often associated with traditionally feminine traits.

Freyr: The Norse god of fertility and warriors, often associated with traditionally masculine traits.

Frigg: The Norse goddess of marriage and the home.

Fylgja: Often referred to as *the fetch* from a Traditional Witchcraft perspective. In this context, we see the *fylgja* as the "lower" or animal aspect of the spirit, as well as being the name used for other guiding spirits detached from humans. There can be big overlaps with familiar spirits. As well as being an aspect of yourself, a *flygjur* can be gifted, created, or formed on its own, separate from a soul. Your own *fylgja* spirit is also sometimes referred to as a *doppelganger;* this appears to others in your image. In pre-Christian times, the *fylgja* took an animal form, but they turned human because having an association with animals in Christian doctrine was thought of as "dirty."

G

Galdrabók: Grimoire, literally magic book.

Galdrahnífur: The knife used in your magic and rituals. Not exclusively for plants, as many use one knife for all purposes.

Galdrakerti: A magically prepared spell candle.

Galdramaður/kona/kvár: A male, female, or non-binary practitioner of magic.

Galdramenn: Wizards.

Galdranisti/Galdragripur: See *Máttargripur.*

Galdraolíublöndur: Magical oil blends.

Galdur: Spell, incantation. More often, specifically vocal magic. All spoken charms and sung words. However, in a more general sense, *galdur* is the ordered and conscious magic of the world. The other side of the coin of what we know as *seiður*.

Gandur/Gandr: A further distinction of some magic that we usually put under the umbrella of seiður.

Glersýn: Scrying on a clear surface. This can be on water, with fire, or on reflective rocks and mirrors.

Grasahnífur: The plant harvesting knife. See *Jurtahnífur*.

Gói: A personification of the month of *Góa*, wife to the spirit Þorri.

Goð: The gods, Norse deities.

H

Hamfari: Shapeshifting; going forth in another form, either spiritual or physical.

Hamhleypa: Shapeshifter. Old Icelandic word for someone who shapeshifts. See *hamskiptingur*.

Hamskiptingur: Modern Icelandic word for a shapeshifter.

Hamstoli: To have one's form or guise stolen or otherwise blocked.

Heillapyngja: A charm bag or pouch.

Helgidagar: Special days, holy days.

Helguð kerti: See *Galdrakerti*. This word is more often reserved for the candle made at Christmas to be burned on Kyndilmessa. Lit. Holy Candle.

Hrafntinna: Obsidian. A volcanic rock occurring naturally in many parts of Iceland.

I

Innrennsli: Infusion.

Innsigli: A seal or sigil, insignia, or mark of something.

Ilmkjarnaolíur: Essential oils.

J

Jónsmessa: The feast day of St. John, the Christianized summer solstice.

Jónsmessunótt: The night before the feast of St. John, a magical night reserved for foraging and rolling naked in the morning dew.

Jötnar: The "giants" of Nordic mythology. Not actually giant in stature, these were a different race of beings from the *Æsir, Vanir,* and *Álfar.* Mentioned in Old Norse material to be "human size" or the same size as the gods.

Jurtablanda: Herb blend.

Jurtahnífur: Like the Neo-Pagan *Boline,* a knife dedicated to the harvesting and preparation of herbs.

K

Kuti: See *galdrahnífur.*

Kerti: Candle.

Kertaspá: Divination using candles. Scrying by fire like this is also called *Eldaspá.*

Kveldríða: Evening rider. See *náttríða.*

Kyndilmessa: Candlemas, February 2. A holy day celebrated in Iceland.

Kyngiveður: Magically influenced or produced weather. Also called *galdraveður* or *görningveður.*

Kölski: The devil.

l

Landvættir: An umbrella term for many spirits, including *genius loci* (spirits of the land) and four cardinal directions within Iceland: South/*Suður,* North/*Norður,* West/*Vestri,* and East/*Austri.*

Læknisfingur: The ring finger on either hand. The leech finger, used for healing and blessing.

M

Máttargripur: A magical talisman, amulet, or object. Can be made of any material.

Megingaskja: A "power box," a spirit home or box designed for magically potent materia, usually for preservation.

Meðal: Medicine. More specifically used in this book to refer to a medicinal potion or magically prepared infusion, philtre, and so on.

Merki: See *Tákn.*

N

Nafnavitjun: Dream visitations where an expectant mother is met by a figure who gives them the name of their future child. Likely Irish/Gaelic in origin.

Norn: Our most frequently us1ed term for a witch.

Náttríða: Night rider, someone who flies by night in spirit form.

O

Olíublanda: Oil blend. Can be either magical or mundane.

Óðinn: The chief God of the Norse pantheon, at least in Snorri's *Edda.* He has many names, guises, and aspects.

Ó

Óhreinn andi: Unclean spirits.

Þ

Pottur: A pot or cauldron, sometimes also called *ketill.*

R

Rauðskinna: An infamous (most likely mythical) grimoire, said to be given by the devil and bound in human skin.

Reykelsi: Incense, suffumigation.

S

Sálarflug: Soul flight, spirit flight. Also known in more New Age contexts as astral projection.

Seyði: To brew, bubble, boil, conjure or create.

Seiðberi: Someone who bears or carries *seiður.* A nice neutral word for someone who practices or carries traditions of *seiður.*

Seiður: Magic and sorcery, too complex to fit into a glossary. In its broadest sense, unconscious and chaotic forms of magic which are hard to quantify and must often be experienced to be understood.

Seiðkonu/karl/kvár: Someone either female, male, or non-binary who practices *seiður.*

Sjónhverfing: Illusions, literally "sight turning."

Skotta: A type of spirit said to haunt and follow victims, able to kill their victims in some cases.

Skuggi: Shadow or shade. Used mostly to describe apparitions of a shadowy or shapeless nature.

Skyggni: The ability to see spirits—mostly those of the dead—apparitions and such.

Smyrsli: Ointment.

Sópur: The broomstick.

Sproti: In a modern context, a magic wand like those worked in Neo-Pagan practices. See *vöndur.*

Spákona/karl/kvár: A seer, diviner. The feminine, masculine, and non-binary terms for this.

Spásögn: General divination. Specific Icelandic names for types of divination are few and far between in the folklore, but we have come up with plenty of new words for them.

Særingamaður/konu/kvár: Spirit commander. Within this context, one who commands and often banishes the spirits.

T

Tákn: A magical symbol, sigil, or marking.

Te: Tea, infusion.

Tinktúrur: Tinctures.

Tröll: Trolls. Both spirits and people can be referred to as trolls. Humans can become trollish in life and after.

Trölljurtir: Troll plants. They should not be disrespected.

Töfra: Magic, enchantment.

Töframaður: Magician, used more in modern times for stage magicians.

U

Urðarmáni: A glowing orb appearing before some natural disaster. In some literature, it is incorrectly conflated with comets preceding some important event.

Ú

Útburðir: The ghost or apparition of an unbaptized or miscarried child. Said to crawl on its elbows and knees, following the mother. One of the more terrifying spirits of Icelandic folklore.

Úburðir: The ghosts of children left outside to die in winter.

Útiseta: the "out-sitting" ritual, a simple rite of sitting out at night with the land spirits. Often in somewhat trancelike states induced by staying seated for long periods of time, as well as other methods. This is one common way we communicate with the spirits in many Northern traditions.

V

Vanir: Nature gods. Freyja and Freyr are two notable *Vanir*. A different race from the *Æsir* and *Jötnar*.

Varnagaldur: Protective magic.

Varnastafir: Emblems, protective staves.

Vaxaspá: Divination using wax, also known as *ceromancy*.

Vindhnífur: A wind knife, a specific tool worked to cut the wind.

Vitki: Most often male practioner. Not a word used all that much in Icelandic tradition.

Vofa: A specter or apparition which takes a human shape.

Völva: A word for a witch, although, within our living tradition, this word signifies an entire role one plays to the community, like the Native American shamans' role. A difficult term to summarise. One does not often become a *völva*. They may well be born with latent magical skills, which can pass down through families, though this alone is not enough, as one needs to be taught skills and deemed worthy of reaching this level and role. As such, within both old and modern contexts, this mostly happens within families and is not something that an "outsider" of the community would be selected for. *Norn* is the more appropriate term for "witch" within Icelandic folk practice.

Vöndur: Wand, short staff, or energy directing implement. Whether this takes the traditional wand form or not is up to the practitioner. See *sproti*.

Vættir: Spirits, wights. *Vættur* is the singular; a land wight is a *landvættur*.

Ý

Ýlir: One of the winter months of the old calendar.

ᛅ

Ævfintýri: Adventures. Within the context of *Þjóðsögur og Ævfintýri,* it refers to folklore and legends.

ᚦ

Þjóðsögur: Folk stories, folktales.
Þjóðtrú: Folk religion, folklore.
Þór: The Norse god Thor.
Þorri: A winter spirit, often personified as a misanthropic old man and the name of the winter month that overlaps December and January.

Ö

Örlög: Fate, destiny, the weave of life and death.

ICELANDIC PRONUNCIATION

Á, á: Pronounced as the "ow" in *cow* and *how*.

Ð, ð: Pronounced as a breathy "th" as in *breath*, with an "e" sound before.

E, e: Pronounced as the "ai" in *air*. Close to the now-common reaction sound "meh," just with no "m" sound.

É, é: Pronounced as if saying "yeah" quickly but with a short "e" sound before it.

F, f: Pronounced as the English "f" when at the start of a word. If it appears before an "I" or a "b," the sound becomes a breathy "p."

G, g: If at the start of a word, it is the same as the English "g." If later, it becomes a soft "g" that is almost the same as the "j" sound in Icelandic.

I, i: Pronounced as the "i" in *sin* and *bin*.

Í, í: Pronounced as an "ee" sound, such as the double "e" in *seen*.

J, j: Pronounced as a "y" most often. Though, if it comes after the letter "y," it is aspirated.

O, o: Pronounced as the "o" in *not* or *lot*.

Ó, ó: Pronounced as a long "o" as in the sound one makes when realising something: "ooh!"

R, r: In Icelandic, the "r" is always rolled. The thicker the accent, the harsher the rolled "r."

S, s: Is always pronounced as an "s" and never as the American "z"; think the British "organi(s)ed" and never "organi(z)ed."

U, u: Pronounced as the beginning of "ooh-la-la." As the "ou" in you but stretched.

Ú, ú: Pronounced as the "ew" in new, yew, and the "u" in *true, blue.*

Y, y: Pronounced the same as the "i."

Ý, ý: Pronounced the same as the "í."

Þ, þ: This letter, called þorn, is where we get the harsh "th" sound in thing or thirst. It is pronounced like the hard "th" in English.

Æ, æ: Pronounced as "eye" as in the "ie" in *tie,* or the "igh" in *sigh.*

Ö, ö: Ö is a tough sound to find in English. It is close to the "ur" of the word *murder,* though more so if said in a Scottish accent. The closest thing I can find that is similar is the way a child will express disgust at something in a dramatic fashion. The harsh "eugh!" of distaste.

Hv: An "h" followed by a "v" sounds closer to a "kf," like the "kf" in thankful. "Hvalur," the Icelandic word for "whale," is pronounced more like "kval-ur."

Hn: The "h" is breathed, and the "n" is nasal. Like you're pushing the "n" out of your nose in a very short, fast exhale. "Hnifur" is pronounced as "h-n-eevur."

Ll: The double "l" in Icelandic is very similar to the double "l" in Welsh. To make this sound, you need to place the tip of your tongue behind your top row of teeth and push air out from both sides of the mouth around the tongue. A good idea would be to Google the pronunciation of the word "Eyjafjallajökull" for many examples of these hard letters.

Au: This is another harder sound to master. Once you can make the "ö" sound, just pronounce "au" as if it is written "öj."

Ei: Pronounced as "ey." "Bacon" in Icelandic is an example of an "Icelandified" English loan word. "Bacon" becomes "Beicon," and these are pronounced the same.

Bibliography

"A Seeress from Fyrkat?". *National Museum of Denmark.*

Agrippa von Nettesheim, Heinrich Cornelius, et al. *The Philosophy of Natural Magic.* L. W. de Laurence, Scott & Company, 1913.

_. *Three Books of Occult Philosophy.* Inner Traditions International, 2021

AM 247 8vo. Copenhagen, 1790-1810.

AM 343a 12mo. Landsbókasafn Íslands Records, Copenhagen, c. 1200.

AM 434a 12mo. Landsbókasafn Íslands Records, Copenhagen, c. 1500.

AM 434d 12mo. Landsbókasafn Íslands Records, Copenhagen, c. 1600.

AM 673a II 4to. Landsbókasafn Íslands Records, Copenhagen, c. 1500.

Árnason, Jón. *Íslenskar Þjóðsögur Og Ævfintýri.* 1862.

Árnason, Jón, et al. *Tröllin Í Fjöllunum: 35 Sögur Úr Safni Jóns Árnasonar.* JPV Útgáfa, 2016.

ATA Ämb. 2, F 16:26. Stockholm, c. 1400-1600.

Bjarnadóttir, Ólöf. "A New Kind of Feminine: The Effects of the Icelandic Conversion on Female Religious Participation and the Image of the Feminine." *University of Iceland,* 2017.

Davidsson, Olafur. "Isländische Zauberzeichen und Zauberbücher." *Magazine of the Association for Ethnology,* 1903, pp. 150–167.

Daviðsson, Ólafur, et al. *Íslenzkar Þjóðsögur.* Vol. 2, Bókaútg. Þjóðsaga, 1978.

Davies, Owen. *Grimoires: A History of Magic Books.* Oxford University Press, 2010.

Davidz, Psalmur. *Lbs 3903 4to.*

Ebenesersdóttir, S. Sunna, et al. "Ancient Genomes from Iceland Reveal the Making of a Human Population." *Science, vol.* 360, no. 6392, 1 June 2018, pp. 1028–1032, doi:10.1126/science.aar2625.

Eiriksson, Leifur. *Egil's Saga.* Penguin Books Limited, 2004.

Gardela, Leszek. "Into Viking Minds: Reinterpreting the Staffs of Sorcery and Unravelling Seiðr." *Viking and Medieval Scandinavia,* vol. 4, 2008, pp. 45–84, doi:10.1484/j.vms.1.100306.

Gårdbäck, Johannes Björn. *Trolldom: Spells and Methods of the Norse Folk Magic Tradition.* Yronwode Institute for the Preservation and Popularization of Indigenous Ethnomagicology, 2015.

Gunnell, Terry, et al. "How High Was the High One? The Roles of Oðinn and Þórr in Pre-Christian Icelandic Society." *Theorizing Old Norse Myth,* Brepols, Turnhout, Belgium, 2017, pp. 105–129. Acta Scandinavia.

Gunnell, Terry. "How Elvish were the *Álfar?*" *Making the Middle Ages,* 2007, pp. 111–130, https://doi.org/10.1484/m.mmages-eb.3.3608.

_. "The Season of the Dísir: The Winter Nights and the Dísablót in Early Medieval Scandinavian Belief ." *Cosmos,* vol. 2, no. 16, June 2005, pp. 117–149.

ÍB 179 8vo. Reykjavík, c. 1700-1800.

ÍB 663 8vo. Reykjavík, 1780.

ÍB 799 8vo. Reykjavík, c. 1600.

Jakobsson, Ármann. "Watch Out for the Skin Deep: Medieval Icelandic Transformations." *Arts,* vol. 12, no. 1, 27 Dec. 2022, p. 5, doi:10.3390/arts12010005.

Janson, Svante. "The Icelandic Calendar." *Isländska Sällskapets Årsbok,* vol. 62, Scripta Islandica, Uppsala, Sweden, 2011, pp. 51–104.

Johnson, Thomas K. *Svartkonstböcker: A Compendium of the Swedish Black Art Book Tradition.* Revelore Press, 2019.

Jónsson, Finnur. *Ynglinga Saga: Særtryk Af Heimskringla.* 1893.

JS 248 4to. Reykjavík, 1846.

JS 313 8vo. Reykjavík, 1750-1850.

JS 375 8vo. Reykjavík, 1800-1820.

JS 379 8vo. Reykjavík, c. 1700-1800.

Kanerva, Kirsi. "The Role of the Dead in Medieval Iceland: A Case Study of Eyrbyggja Saga." *Collegium Medievale, vol.* 24, Nov. 2011.

Kreager, Adèle. "Lapidaries and Lyfsteinar: Health, Enhancement, and Human-Lithic Relations in Medieval Iceland." *Gripla,* vol. 33, Dec. 2022, doi:10.33112/gripla.33.4.

Konráðsson, Þorsteinn. *Lbs 3902 4to.* 1934.

Lbs 143 8vo. Reykjavík, 1670.

Lbs 143 8vo. 1860.

Lbs 489 8vo. Reykjavík, c. 1700-1800.

Lbs 627 8vo. Reykjavík, 1820.

Lbs 764 8vo. Reykjavík, 1780.

Lbs 977 4to. Reykjavík, 1818-1820.

Lbs 1140 8vo. Reykjavík, 1820.

Lbs 1593 a 4to. Reykjavík, 1859-1879.

Lbs 1861-69 4to. Reykjavík, 1859-1879.

Lbs 2413 8vo. Reyjavík, c. 1800.

Lbs 3902 4to. Reyjavík, c. 1800.

Lbs 4375 8vo. Reykjavík, 1900-1949.

Lbs 4627. Reykjavík, c. 1900.

Lbs 5472 I-IV 4to. Reykjavík, c. 1800.

MacLeod, Mindy, and Bernard Mees. *Runic Amulets and Magic Objects*. Boydell & Brewer, 2006.

Marbode, and Johannes Cuspinianus. *Libellvs de Lapidibvs*. 1511.

Mitchell, Stephen A. *Witchcraft and Magic in the Nordic Middle Ages*. University of Pennsylvania Press, 2013.

Page, R. I. "The Icelandic Rune-Poem." *Nottingham Medieval Studies*, vol. 42, 1998, pp. 1–37, doi:10.1484/j.nms.3.276.

Prehal, Brenda. "Handbook for the Deceased: Re-Evaluating Literature and Folklore in Icelandic Archaeology." *CUNY Academic Works, City University of New York*, CUNY, 2021, Accessed 2023.

Rich, Ellora Nimbkar. "Seið the Magic Words: Two Case Studies in Old Norse Etymology." *University of Iceland*, 2023.

Saemundsson, Matthías Vidar. *Galdrar Á Íslandi: Íslensk Galdrabók*. 2nd ed., Almenna Bókafélagið, 1992.

Shiell, Albert. *Icelandic Plant Magic: Folk Herbalism of the North*. Crossed Crow Books, 2023.

Skuggi. *Galdra-Skræða*. Lesstofan, 2013.

Smith, Christopher Alan. *Icelandic Magic: Aims, Tools and Techniques of the Icelandic Sorcerers*. Avalonia, 2015.

Smith, Kevin, and Guðrún Sveinbjarnardóttir. "The Colour of Belief: Objects of Jasper, Opal, Chalcedony, and Obsidian from the Reykholt Churches." *Reykholt: The Church Excavations*, University of Iceland Press, Reykjavík, 2016, pp. 230–242.

Steffensen, Jón. "Aspects of Life in Iceland in the Heathen Period." *Saga-Book*, vol. 17, 1966, pp. 177–205. *JSTOR*.

Stefansson, Vilhjalmur. "Icelandic Beast and Bird Lore." *The Journal of American Folklore*, vol. 19, no. 75, 1906, p. 300, doi:10.2307/534436.

Sturluson, Snorri. 1179?-1241. *Edda Snorra Sturlusonar.* ed by Jónsson, Þorleifur Kaupmannahöfn, Gyldendals Bóokverzlun, 1875. Pdf. Retrieved from the Library of Congress.

_. *Egils Saga Skalla-Grímssonar.* Reykjavík :Hið Islenzka Fornritafélag, 1933.

Spare, Austin Osman, et al. "The Zoëtic Grimoire of Zos." *Zos Speaks! Encounters with Austin Osman Spare,* Fulgur, Somerset, 1998.

Vigfússon, Geir. *Huld Manuscript (ÍB 383 4to).* Reykjavík, 1860.

Waggoner, Benjamin M. *Norse Magical and Herbal Healing: A Medical Book from Medieval Iceland.* Troth, 2011.

Westcoat, Eirik. *Viking Poetry for Heathen Rites: Asatru Liturgy in Traditional Verse.* Skaldic Eagle Press, 2017.